READINGS ON EQUAL EDUCATION
(formerly *Educating the Disadvantaged*)

MARGUERITE ROSS BARNETT is Chancellor of the University of Missouri at St. Louis.

CHARLES C. HARRINGTON is Professor of Anthropology and Education, and Director of the Institute for Urban and Minority Education at Teachers College, Columbia University.

PHILIP V. WHITE is University Associate Dean for Academic Affairs at the City University of New York.

READINGS
ON EQUAL
EDUCATION

Volume 9

EDUCATION POLICY
IN AN ERA OF CONSERVATIVE
REFORM

Edited by

Marguerite Ross Barnett   Charles C. Harrington

Philip V. White

AMS PRESS, INC.
NEW YORK

TABLE OF CONTENTS

IV.

PREFACE

Most of the essays in this volume originated as presentations made as part of a year-long lecture series sponsored by the Politics and Education Program and the Institute for Urban and Minority Education at Teachers College, Columbia University. The lecture series was organized to provide a forum for exploration of the implications of fiscal retrenchment, to assess Reagan administration proposals for block grants in education, and to explore other proposed educational reform measures. In revising their presentations for publication, the authors have expanded the initial concerns to encompass some of the broader policy themes, dynamics, and conundrums inherent in the somewhat contradictory, even oxymoronic, notion of conservative educational reform. The result is a lively set of contributions reflecting both the passion of public debate and the exactitude of impartial scholarly analysis.

We want to thank Lawrence Cremin, then President of Teachers College, who lent his support to this lecture series; the lecture series participants, all of whom gave generously of their time and energy to make the series a success; the faculty and staff of the Politics and Education Program and the Institute for Urban and Minority Education at Teachers College; and chapter contributors who were not able to participate in the lecture series but who agreed to write original articles appropriate for inclusion in this volume.

Marguerite Ross Barnett
Charles Harrington
Philip V. White

ACKNOWLEDGMENTS

BOWLES, SAMUEL, DAVID M. GORDON, and THOMAS E. WEISSKOPF. "The Arithmetic of Economic Decline," excerpted from Chapter 2, Chapter 16, and Appendix A of *Beyond the Wasteland* by Samuel Bowles, David Gordon, and Thomas Weisskopf. Copyright © 1983, 1984 by the authors. Reprinted by permission of Doubleday & Co., Inc.

MINTER, THOMAS K. A revision of "The Importance of the Federal Role in Improving Education Practice: Lessons from a Big-City System," *Harvard Educational Review*, 52:4, 500-513. Copyright © 1982 by President and Fellows of Harvard College. All rights reserved.

INTRODUCTION:
EDUCATION POLICY
IN AN ERA OF CONSERVATIVE REFORM

Since coming to power in 1981, the Reagan administration has claimed a sweeping mandate to dramatically alter the nature and structure of power between the federal government and the states and to restore the compact between the people and the government regarding its role and responsibility. Responding to what it perceives as a broad-based constituency, the administration has sought "to take the federal government off the backs of the people and out of their pockets" by reducing taxes, sharply curtailing the growth of and expenditures for social programs, and reducing federal regulation of the economy. Within the first eight weeks of assuming office, President Reagan unveiled eighty-four proposals to eliminate or reduce federal programs; eventually, more than half were enacted in one form or another. Significant changes were instituted in social security, education, health care, civil rights, agriculture, environmental action. So-called "safety net" programs to protect the poor and disadvantaged sustained deep budget cuts. If the Reagan administration has not yet managed to enact fully its public policy "revolution" thus far, it has at least managed to drastically change the terms of debate.

Prompted largely by a perception of failure on the part of the nation's public schools, education has emerged as an important element in this debate. This perception has been fed in large measure by the same kind of commercial and military considerations that inspired educational reform in the late 1950s and 1960s. Then, as now, there was general uneasiness about the possibility that the United States might lose its competitive edge—economically and militarily—to other nations. Critics of today's schools, however, also point to the loss of U.S. dominance in important manufacturing and industrial markets and to reduced worker productivity as concrete evidence of our educational shortcomings. Furthermore, heightened tensions in East–West relations add an extra measure of concern about the educational preparation of military personnel who may be called upon to operate and maintain sophisticated armaments.

The concern about education is also prompted by a kind of cultural reaction to what is viewed as the "permissiveness" of the 1960s which led to the challenging of authority and tradition and the establishment of what many viewed as educational and moral relativism. One of the hallmarks of the 1960s, after all, was campuses in tumult, with college students playing lead roles in the civil rights movements, anti-war protest, free speech, and establishment of alternative types of schooling, non-traditional lifestyles, and sexual experimentation. The power of traditional authority—whether in the classroom or administration building, in the family, or in the government—was under attack, and many Americans have seized upon the educational system as both symptom and cause of these challenges.

The most striking difference between education reform of a generation ago and that of today is the *Brown v. Board of Education* decision which in the 1950s set the stage for the pursuit of policies aimed at achieving equal opportunity in education. (See Volume VIII in this series.) Some of these efforts involved school desegregation and busing, while others involved improvements in on-site education for low-income minority childen. Educational excellence and equity were not viewed as antithetical or as products of a zero-sum contest; educational excellence was to be fostered by raising the performance of all students, but especially by concentrating on the needs of low-income minorities.

Today, however, the official theme of excellence in education is often viewed as incompatible with educational equity, especially in a period characterized by severe fiscal constraints. Indeed, many argue that the educational experiments to achieve a greater measure of equality, particularly through intervention in the early childhood education of low-income minority students, were failures. This conclusion, while politically useful, flies in the face of years of research findings. Both direct and indirect evidence from the 1982 National Assessment of Educational Progress report substantiate findings of educational gains recorded in the 1970s in cities and in schools where Title I money has been concentrated. The narrowing of the gap between black and white students in SAT and other national achievement scores during the 1980s also attests to the positive effects that massive federal intervention can have on the education of disadvantaged children in the elementary and secondary schools.

Education policy is currently being made in a society undergoing massive technological and structural transformation, especially in the economic system. A brief contrast with the 1960s, when massive federal intervention in education was initiated, reveals how far we have moved from a period of enlightened social policy concerning education. During the 1960s the struggle for minority advancement coincided with American economic interests. The economy was booming, there was a shortage of labor, and businessmen believed that Blacks, minorities, and women represented a new and untapped potential source of semi-skilled and skilled workers. In this tight labor market, big businesses sought the expansion of a skilled labor force through education and affirmative action.

By the time a few gains were registered, however, the global economy had begun to change, and the United States was not immune to these changes. Facing strong competition in the world market from other capitalist nations, especially Germany and Japan; the decline of the dollar as the stabilizing currency in the world economy; increasing independence of nations in the Middle East, Africa, Asia, and Latin America which were controlling and setting prices for their own raw materials; and greater demands for higher wages and lower prices from both organized and unorganized workers, the United States slipped into protracted economic crisis. Economic stagnation limited the availability of and increased competition for educational opportunities, and resulted in cutbacks in social services. There was also more competition for jobs as the nation entered a period of persistent downturn, decremental planning, and truncated expectations. Hardest hit were Blacks and other minorities.

These economic changes are also mirrored in the character of what some commentators have called the public policy revolution in education. What, in fact, is this public policy revolution? Though seemingly disparate and unrelated, an underlying unity of perspective does in fact link the key education policies of the current administration: tuition tax credits; budget reductions; support for Internal Revenue Service grants of tax exemption to schools that discriminate; opposition to busing to achieve racial balance; transformation of the Department of Education into a foundation; opposition to affirmative action; emphasis on educational excellence and freedom for the educational consumer; and, most importantly, the new federalism. Three themes converge in these issues and unite them: (1) contraction of the public sphere and of the definition of what constitutes legitimate public interest; (2) social triage; (3) and finally, individualism and the privatization of public interest.

Contracting the public sphere and limiting the number of legitimate subjects for public deliberation has been a major thrust of the Reagan Administration. This becomes clearly evident in the formulation of the new federalism concept and the principal way in which it is to be implemented—block grants accompanied by budget reductions. The new federalism helps establish the necessary preconditions for contracting the public sphere. It removes the debate on many pressing issues of political and social change from the federal level, where press and public can monitor, mobilize, and organize for national solutions to national problems, and places the locus of the discussion in separate states, where attention and mobilization are necessarily fragmented. Such a strategy lowers expectations about what the federal government can and should legitimately do. It shifts political conflict from the federal arena where a broad array of groups have already mobilized to lobby for what they define as public interest issues to state arenas where it is more difficult for groups with universal, public interest concerns, such as equity in education, to mobilize an effective presence. The initial decisions to include most of the major educational programs for the disadvantaged in block grants and to transform the Department of Education into an educational foundation are therefore best seen as part of the general effort to delimit the scope of federal policy and public action.

Social triage, a second element underlying current national educational policy, holds that students can be divided into three groups: those for whom middle- and upper-class status is assured; those for whom it is possible; and those for whom it is virtually impossible. Since some believe resources spent on the third group are largely wasted, as triage advocates view the example of programs for the educationally disadvantaged, they believe it makes more sense to help those of the second group for whom success is at least possible. There are two current examples of the expression of triage in education policy. One example is the popular interpretation of the report of the National Commission on Excellence in Education according to which the federal and local government ought to be selective in educational innovation, for example by focusing solely on improvement in mathematics and science and emphasizing programs for the intellectually gifted.

Perhaps the *best* current example is tuition tax credits. To the extent that tuition tax credits will benefit the poor, in contrast to the middle- and upper-class who clearly will be helped, the poor children most likely to benefit will be those with the best potential for upward mobility. Administration analysts and conservative thinkers believe it is the more motivated children and parents who are likely to use their tax credits to leave ghetto schools. Nathan Glazer has written: "Do those who wish to escape have the duty to stay behind with the worst? And does society have an obligation to force them to? I think the answer to both questions is no. To me, freedom is a higher value than those advanced by the forced association of the aspiring and achieving with those who create an environment in which they can neither aspire nor achieve."

The third element that runs through the Reagan administration educational policy—the priority of individualism and individual choice over group goals and social or public choices in areas where individual and private action is possible—is so central that individual choice is often equated with freedom and justice. Since we are ending an era of public dialogue on education in which justice was sometimes proximately equated with equity, the equation of justice with choice sounds innovative. But in actuality this equation simply recapitulates the confusion between personal freedom and individual choice in the market place which is so typical of conservative writing.

Civil rights issues are those which have evoked the most articulate expressions of the priority of individualism and private choice over public and social goals. Publicly-stated presidential opposition to busing, to affirmative action, and support of tax exemptions for schools that discriminate have all been jusitified or rationalized through the juxtaposition of individual to group rights; the denial of virtually all group rights as illegitimate; and the further denial of public responsibility to redress group discrimination, deprivation, or exploitation. Instead, efforts to redress these problems are themselves attacked as inimical to the rights and essential freedom of the individual.

These ideological themes are also sustained by a pragmatic political reality: minorities, big cities, and the educational establishment (particularly the National Education Association) are all closely tied to the Democratic party. They did not support Ronald Reagan's election in 1980. Minorities are now the chief clientele of the large urban school districts, and the NEA has always favored and benefited from the Great Society-type programs that funded improvements in urban education during the 1960s and 1970s. Proposals such as creating a corps of master teachers, promoting differential pay, and abolishing job guarantees are all measures that would weaken the power of the NEA. Many politicians feel that neither minorities nor the education establishment can call in debts that would act to moderate the thrust of Reagan policies.

In addition to the ideologically explicit themes of retrenchment, erosion, and contraction in the public sector; social triage; and the primacy of individual choice over group claims and goals, there is an implicit, encompassing dynamic of American society that also shapes the environment for current educational policy.

That characteristic is progressive loss of a substantive, consensual core of American values and symbolic referents. It is precisely because of this loss that we now witness the revival of a colorful but substantively empty notion of patriotism, the promotion of a nostalgic, roseate past, and the elevation of local and regional mores and practices. Although it might be argued that the heterogeneity and complexity of American life has always generated great cultural and subcultural differentiation as well as an unresolved American identity, nevertheless there was always a proximate consensus on common national direction, an overarching American purpose.

This proximate consensus is important because it provides the most general frame of reference and purpose for the educational system. For example, on one level during the early 19th century the myth of the melting pot encapsulated a real cultural emphasis on ethnic assimilation that was reflected in school curricula. Another way of making this point is to say that the educational system is not autonomous but is shaped in fundamental ways by the economic, political, social, and cultural context.

Now we are in a period in which both a unifying and compelling national purpose and a homogeneous, contained cultural core are lacking, which leaves educators and educational systems open to the vicissitudes of reform faddism. Under these circumstances education becomes increasingly like popular culture. One year hemlines are up and hula hoops are "in." The next year hemlines fall and punk rock defines the accepted social style. One year the educational focus is on open classrooms, and another year it is back to the basics. One year physical education and exercise are in. Another year, mathematics and science are emphasized.

Because of the vacuum in values in American life, we embrace a succession of fads in goods and in education, making individualism and social triage more acceptable. Without a strong sense of the public sphere, public interest, collective goals and direction, the seemingly natural impulse is to raise the private and the individual to the level of the public as a substitute for a public interest. Since no private value, symbol, or interest has intrinsic primacy over any other, continual substitution of successive fads and fashions becomes possible. Erosion of resources has seemingly only exacerbated this societal dynamic.

The essays that follow introduce the reader to new ideas related to those mentioned in this brief introduction and further elaborate on some that we have only touched upon here. The book is divided into four parts. Part I provides a theoretical overview detailing the fortunes of the U.S. economy over the past generation that have paved the way for the radical retrenchment that the Reagan administration has been effecting, and elaborates how affirmative action, a key public policy goal in education and employment, has evolved and been undermined by the changing socio-political and ideological climate. Part II provides a direct assessment of the political and economic consequences of retrenchment and block-grant strategies at the state level and at the level of the large urban school district. In Part III we examine criteria by which to judge the effectiveness of block grants in achieving public policy goals, and compare their success to enhanced federal involvement as a means of implementing policy. Finally, the concluding essay in Part IV looks at how those with few resources attempt to influence policy without resort to protest when the kinds of public policy they favor are clearly out of fashion. It raises some interesting questions about how the American political system really operates.

While dealing with two issues seemingly quite different from block grants and retrenchment in educational expenditures, these introductory chapters by Bowles, Gordon, and Weisskopf and Barnett and Williams provide the reader with a useful, overarching theoretical context in which to view the economic and ideological underpinnings for both the expansion and contraction of federal aid to education during the past generation. Situating the beginning of the decline in economic fortunes for the United States in the mid-1960s, Bowles et al. argue that fundamental structural changes are necessary to remedy the low productivity, tendency toward inflation, ever higher levels of unemployment, and other problems bedeviling the American economy. Their diagnosis supplies the material basis for the electorate's receptiveness to the "supply-sided juggernaut" in 1980 and suggests the limits of constraint within which a changed political climate might renew the kinds of increasing federal commitment to education that developed in the 1960s and 1970s.

In the era of retrenchment, affirmative action as a process to expand educational and job opportunities for Black Americans has sustained critical assault. Understanding the economic climate, for Barnett and Williams as for Bowles et al., is a key to understanding the emergence of affirmative action and the dynamics of its evolution. But equally as important is comprehending the social, political, and ideological factors that they scrutinize. Analyzing affirmative action as a form of racial public policy which provides benefits to individual Black Americans by changing the rules according to which certain institutions operate, Barnett and Williams also underscore the contradiction which the hierarchical, collective domination of Blacks represents in a society premised on a radically individualistic egalitarianism. Both the limits of affirmative action to redress the generations of discrimination that Blacks as a group have suffered and the internal dynamics that undermined its effectiveness as a policy are shaped by this contradiction.

In analyzing this policy that has been crucial to expanding access for Blacks to higher education, Barnett and Williams throw into sharp relief the dynamics of an important dimension of conservative reform.

THE ARITHMETIC OF ECONOMIC DECLINE

Samuel Bowles,

David M. Gordon,

and Thomas E. Weisskopf

The economy is basically healthy; the problems we have now are less economic than emotional.
-Chief economist, Bank of America, 1977[1]

Things are going much better in the economy than most people realize. It's our attitude that is doing poorly.
-Chair, Federal Reserve Board, 1978[2]

Most people in the United States now recognize that our economy is a mess. Some still believe that quick fixes and magic potions will be enough, that a few tax cuts here and a little exhortation there will turn the economy around. Others believe that the economy could return quickly to full health if only the government would get off its back. Increasing numbers of people are prepared to make more significant changes in economic organization to resolve our most critical problems—which helps explain why so many were prepared to countenance the supply-side juggernaut in 1981.

Those varying attitudes reflect major uncertainty about the proper diagnosis of our economic disease. Some, pointing to the

3

continued rise in per capita gross national product, deny the existence of serious economic problems altogether. Others, pointing to bad harvests and soaring oil prices since 1973, concede the reality of the crisis but nonetheless attribute it to accidental external events of relatively little enduring importance. Still others suggest much deeper causes requiring much more fundamental solutions.

Standard measures of economic performance can help us choose among such conflicting views. The data suggest a stark conclusion. Two results are most important. First, our economic fortunes began to decline in the mid-1960s; the deterioration of the U.S. economy has been unfolding for at least a decade and a half. Second, that deterioration has continually intensified ever since: far from receding, our problems have persisted and deepened.

These factual conclusions are not simply fodder for trivia-mongers and number crunchers. They carry profound implications for debates about program and strategy; our problems are long-standing and fundamental. Those who attach later dates to the onset of decline are likely to miss the first moments of reversal and, as a result, the first causes of economic deterioration. Those who regard our current problems simply as cyclical downturns or the result of accidental jolts to a healthy economy are likely to prescribe Band-Aids for much more fundamental ailments. The persistence and severity of our economic problems should persuade us that those problems stem from structural faults in the foundations of the postwar corporate system. They are not temporary aberrations. They will not disappear by themselves. They require fundamental structural solutions.

HOW RECENT?

Few would disagree that there was a turning point at some time during the past decade or two. The history of the United States economy (as well as the world economy) appears to encompass two different periods since World War II.

The first, beginning shortly after the war and continuing at least through the early 1960s, created "boom" conditions for most people in the United States. There were obvious flaws in the vessel of expansion: Many continued to have difficulty finding a steady job, even in conditions of relatively full employment. Income inequalities persisted—between rich and poor, men and women, whites and blacks—and some even widened. Working conditions were often unhealthy, public services were often inadequate, and economic priorities were often inappropriate to meet people's real needs. As John Kenneth Galbraith argued in the late 1950s, the "affluent society" was far from perfect; Michael Harrington's *The Other America* was the flip side of postwar prosperity.

Yet, in spite of these continuing problems, there was a real sense in which the economy was working. Total output and total income were growing so rapidly that most people in the United States could realistically anticipate a brighter economic future. The expanding pie helped moderate some of the tensions inherent in an unequal society and cushioned the blows of misplaced priorities and irrational economic allocations.

Those years of optimism now seem like a distant and receding past. Economic welfare has been stagnating or declining for large proportions of the U.S. labor force and U.S. households. Economic anxiety has been spreading like the plague— infecting more and more of us, reaching from Wall Street to Main Street. "It would be necessary to go back to the 1930s and the Great Depression," pollster Daniel Yankelovich concludes, "to find a peacetime issue that has had the country so concerned and so distraught."[3]

How do we measure this reversal of economic fortunes? And when did this reversal begin?

Inflation and unemployment are the symptoms of economic deterioriation to which economists and the media have devoted most of their attention. From the early 1950s through 1965, the annual rate of price increase fluctuated around an average of 2 percent. It neither showed a noticeable tendency to rise nor displayed sharp fluctuations; indeed, the more striking feature of the first part of this era was the *stability* of a relatively low inflation rate through the early 1960s.

From the mid-1960s to 1981, however, the rate of inflation increased dramatically—climbing to double-digit levels from 1979 to 1981. Each of its peaks was higher than the previous business-cycle peak, and each of the troughs was higher than the rate of inflation in the previous trough. The acceleration of inflation began well before OPEC and got its act together in 1973.

The rate of inflation dropped significantly in 1982—thanks in large part to the highest unemployment rates since the Great Depression. Even with more than 10 million jobless, however, inflation was still more severe in 1982 than it was in 1976, the previous cyclical low in the inflation rate. This can hardly be considered a permanent cure for accelerating inflation, since the pattern of higher inflation rates at each cycle trough has continued. And who knows how many more million unemployed must lose their jobs before such hard-times strategies could permanently reverse the inflationary dynamic?

Unemployment is itself subject to sharp cyclical fluctuations, but joblessness began to move significantly upward from the late 1960s through the 1970s and into the 1980s. The data for 1948 to 1965 show no obvious trend. After the mid-1960s, as with the inflation data, each peak is higher than the previous one and each trough is higher than the previous trough as well.

Dismal though they are, these data on unemployment disguise much of the problem. Women, minority workers, and teenagers all experience higher rates of unemployment; their relative disadvantages in the labor market, by this measure, have been intensifying throughout the years of economic decline. Equally important, the official overall unemployment rate excludes many in the labor force who nonetheless have serious employment problems—those who have grown discouraged and abandoned their search for work and those who want full-time work but must settle reluctantly for part-time jobs. The official data further understate the extent of joblessness as well, because they measure unemployment only at a particular moment. In 1981, for example, unemployment was recorded at 8.3 million persons, but the Bureau of Labor Statistics estimates that 23.4 million were unemployed *at some time or another* during the year.[4]

Those who were able to find and hold jobs were more fortunate, of course, but they hardly escaped the effects of economic decline. Roughly 90 percent of U.S. households depend on wage and salary income for their survival.[5] For this vast majority, two principal trends determine the level of income available to their households: Take-home pay per hour of work and the total hours worked to support household members. What has happened to hourly earnings, and what has happened to hours worked?

Production workers comprised 81.3 percent of total employment in 1980 and represent that group in the labor force which is most clearly dependent on wage and salary income.[6] Spendable hourly earnings measure the average worker's hourly wage and/or salary income plus other compensation—for example, medical benefits—minus personal income taxes and Social Security taxes. These earnings are expressed in constant (1977) dollars in order to adjust for the effects of inflation on the cost of living.

The data show a clear pattern: The average worker's real after-tax pay grew rapidly through the mid-1960s. Its growth then slowed, with some fluctuations, until 1978, and then declined precipitously after 1978. By 1981, average real after-tax hourly earnings had fallen back to their lowest levels since 1961, twenty years earlier. Average annual growth in real spendable earnings was 2.1 percent from 1946 to 1966, slowed to 1 percent between 1966 and 1973, and then dropped by 1.9 percent a year from 1973 to 1981.

The average annual *hours worked per capita* by the U.S. population is the measure that reflects the total amount of labor which U.S. households commited to the economy in order to support themselves and their dependents. Average hours per capita declined fairly steadily until the early 1960s—as workers and households were able to take advantage of rising wage and salary income. They rose in the mid-1960s as the growth of real earnings began to slow. They have risen most rapidly since the mid-1970s as households have tried to stave off the squeeze of declining real earnings.[7]

This increase in average annual hours per capita reflects an increase in the number of household members working outside the home, and not an increase in average hours per week. Faced with stagnating and then declining real spendable earnings, additional family members, particularly married women, have sought work. The percentage of the adult population working or looking for work outside the home—a figure which had been roughly constant over the postwar period—began to rise in the mid-1960s, climbing from 59 percent in 1966 to 64 percent in 1981.[8] This extra labor helped sustain total household earnings, making possible continued increases in household consumption levels. As the 1970s progressed, *Business Week* noted, it became more and more important to take into account "the sweat that goes into producing (household) income."[9] "Everybody is working harder to maintain their standard of living," University of Massachusetts economist Leonard Rapping concludes, "but most of them are not making it."

Since the mid-1960s, through both the stagnation in real spendable earnings and the added hours necessary to compensate for that stagnation, working households have felt the pinch. There is more to the crisis, of course, than the symptomatic erosion of real earnings and leisure time, much less the acceleration of inflation and rising unemployment. No statistical measures can adequately reflect the real personal impact of heightened insecurity, personal anxiety, and social tension which result from economic decline. Nor can our data series begin to capture the loss in popular power resulting from continuing erosions in labor union vitality and leverage, declining citizen support from social programs and personal entitlements, or the spreading power of corporate political action committees (PACs) and business money in electoral politics. But even simple statistical measures *are* sufficient to shift the terms of discussion. According to relevant measures and available government data, our economic fortunes began to deteriorate in the mid-1960s, not later. We have now experienced almost two decades of economic decline.

HOW DEEP?

We have focused on aspects of economic decline which people have experienced more or less directly. But in order to assess the depth of our economic problems, we must move from measures of personal distress to more fundamental indicators of basic economic performance.

Periods of Growth and Decline

The first task is to distinguish between the short-term business cycle and more persistent trends in the economy. Most indicators of economic distress move up and down over the business cycle, riding the roller coaster of expansion and contraction every few years. If we want to probe the depth of the current economic crisis, we should make comparisons which avoid confusing short-term movements with more persistent trends.

One common method of controlling for short-term oscillations concentrates on *comparable stages* of successive business cycles. If we compare rates of growth from one business-cycle peak to another, for example, we can highlight the economy's performance between years when it is at the same stage of each cycle.

In the discussions which follow, we use this standard peak-to-peak method of controlling for the effects of the short-term cycle. We identify the business-cycle peak years by looking at the ratio of actual gross national product (GNP) to the corresponding "potential" GNP; potential GNP is an estimate of what the economy was capable of producing with what is somewhat arbitrarily termed "full utilization" of available resources. The ratio of actual to potential GNP reaches a cyclical peak at the state of an expansion when the economy's productive potential is more *fully* utilized.

By this measure, there were seven business-cycle peaks in the postwar period up to the 1980s: 1948, 1951, 1955, 1959, 1966, 1973, and 1979. Since everyone seems to agree that the boom period lasted at least until 1966, we study the economy's performance during the years of stable prosperity by examining the *entire* period from 1948 to 1966, ignoring the several short-term cyclical fluctuations in between. Then, in order to sharpen our focus on the contours of subsequent decline, we consistently compare two stages of deterioration: from the cyclical peaks of 1966 to 1973 and 1973 to 1979.

Much of our analysis will focus, in short, on data for just three key periods between bench-mark years: the boom period, from 1948 to 1966; the first phase of decline, from 1966 to1973; and the second phase, from 1973 to 1979. Where possible, we will also introduce data for more recent years, although economists cannot yet agree on whether or not the sustained decline since 1979 was punctuated by a feeble cyclical peak in 1981.

Measures of Growth and Decline

Our second task is to choose an indicator of the economy's overall performance. Economists often focus on "per capita GNP"—a society's gross national product divided by its total population. The rate of growth of per capita GNP, adjusted for inflation, is thought to reflect the rate of improvement in the average citizen's well-being. However, we prefer an alternative measure which we label "hourly income"—real net national income per hour of work.

Hourly income differs from per capita gross national product in three respects: (1) in accordance with widely accepted economic reasoning, it removes from gross national product the amount spent on "depreciation," that is, the output needed to replace deteriorated structures and equipment; (2) it adjusts for inflation with a price index reflecting changes in the prices of *purchased* rather than *produced* commodities, allowing us to take into account changes in international terms of trade; (3) it substitutes total hours of work for total population as the standard against which real income should be measured.

None of these modifications is particularly controversial, but the third one—dividing by hours of work rather than population—is quite important. Many agree that the current problems of the U.S. economy involves its productive capacity and efficiency. By focusing on *hourly* income, we can sharpen our attention on the standard of living we attain *in return for the amount of work we must perform to achieve that standard of living.* Increases in per capita GNP may not be desirable if we must work too many additional hours to achieve them. And, as we have already seen, hours of work per capita have been rising dramatically, accounting for a substantial portion of recent increases in per capita GNP.

Dealing with the average annual rates of growth of *hourly income*, we find that data for our three main periods of comparison and for the most recent available trends from 1979 to 1981 confirm the impressions we have already formed: hourly income grew rapidly from 1948 to 1966; slowed noticeably from 1966 to 1973; and declined even more dramatically from 1973 to 1979. Hourly income essentially stagnated between 1979 and 1981.

There is one obvious source for these dramatic declines in hourly income—the slowdown in the rate of growth of *productivity* (that is, real output per hour of work).[10] Hourly *income* did not grow as fast after the mid-1960s largely because hourly *output*—another term for productivity—did not rise as rapidly as during the two decades following World War II. Using the same bench-mark years, we find that the average annual rate of growth of hourly output in the private-business economy of the United States slowed from 3.2 percent in 1948–1966 to 2.3 percent in 1966–73 and then again to .8 percent in 1973–79. Productivity growth has slowed even more since 1979—according to data available at the time of writing—falling to an annual rate of .4 percent from 1979 to 1981.[11]

Some observers have suggested that the productivity slowdown is little more than a statistical artifact. For example, Harry Magdoff of the journal *Monthly Review* has (correctly) emphasized the difficulty of measuring output in a wide variety of industries. Others have (incorrectly) supposed that the measured productivity slowdown in the aggregate economy simply reflects the shift of labor from higher-productivity goods-producing sectors into lower-productivity service-providing sectors.

We think that the productivity problem is real and severe. Whatever the problems in measuring output, the extremely close correspondence between our series for hourly income and hourly output suggests that slower growth in hourly output is the likeliest factor to explain the more easily measured income trends. Moreover, slower growth of productivity has been pervasive, affecting nearly every sector in the U.S. economy. The trends in hourly output growth for eleven separate industries covering the full breadth of the economy show almost all of the sectors following the same two-step decline we have already seen in the total private business economy.[12] The most important exception to this pattern is manufacturing, which did not begin to experience the productivity slowdown until 1973–79. But this exception largely reflects the unusually rapid rate of capital investment in manufacturing during the Vietnam years. And the general pattern seems clear enough. It is hard to write off the general overall decline in productivity growth as a statistical mirage.[13]

Deterioration

Some may not find the drop in hourly-income growth from 1948–66 to 1966–73 particularly striking; it is certainly true that the later drop to 1973–79 is more substantial both absolutely and relatively. But this is not the relevant standard of evaluation. The slowdown in hourly-income growth in 1966–73 would be extremely important *if* it created stresses and strains which the economy was unable to overcome and thereby led to even more severe problems in subsequent years. And this is exactly what happened. An example of this point may help to clarify our argument.

When the postwar corporate system was working well, at least from the viewpoint of corporations, profitability recovered from short-term recessions and achieved levels more or less comparable to its pre-recession peaks. Despite the depths of the 1957–58 and 1960–61 recessions, for example, the after-tax rate of corporate profits was far higher in 1965 than it had been in 1955, before those two recessions.

After 1966, however, corporate profitability did not recover from the stresses of economic downturn. After the recession of

1969–70, the after-tax profit-rate peak in 1972 was one-third lower than it had been in 1965. After the recession of 1974–75, once again, the after-tax profit-rate peak in 1977 had fallen below its 1972 peak.

This observation echoes our earlier comments. There we noted that with each successive business cycle since 1966, rates of inflation and unemployment have become worse. The pattern of deterioration of profitability runs parallel to this: it has declined from cycle to cycle since the mid-1960s. Operating through its normal cyclical mechanisms, *the economy has been unable to reverse this process of decline by itself.*

Domestic and International Decline

This pattern of economic deterioration has affected not only the U.S. economy but also the world economy.

The domestic dimensions of the crisis have become painfully familiar by now. The U.S. economy has lost much of its initial competitive advantage, falling from its lofty pinnacle in the earlier postwar decades. In 1951, for example, the U.S. economy accounted for 30 percent of the world trade of the sixteen leading industrial nations; by 1971, the U.S. share had fallen to 18 percent.[14]

Even more dramatically, the U.S. economy has taken a nose dive in the international rankings by per capita gross domestic product. The United States, as we were frequently reminded, was number one in 1950, in 1960, and again in 1970—still over 20 percent ahead of its nearest competitor. By 1980, the original land of plenty had dropped to number eleven (not counting the oil-rich Middle Eastern states), trailing Switzerland, Sweden, Norway, Germany, Denmark, Luxembourg, Iceland, Finland, the Netherlands, and Belgium in that order.[15]

Despite these relative advances, however, other countries have been suffering economically as well. All of the advanced countries have experienced significant declines in the growth of output and productivity. Even Japan, that economic wonder held up for all to emulate, has been growing less than half as rapidly since the early 1970s as it did during the 1950s and 1960s.

This world-wide character of the economic crisis serves as a potent reminder of the complexity of its causes. When and if we in the United States begin to move toward promising economic solutions, we must be certain to review their international implications. The U.S. economy, despite its great internal resources, is tightly bound to the world economy. We can gain much greater control over our own economic destinies, but we cannot afford to neglect the impact of our own actions on the rest of the world and, in turn, the effects of international trends on our domestic margin for maneuverability.

SHORT MEMORIES

It is unfortunate, perhaps, that so few economists and policy makers still remember the interwar years—the years of persistent instability from the 1920s through the Great Depression. Many of us learned our practical economic lessons during the period of unprecedented boom and social progress from World War II through the mid-1960s. We came to take expansion for granted, regarding rapid economic growth, relative social harmony, and continuing political stability as the expected norm. There were occasional recessions, to be sure, but the steady waves of expansion carried us over and beyond their troughs to new highs.

We must discard such rosy expectations. The 1950s and the 1960s will not provide a fruitful model for the coming decade or two. The 1920 and 1930s, with their economic gyrations, political instability, and social unrest, may well be more pertinent. We have not experienced the soup lines and massive unemployment of the Great Depression, of course, and the impact of decline has been much more varied and diffuse than it was during the 1930s. But institutional sclerosis and continuing economic instability indicate that we are in an economic crisis nonetheless.

Others, apparently, have reached similar conclusions. Few used to speak about "capitalism" during the boom years because most took "capitalism" for granted. The word has since been re-admitted to polite company. Magazines ask, "is capitalism in trouble?'' Business executives worry out loud about its future. More than three fifths of those polled in 1970 agreed that the economy was in "a real crisis."

Economic decline has continued for nearly twenty years. It is time for analysis both of its causes and programs for revival to catch up with the true dimensions of the crisis.

TOWARD A DEMOCRATIC ECONOMY

Down in the country, we used to have to ring the bell if there was trouble or we'd ring it for dinner. You used to pull this rope. Sometime, especially if it was cold, you'd keep pullin' and keep pullin' the bell. You'd think you'd never hear a sound. Maybe by the time your hands got raw almost, you'd hear a little tinklin' of the bell. That's just the way I visualize the community. We all keep pullin' at the rope and our hands are gettin' raw, but you do hear a little tinklin.' It does give you some hope that after a while the bell is gonna ring. We gotta do it, we must do it, we have no other choice. As my father said, "If you're the only one doin' it, the only one left in the world to do it, you must do it." We gotta keep pullin'. And I believe the bell will ring.
—Retired community organizer in Chicago[16]

If there's ever gonna be change in America, it's gonna be cause every community in America's ready for it and—boom! There's gonna be a big tidal wave, and it's just gonna crash down on Washington, and the people are finally gonna be heard.
—Community organizer[17]

Our Economic Bill of Rights cannot be separated from the analysis on which it rests. We have argued that symptoms of economic decline in the United States reflect a real structural crisis—a crisis resulting from the erosion of the postwar corporate system and its relations to domination. Some kind of restructuring of the U.S. economy is necessary before real and lasting economic recovery can begin.

We now face two distinct paths toward restructuring. *Pro-business* programs share three basic principles: profit-led growth, market-based allocation, and arms for economic power. At their best, these principles force the majority who can least afford it to finance and sustain future economic recovery. At their worst and most likely, these pro-business strategies will dramatically increase the costs of corporate power in the U.S. economy and pose serious threats to our political democracy. Many readers will find these criticisms plausible. Some will have directly experienced the recent costs of corporate efforts to restore their own power—through unemployment, falling wages, supervisory harassment, safety hazards on and off the job, or the insecurity of soaring prices and interest rates. But most have hesitated in recent years to express and act upon their frustration and anger. "Have they an alternative?" President Reagan asked of his critics.

The answer is yes. We have outlined a detailed *democratic alternative* to trickle-down economics. For all its twenty-four points and detailed proposals, our Economic Bill of Rights is based on a simple set of underlying strategies:

- A program for economic recovery must make use of *all* our resources and *all* our economic potential. With a clear commitment of *economic security and equity*, we can make the economy work for all of us. Without such a commitment, we fight with each other over the crumbs.
- Work commitment is a serious problem. Our approach is to lay down the whip of unemployment, to find more productive work for the armies of supervisors, and to provide workers with a real and lasting stake in their performance and output by moving quickly toward fundamentally *democratic and productive work relations*. A democratic alternative offers workers a real opportunity to determine their economic fate.
- We cannot pursue full employment or workplace democracy without being able to control the resources we need.

Private profitability is not a safe or reasonable guide to a healthy and decent economic recovery. Effective mechanisms are required for *democratic planning in a democratic economy*—mechanisms for determining our needs and investing to meet them.

- We must be able to gain control over what we consume as well as how we produce it. This requires that we ensure our *right to a better way of life*—beating swords into good food and a safe environment, creating right and supportive opportunities for free time, supporting our communities instead of tearing them apart. Sector by sector, industry to industry, there are specific and practical steps we can take to improve the usefulness of available goods and services. We do not need more guns. We do not even necessarily need more butter. We need living conditions and social relationships more supportive of our growth as people. Our proposals for more useful goods and services can begin to realize those ambitions.

The four key principles—economical security and equity, democratic and productive work relations, democratic planning, and the right to a better way of life—are clearly attractive. Equally important is that our Economic Bill of Rights *holds together as a whole*. It is internally consistent in that its proposals are mutually reinforcing and the program as a whole can pay for itself. It aims to mobilize and unify progressive groups not by aggregating the particular demands of each group, but by proposing a new approach to economic revitalization which by serving our common interests would heighten our sense of unity.

LOOKING AHEAD

The economic payoff to our program is what makes it possible, not what makes it desirable. The reason why we need a democratic economy has more to do with the quality of life than with the calculus of taxes and expenditures. The easiest way to dramatize the need for a democratic economy and to illustrate the differences among economic alternatives is to give each the benefit of the doubt and project its programs forward. Suppose the monetarist or corporatist or democratic strategy took hold. What would the economy look like in 1990 in each case? How would we experience the fruits of these different plans for economic restructuring? While such projects cannot possible pretend complete accuracy or anticipate all possible developments, this exercise can at least clarify and help concretize the choices we face.

The *monetarist* program is at least comprehensive, so there is the least to project. Between 1983 and 1990, there would be a long period of continued deflation and high unemployment while we waited for the cold bath to take final effect. Not even the monetarists are willing to predict how long it will take, but the Thatcher program had been in place for more than three years by the end of 1982, and it had succeeded in doing little more than flattening the British economy. While we wait—until 1986 or 1987 or beyond—unemployment would continue to be the lot of between 20 and 30 million people a year (nearly 25 million were unemployed at some point during 1982). It is highly likely, under monetarist auspices, that we would build more prisons to contain those who can least tolerate the consequences of continued stagflation; even if we simply project recent (1979–81) rates of increase in incarceration, without assuming any further accelera- tion as a consequence of sustained monetarist ice water, there would be more than 750,000 people in prisons and jails in the United States in 1990, a 50 percent increase over the present population. Similar projects suggest that there would be roughly 3.5 million under correctional jurisdiction—including prisons, probation, and parole—the equivalent of the total size of the army at the peak of the Vietnam War.[18]

Under the monetarist program, there would undoubtedly be more cuts in social programs—leaving millions in 1990 without any kind of public support. Women and minorities would be especially hard hit by these cuts. The feminization of poverty would accelerate. The decay of schools and parks and the eclipse of public life would usher in the era of the shopping mall as our most vibrant social and cultural institution. Withering public support for the arts, and for any but the most applied research, would increasingly reduce both beauty and wisdom to marketable commodities.

Although the monetarists claim to support small business, large corporations would be much more likely to weather a continued monetarist deflation than small firms; it is therefore likely that large corporations would have even greater economic power in 1990 than today, with virtually no government restraints on how they spend their money or what they do with their power.

Perhaps the most pertinent project is the most speculative: A monetarist United States in 1990 would be tough and acrimonious, threaded with hardship and divisions, girding for outbreaks of social protest, mean-spirited in public policy and tough-handed in treating (and confining) those who protest. Foreign policy, we can assume, would be no less "firm." Ours would be a bitter, distrustful society, full of contention and selfishness. Monetarists promote a reign of creative individualism. We project a world of grief, strife, and shame.

What would a *corporatist* United States look and feel like in 1990?

The (roughly) two hundred largest corporations would have enormous power—probably controlling something like 70–75 percent of total industrial assets.[19] A cozy circle of the national "leadership" from corporations, those unions included in the new social contract, and the ruling political elites—would tightly control economic decisions and economic debate. More than 20 percent of all employees would probably occupy managerial and supervisory positions, with more than a quarter of national income devoted to their salaries. Probably only about one sixth of the work force would be unionized.[20]

A national investment agency—the child of the Reconstruction Finance Corporation—would play a central role in determining which industries received the most public support. Those decisions would themselves be based on an analysis of the world market, not of domestic needs. Trade would probably have increased to nearly one fifth of total national product, exposing us even more to the vagaries of world trade patterns and world prices beyond our control. There might be a fairly decent program of income maintenance to support those who could not find stable employment at adequate wages, but there would probably be relatively few other public programs to provide for social needs. Between now and 1990 family and neighborhood ties would be sundered as people continually moved around in search of work during a period of transition and restructuring. We would know far less about the people around us—both on and off the job—and far more about the daily television fare.

Most of our lives would bear the imprint of the top-down approach of corporatism. Most of us would work in large bureaucracies with elaborate rules and standards. Leaders would make decisions for us, filling the air with somber appeals for our support in the "national interest" or a "forward-looking America." The corporatist program would inaugurate the era of Big Brother in a pin-striped suit.

Is it possible to make parallel kinds of projections about a *democratic* economy in 1990?

Economic life would be more decentralized than now, organized more around community institutions. There would be more concentration on the projection of basic goods and services, responding to local community needs—both because there would be a much more equal distribution of income and because private profitability would play a much smaller role in investment allocation. Both private and community enterprises would be turning, for example, toward safe and inexpensive food packaging, small-scale computer production for home and business needs, decent and much more varied housing, development of new kinds of equipment for tapping renewable energy sources, and a wide variety of goods and services for entertainment and recreation. Public funds would provide more services for child care and the elderly, for recreational facilities, for community health care and preventive health training, for lifelong education and skills training, and for serving people's transport needs in more flexible ways.

Much more important, we think, people would be actively involved in a much wider variety of institutions affecting economic decisions—in work teams implementing cooperative work agreements, in union investment boards allocating both pension funds and collective profit shares, in the boards of community enterprises and community investment agencies, in hearings on consumption needs, and in a wide variety of public agencies aimed at determining priorities for public programs. Many more economic decisions would be made at the local and community level, with active—and, we assume, lively—political debate about their directions. Communities would begin to acquire much more focused definition in people's lives—both because they constituted much more of a locus of economic activities and because there would be much less economic pressure to move around from place to place.

The average work week would have fallen considerably; correspondingly, a boom may be anticipated in sports, cooking, dieting, block parties, local politics, and the pursuit of self-understanding. Complaints would be heard that reduced work hours have been offset by more meetings. Flexible work-time options would have opened new opportunities for the sharing of child-rearing tasks and for making more productive use of the creative energies of older people.

Perhaps most important, a democratic economic program would have begun to transform the waste in our present economy into useful goods and services. Substantial progress would have been made toward the full-employment goal of 2 percent, making the right to a job at decent pay a reality. An adequate program of child care and payment for single-parent home child care would have begun to broaden options facing parents. People would be able, in short, to move beyond nagging worries about where the next paycheck is coming from and to pay more attention to improving the quality of their lives. A democratic economy could be on track, by 1990, because all of us would be contributing to its direction.

THE POLITICS OF A DEMOCRATIC ALTERNATIVE

We image that this portrait of a democratic economy, however schematic, will look attractive to many readers. But is it a serious possibility? Could we actually achieve such a dramatic shift in the direction of our economy between now and 1990?

We would be quite unrealistic if we *promised* such a prospect. Too many people believe that it is necessary to tighten our belts, and corporations have too much power in this country, for us to be wildly optimistic about the prospects for our Economic Bills of Rights.

We want to emphasize, instead, that popular mobilization around a democratic alternative like ours is *essential* to improve the prospects for any kind of progressive change and any kind of progressive movement in the United States. We base this conclusion on our evaluation of both the possibilities for real progressive change and the problems which such a mobilization would face.

We think there are realistic possibilities for widespread mobilization around our Economic Bill of Rights for three important reasons.

First, we think that there is already widespread popular support for many of the specific proposals included in our program. Consider the following poll results:[21]

- As many as two-thirds of respondents have consistently favored price controls if they would help curb inflation.
- Two-thirds responding to a 1975 poll said they would prefer to work in an "employee-controlled company" while only 20 percent preferred an "investor-controlled" company. In a 1976 survey, half of workers answered yes when asked whether it was a good idea for corporations in America to become more like what they are in Europe, in offering workers more involvement in corporate governance. In 1979, 74 percent answered yes. More than half have said that they would "definitely" or "probably" support a presidential candidate who "advocated employee ownership and self-management."
- Almost twice as many in a 1982 poll said there was "too much" defense spending as said there was "too little."

These results are not really surprising, but they get little attention because questions are so rarely asked.

There is comparable evidence to suggest that people are ready for a change.[22]

- In 1966, 26 percent of U.S. adults felt that "people running the country don't care what happens to people like me." By 1977, that figure had soared to 60 percent.
- In the early 1960s, 28 percent agreed that "government is run for the benefit of a few big interests." By the late 1970s, the percentage had climbed to 65 percent.
- In a 1975 poll, 41 percent agreed that there should be a "major adjustment" in the economy, and only 17 percent thought that we should "keep it as it is." (We do not think they got the adjustment they were looking for.)

Second, our analysis of the waste burden casts new light on the latent potential of the U.S. economy. If there were not so much waste, we would face some very tough zero-sum choices about who sacrifices for whom in a program of economic restructuring. But we have argued that there was more than a trillion dollars of waste in the U.S. economy in 1980—almost half of useful output in that year. The opportunity to transform that waste into useful output or increased free time provides plenty of margin with which we could chart new directions and institute new programs. Pro-business strategists argue the need for regressive redistribution. We argue the possibility of moving beyond the waste land.

Third, we think that clear discussion of and mobilization around a *comprehensive* democratic economic program could help solve some critical problems which have recently hampered progressive movements in the United States. One problem has been our hestitation and uncertainty; some have doubted the feasibility of a democratic alternative, while others have assumed that it would be too costly. Our program lifts the burden of defensiveness under which proponents of progressive change have had to labor in recent times. Progressive political activists have continually run up against the charge that their proposals would be costly to the economy in terms of economic efficiency or growth. We have shown that there need not be such a discouraging tradeoff; building a more humane society is part and parcel of the process of revitalizing the economy.

Another problem has been our fragmentation, bred in part by the persistent and nagging fear that what one group gains will come at another group's expense. We do not pretend that such suspcicions will disappear overnight. But we do think that mobilization for a comprehensive democratic economic program such as the one we have elaborated here will provide the most favorable possible opportunity for beginning to overcome some of those divisions and mutual recriminations. Simply knowing that there is a democratic alternative to regressive distribution, in the first instance, makes an enormous difference. Much more important, the possibility of real job security through active full-employment policies helps remove the occasion for much of the fragmentation and mutual suspicion. Given employment security, for example, union members could recognize that job opportunities for everyone can help sustain rapid growth and do not pose a threat to their own employment. Given a more securely protected natural environment, correspondingly, environmentalists will be less likely to see the insistent demands of lower-income people for jobs and for a higher material standard of living as a drain on limited natural resources and as a threat to ecological balance.

The more an economic program recognizes the needs of disparate groups as *interdependent*, in short, the greater the likelihood of building a strong economic movement among a broad majority of workers and citizens. The key is rather like the solution to the famous prisoner's dilemma: if everyone acts individually, then each individual's gain comes at someone else's expense and rational behavior leads to a suboptimal outcome. If people perceive, in contrast, that common efforts can make everyone better off, then it is possible to cooperate in attaining the best solution for all.

If this is the promise, there are also clearly problems in pursuing something like our Economic Bill of Rights.

One is that corporate opposition will accelerate with every flicker of interest in taking democracy seriously. Corporations will warn grimly about chaos and inefficiency, about disruption and short-sightedness, about the primacy of profitability in any program for restructuring. They will blackmail us by threatening to move their businesses. They will warn of capital flight overseas. Financial speculation may spread ripples of destabilizing effects. Capital may even consider, as mobilization around a democratic alternative mounts, moving politically to curtail popular rights and abridge democratic freedoms. While we are disinclined to warn of such a political Armageddon, we think it is equally foolish to ignore the lessons of history and the evidence of recent corporate concerns: corporations value profits more than democracy, and it is certainly possible that they will move to curtail the latter before they will agree to reduced priority for the former.

The best defense of democracy is more democracy. By revitalizing local, state, and federal government functions as well as promoting the proliferation of community organization and the expansion of union membership, we think our program would be an essential part of a viable strategy for turning back corporate encroachments on democratic rights.

The defense against capital strike (noninvestment) and capital flight is more complicated. Both capital strike and capital flight, if not countered, result in short-run declines in employment and long-run declines in productive capacity. But they can be countered. The runaway shop does not itself move to greener pastures; what moves is the management and the money. But neither management nor money produces output: machines and labor do. The plant and equipment as well as the work force which knows how to use it generally stay put. Our program would greatly facilitate workers in assuming ownership and democratic control of plants threatened by closedowns. Our public-investment programs at local and federal levels could compensate for shortfalls in private investment, while our subsidies to selected private investments would discourage capital strike in strategic economic sectors. The increased unemployment stemming from short-run declines in the demand for goods and services resulting from an investment strike can be countered by familiar short-run fiscal and monetary policy, as well as by the expansion of public employment.

The disruptive effects of a capital strike could be tempered; but a massive refusal to invest would most likely promote a serious economic and political crisis, the resolution of which might require a considerable expansion of the public sector of the economy. Whether capitalists would willingly provide such a crisis depends of course on their estimate of the chances that the democratic economic program could thereby be discredited. We think the vast majority of the people of the United States would be at least as likely to blame the capitalists and press for further democratization of investment.

Another problem likely to confront a democratic economic restructuring is that the bases for division among different popular groups are deeply rooted and will not evaporate as soon as we mobilize around a common economic agenda. Sexism is real, creating a vast legacy of suspicion and conflict among men and women. Racism is real, posing huge barriers to cooperation among whites, Blacks, Hispanics, Asians, Native Americans, and other minorities. Ageism, a less familiar source of problems, is also real, fostering sharp and increasing divisions among the young, the old, and those in between.

Moderating these problems will take time and commitment. Our economic proposals do not address all of their roots. We do not offer an exhaustive social program here. We have focused on but one problem—the poor performance of the U.S. economy—and have presented concrete and comprehensive proposals for a democratic approach to solving those problems. Our program in this sense is not exhaustive but essential. It does not deal with all our needs, but it provides a basis for dealing successfully with one of the most important. Mobilization around the democratic economic alternative, we think, can provide the most favorable possible position from which to deal with the rest of our problems.

Many will hesitate, wondering if less sweeping programs could do the job. We wish it were the case. We do not enjoy confrontation for its own sake. We do not relish such sweeping challenges to the established economic powers. We, like many others, are pushed in these directions quite simply because the imperatives of the pro-business strategies leave so little room for compromise. They want more wealth and more power. Their strategies for serving those ends require that the rest of us sacrifice our welfare and our rights to augment theirs. The pro-business strategies insist that we act out the zero-sum illusion. They call for subordinating other economic interests to their own bottom line. Their bottom line, as we have seen throughout the book, does not pay much attention to the needs or concerns of the great majority of us.

The economics of greed has reigned long enough. Large corporations dominated the postwar era and we are now paying the price. It is time to assert our own priorities, to propel the economy in a more rational and democratic direction. We could succumb once again to the costs of corporate power—moved either by the spirit of compromise or by a sense of political weakness—but these costs will simply recur and undoubtedly rise if we do. It is time instead for a *real* change in the way we run our economy.

We are committed to traditional popular values of democracy, equality, community, security, efficiency, and liberty. We refuse to believe that these values must be abandoned or compromised in the search for economic revitalization. Our analysis of the possibility of moving beyond the waste land convinces us that a successful and effective program for economic recovery can advance these traditional popular values, not suppress them. Popular groups can build a decent society without undercutting its economic viability. Democracy is not a cost but an essential ingredient of economic recovery.

APPENDIX: THE RELEVANCE OF HOURLY INCOME

Economists generally measure the average level of well-being in a society by its real per capita GNP—the gross national product divided by total population and expressed in terms of the (constant) prices of a particular year, so that year-to-year changes reflect changes in real output rather than just changes in prices.

It is well known that there are serious shortcomings to the use of real GNP as a measure of total well-being. For example, this measure does not take into account many factors affecting our standard of living because these factors are not readily quantifiable in dollar terms. Excluded are such important considerations as the amount of free time available to people, the quality of community life and working conditions, the condition of the physical environment, and the degree of people's personal security. Moreover, the GNP does include many goods and services that make no significant positive contribution to our standard of living—notably military weapons. Indeed, the true benefits of many goods and services—their "use values," in Marxian terms—are poorly reflected by the prices—or "exchange values"—at which they are measured in the national accounting system.

Dividing real GNP by total population to measure average well-being is also subject to serious reservations. Real per capita GNP tells us how much real GNP is available on average for each person in the society, but it takes no account of the amount of time or effort that went into production of the output. The same level of real per capita GNP might be achieved—under different circumstances—by people working an average forty-hour week or an average thirty-hour week. Surely a society would be better off in the latter case, for then people would have much more time to engage in other pursuits such as child care, education, recreation, or home improvement. And even if a given level of per capita GNP were produced by the same number of hours of work, the amount of effort required by the work could vary widely depending on the nature and pace of the average job.

An ideal measure of average well-being would meet these shortcomings of real GNP per capita first by reevaluating the numerator—real GNP—in terms of the use value of the goods and services produced, also taking into account any changes in the social and physical environment that affect the quality of life. Second, the denominator—population—would be revised to take account of the sacrifice of time and effort actually involved in producing the (broadly defined) output of the society.

Such a task of reevaluation was well beyond the scope of our project.[23] But to avoid some of the most serious biases in the conventional measure, we made three adjustments in real per capital GNP to arrive at our preferred concept of "hourly income."

First, we subtracted from GNP that portion accounted for by the "capital-consumption allowance" to obtain what economists call the "net-national product" (NNP). The logic of this correction is that the output corresponding to the capital-consumption allowance does not add to society's welfare. It serves instead to maintain at its previous level the society's stock of physical structures and equipment, by making up for deterioration through wear and tear during the year. NNP measures the amount of output available for consumption (private and public) and net investment (net additions to the society's stock of structures and equipment).

Second, we used a different price index from the conventional one to adjust for the effects of price inflation and thus to express NNP in real terms. The conventional "implicit price deflator" for NNP reflects changes in the prices of the components of output produced in the economy. But to measure the value of the output from the point of view of those who use the corresponding income for consumption or investment, it is preferable to use an index that reflects changes in prices of the goods and services *purchased*. Since some produced output is exported and some purchased goods and services are imported, the purchase price deflator can differ from the conventional product price deflator if the terms of trade between exported and imported goods (i.e., their relative prices) change over time. To underline our use of a purchase price rather than a product price deflator, we refer to our resulting measure as real net national *income* rather than product.

Finally, we chose to divide real net national income by the total number of hours that people were at work in the economy rather than by the total number of people in the society. The logic of this approach was suggested above. Increases in real income achieved without any increase in work time—i.e., increases in real income per hour of work—are clearly beneficial (assuming no deterioration in working conditions). But increases in real income achieved by increasing average work time—which will show up in increased real income per capita—are not so unambiguously beneficial, for they involve the sacrifice of time for other activities. Dividing by work hours thus provides a better measure of the welfare implications of a rise in real income than does dividing by population.

The three steps just described can be readily applied to convert real GNP per capita into our preferred measure of real net national income per hour of work, or—for short—hourly income.[24] Hourly income is still far from a perfect measure of people's average well-being, but we are convinced that it represents a significant improvement over the conventional measure.

NOTES

1. Quoted in New York *Post*, January 23, 1978, p. 29.

2. Quote in *Business Week*, January 15, 1978, p. 64.

3. Quoted in William Bowen, "The Decade Ahead: Not So Bad If We Do Things Right," *Fortune*, October 8, 1979, p. 88.

4. Data on 1981 unemployment during the year are from U.S. Bureau of Labor Statistics, "One in Five Persons in Labor Force Experienced Some Unemployment in 1981," USDL 82-255, July 20, 1982.

5. See Institute for Labor Education and Research, *What's Wrong with the U.S. Economy?* (Boston: South End Press. 1982), p. xi and notes, for analysis of the income sources of the bottom 90 percent of U.S. households in 1980. Underlying data are from Internal Revenue Service, *Statistics of Income, Individual Income Tax Returns*.

6. Based on *Employment and Training Report*, 1981, p. 213.

7. Some might argue that a series on hours should use adults of working age in the denominator, not total population. We would argue theoretically that our measure is the correct one, since the working responsibilities of employees in the economy as a whole are to provide output for the economy as a whole, not

just themselves. If more people within a household must work in order to sustain household living standards, then the welfare of that household has probably declined. For our measure of aggregate hours for 1980–81.

8. *Economic Report*, 1982, B–28, B–31.

9. *Business Week*, January 28, 1980, p. #73. Following quote from Rapping is from the same source.

10. Hourly income—defined as real net national income per hour of work—is very closely related to productivity—defined as real net domestic output per hour of work. The only differences involve three technical distinctions:

　　a. Real net national *income* is the nominal value of net additional income/product divided by a *purchased*-output price index, while real *output* is the same nominal value of net national income/product divided by a *produced*-output price index;

　　b. *National* income includes income received by U.S. nationals from their activities abroad (e.g., foreign investment) and excludes income received by foreigners from their activities within the United States; domestic output includes output produced by foreigners in the United States but excludes output produced by U.S. nationals abroad; and

　　c. The denominator in hourly income is hours of work by U.S. nationals anywhere, while the denominator in productivity is hours of work by all people within the United States.

11. These productivity-growth rates were calculated from annual data tabulated in *Economic Report*, 1982, Table B–40. Note that the productivity figures apply to persons at work in the private business sector, while the hourly-income figures cited earlier apply to the whole U.S. national economy; the difference is accounted for primarily by the government sector.

12. The industries include agriculture, mining, manufacturing, transportation, government, utilities, finance and real estate, trade, communications, construction, and other services.

13. Although this information is compiled by U.S. Department of Commerce largely on the basis of information collected by the Bureau of Labor Statistics, some scholars argue that (1)

the index of manufacturing productivity compiled by the Federal Reserve Board (FRB) is more reliable because it is based more fully and directly on physical measures of output growth, as opposed to dollar measures deflated by estimated price indexes, and (2) the measure of hours (in the denominator of productivity estimates) should reflect hours worked by production workers only—not supervisory and nonproductive personnel. But even if we use the FRB index of real manufacturing output, and divide it by hours of production workers in manufacturing to arrive at an alternative manufacturing productivity index, we find that projectivity growth still shows a definite pattern of slowdown: from 4.3 percent in 1948-66 to 4.1 percent in 1966-73 to 2.8 percent in 1973-79 (as compared with the Department of Commerce figures of 2.9 percent, 3.3 percent, and 1.5 percent). Because FRB data are available only for the manufacturing sector, we could not make use of their series for our analysis of overall productivity growth. But we have made a point of analyzing productivity in terms of real output per hour of production workers rather than all workers.

14. OECD, *National Accounts, 1950-1980*, Vol. 1 (Paris OECD, 1982).

15. OECD, *National Accounts*, Vol. I (1982), p. 88. The comparisons are in current prices at current international exchange rates.

16. From Studs Terkel, *American Dreams Lost and Found* (New York: Pantheon, 1981), pp. 276-77.

17. From Terkel, p. 312.

18. These estimates are based on straight line projections of the increase in two categories—those in federal and state prisons and local jails and those on parole and probation—from 1979 to 1981. The data come from Department of Justice, Bureau of Justice Statistics, *Bulletin*, 1982.

19. This projection is based on the assumption that the increase in the concentration of large corporate ownership between now and 1990 will be comparable to the increase after the last two crises.

20. These two projections are based on a projection of the recent data on the trend in the union membership share of the nonagricultural labor force.

21. These poll results come, respectively, from the *New York Times*, November 8, 1979, p. A16; Jeremy Rifkin, *Own Your Own Job* (New York: Bantam, 1975), p. 176; *In These Times*, April 4–10, 1979, p. 8; and the Gallup Poll, Survey 191–G, Q.10, conducted March 12–15, 1982.

22. A summary of these and other related results may be found in Daniel Yankelovich, *New Rules* (New York: Random House, 1981), pp. 95 ff.

23. For an interesting effort along these lines to develop a measure of "net economic welfare," see W. Nordhaus and J. Tobin, "Is Growth Obsolete?," in the National Bureau of Economic Research, *Fiftieth Anniversary Colloquium* New York: Columbia University Press, 1972), Vol. V.

24. We calculated annual figures for hourly income in the U.S. economy as follows. First, we divided GNP (NIPA, Table 1.1) by the implicit price deflator for gross domestic purchases (NIPA, Table 7.3). Then we subtracted the constant-price value of capital consumption allowances with capital consumption adjustment (NIPA, Table 5.2). Finally, we divided the resulting real net national income by the total hours worked by persons engaged in production (NIPA, Table 6.13). The total hours figures for 1980 and 1981 were obtained by extrapolation from the 1979 figure in the same proportion as the "manhours of employed labor force" series published by *BLS*.

AFFIRMATIVE ACTION AND THE POLITICS OF THE CONTEMPORARY ERA

Marguerite Ross Barnett
and Linda Faye Williams

INTRODUCTION

Affirmative action has been one of the most widely controversial and, ultimately, most important concepts in contemporary American public policy. Critics of affirmative action define it as a quota system, but implementation of affirmative action policy has actually fallen far short of imposing fixed occupational allotments or quotas. A more accurate understanding of affirmative action should focus on two key elements: the normative emphasis on equality and nondiscrimination and the administrative emphasis on implementation through more targeted (goal-oriented), careful, and institutionalized recruitment procedures. Affirmative action, therefore, is a generic name given to a range of approaches in the public and private sector designed to eliminate discriminatory practices and to correct the effects of past biased practices by using specific planning and recruitment mechanisms and procedures such as goals, timetables, affirmative action committees, and so on.

Affirmative action, in the most general sense, has substantial legal underpinning. The Civil Rights Act of 1964 was the first enforceable federal law against job discrimination. Title VI and Title VII of that Act provided concrete enforcement powers to a

35

newly created, but limited, Equal Employment Opportunity Commission. Executive Orders 11246, 11375, and 11478 and the Equal Employment Act of 1972 all furthered and expanded affirmative action. In 1978, President Carter's Reorganization Plan No. 1, 43 Federal Register 19807, abolished the EEO Coordinating Council and transferrred its function to a, by then, stronger Equal Employment Opportunity Commission headed by Eleanor Holmes Norton. In addition, a number of significant court cases, although originating as challenges to affirmative action on the part of white males charging reverse discrimination, have upheld certain forms of voluntary affirmative action plans.

Despite the importance and the controversial nature of affirmative action policy, the literature on the subject has focused mainly on philosophical questions and analysis of affirmative action in relationship to concepts of democracy, justice, and/or equality; attitudes toward various plans on the part of employers and employees and other groups; and discussions of the success or failure of affirmative action plans in relationship to their method of implementation and/or their impact on statistical representation of minorities and women. While all of these approaches have produced valuable insights, they have not enriched our understanding of affirmative action in relation to the dynamics of political, economic, and social change. Furthermore, very little literature in this area has contributed to a more general understanding of affirmative action as an aspect of racial public policy. This is particularly distressing for those interested in the interface between affirmative action and other racial public policy issues and processes. Finally, there is very little in the literature that could be used as a "theory" of affirmative action.

Richard Burkey described four types of racial public policy in his study of the subject.[1] Although Burkey's typology provides a useful way of categorizing racial public policies, it is a static framework. Also, it focuses on specific policies such as affirmative action as ends in themselves rather than as examples of *types* within more broadly conceived categories.

In contrast to the Burkey perspective, Barnett has suggested a categorization of public policy in this area into "ethnic" policies, "collective" policies, "institutional" policies and "structural" policies.[2] Central to this distinction among types of public policy are the concepts of divisible and indivisible benefits as developed by Robert Dahl:

> Certain benefits are divisible in such a way that they can be allocated to specific individuals; jobs, contracts, and welfare payments are examples of divisible benefits. Other benefits are more clearly indivisible; parks, playgrounds, schools, national defense and foreign policies, for example, either cannot be or ordinarily are not allocated by dividing up benefits piecemeal and allocating various pieces to specific individuals.[3]

Ethnic policies are those which provide divisible benefits, that is, benefits to individuals. The emphasis is on individual access. Collective policies provide indivisible benefits to an entire racial group.

In addition to differentiaing racial policies according to their locus of impact (divisible versus indivisible), they may also be usefully distinguised by the type and degree of change the policy creates in the total socioeconomic system. Incremental changes are defined here as those changes that do not create differences in the *regime* (kind of government); the *political community* (the people included in the legitimate body of people with whom one solves problems); the organizing principle of the *economic system*; or the *political system* itself. Incremental policies may marginally change the way in which resources are distributed or the authorities who distribute political benefits, but do not change the nature of what is defined as a political benefit or the "rules of the game" governing the overall process. Systemic, fundamental, or non-incremental change, in contrast, transforms significant structures or systems in society.

By examining the two dimensions (divisible vs. indivisible benefits and incremental vs. systemic impact) together, we derive a table with four major types of racial public policy.

TABLE I

Types of Racial Public Policy
Public Policies

Locus of Benefits

	Divisible Benefits	Indivisible Benefits
Incremental	Ethnic Policies I	Collective Policies II
Systemic	Institutional III	Structural IV

Ethnic Policies. Ethnic policies are divisible, incremental policies based on the premise that the ethnic political experience and policy is a model for racial public policy. An example would be the Great Society program, which distributed material benefits to individuals without changing social, political or economic systems or basic structures. In that sense it was analogous to machine politics, which distributed material benefits to ethnic groups to win their loyalty and support.

Collective Policies. Collective policies provide indivisible benefits to racial group members because of their racial group membership. These policies, however, do not change the system in fundamental ways. Benefits from these policies are not divided and allocated to separate racial group members although individuals can derive benefits from these polices. Civil rights legislation mandating nondisrimination would come under this category.

Institutional Policies. Institutional policies are policies which have the potential of changing the "rules of the game," restructuring some fundamental aspect of the system itself and in so doing providing benefits to individuals. We shall argue that affirmative action policy fits into this category. Institutional policies have the potential of changing the life chances for individuals and changing subsystems or modifying system behavior at a level short of total restructuring.

Structural Policies. Structural policies challenge, confront, attack, and would fundamentally alter the structure of racial hierarchy and provide benefits to a racial group as a collectivity. The termination of black slavery and passage of the 13th, 14th, and 15th Amendments together were a set of structural policies which transformed the position of Blacks as a collectivity. Structural policies change the life chances for all members of a racial group and alter basic aspects of the political system

In the American political system structural public policy is a rare phenomenon because American politics is usually characterized by incremental policy and demands for divisible political benefits. Racial public policy has been an exception to the normal public policy pattern because it has been shaped by continuing Black demands for fundamental change. Demands for change from slave status to free status, dismantlement of the system of legal segregation, incorporation of Blacks into the economic and political systems, all require change in the regime (rules of the game) and political community. They go beyond demands for isolated rule change or for an alteration in conceptual understanding by an individual or individuals making up the political leadership (i.e. political authorities). Our theory of affirmative action leads us to hypothesize that because institutional and structural policies are rare policy forms within the American context, efforts to implement them are (incorrectly) modeled on the more commonly found ethnic policies. This process, we believe, leads to the destabilization of institutional and structural policies.

In order to begin what we hope is a more penetrating and theoretically useful dialogue regarding racial public policy, we shall suggest an interpretation of the origins, mode of implementation, and decline of affirmative action. As mentioned previously, we see affirmative action as a form of *institutional racial policy*. We begin by briefly discussing the structure of U.S. racial hierarchy, trace the political origins of affirmative action, discuss the impact of affirmative action in the labor market as a whole, and conclude by suggesting what affirmative action indicates about racial public policy in general and institutional types of racial policies specifically. Our discussion of affirmative action will focus primarily on the Afro-American experience.

STRUCTURAL DIMENSIONS OF RACIAL PUBLIC POLICY

Historically, American racial public policy toward Blacks has been concerned with three major problems: (1) defining the meaning, rights, and obligations of a slave class within a political setting ideologically influenced by philosophies stressing the equality of free individuals; (2) definition of citizenship status of the freed slaves, including "Black codes" and various forms of legal segregation; and (3) dismantling of legal segregation and destruction of dual citizenship. The above three issues indicate how American public policy has been historically shaped in fundamental ways by the Black presence. In each historical period, Afro-Americans have been at the cutting edge of social transformation, highlighting underlying contradictions through crises raised by their very existence as part of the social fabric.

Blacks were slaves in a "free" society; a stigmatized collectivity in a society emphasizing individualism; and a hierarchically-ranked, supposedly inferior racial group in a society of substantial white ethnic egalitarianism. Certainly, no other group in American society has been subjected to the extreme form of economic exploitation suffered by Blacks. Each change in the relationship of Blacks to the economic system has been a transmogrification of the form but not the substance of economic subjugation: slave to cash tenant and sharecropper; cash tenant/sharecropper to low level rural laborer, and finally, urban worker, plagued by low wages and high unemployment. Sadly, many of the Black poor "progressed" from slave labor to cheap labor (and many to no labor at all).

In one period of American history after another, controversy over the direction of the nation has been intrinsically linked to conflict over the fate of Blacks: the debate among the framers of the Constitution involved the question whether Blacks were men or merely property; the "free soil" conflict was related to slavery and finally to the Civil War; the inconclusive Hayes-Tilden election and the Compromise of 1877 restored Southern white political hegemony and the Democratic party to the Reconstruction South; and recently, the "massive resistance" and states rights movements led by Southern elites against the national government's civil rights efforts in the post-World War II era posed basic questions regarding the distribution of power among national and state and local governments.

This admittedly truncated discussion of the historical relationship between race and public policy underscores our starting point: the Afro-American presence has continually raised fundamental questions regarding the nature of the regime, the composition of the political community, and even the very persistence of the American political system. Analysis of the structural relationship of Afro-Americans to the society as a whole suggests why their presence has been problematical and system-challenging for the U.S.

Barnett has argued that Afro-Americans are structurally differentiated, that is, their group position has been fundamentally different from that of white ethnic groups:

In structural terms, Blacks are qualitatively different from white ethnic groups. For white ethnic groups there is no nationwide ideology that ranks specific groups. In contrast, racism is a pervasive ideology that ranks Blacks as a group below all others because it assumes the inherent genetic inferiority of Blacks. The stress on phenotypic differences (in this case skin color) and its expression in racist ideology determines the character of white–black interaction in every part of the country. From the earliest days, definitions of humanness were crucial to decisions about the composition of the political community. Racism, therefore, is a fundamental factor that makes the black situation distinctly different from that of all white ethnic groups.[4]

Structural differentiation of Afro-Americans is hierarchical and collective:

... hierarchy specifically means the existence of a principle (racism) that ranks groups consistently and pervasively, *and is enforceable through social control*. Collectivism means that each individual member of a group is treated according to some principle that defines the whole. Ultimate meaning resides in the definition of the characteristics ascribed to the group as a whole.[5]

Related to, buttressing, and profoundly integrated with the sociological aspects of differentiation outlined above are elements of class exploitation. In economic terms, Blacks are the most superexploited sector of the working class. To expand on this point, we must begin by asking what are the current requirements of the capitalist mode of production in the United States and what is the relationship of Blacks to that mode of production? This issue is extremely complex but we shall attempt to be succinct.

An important key to unraveling this problem is analysis of the virtually uncontrolled inflation characteristic of capitalism today. This inflation results from two major factors: the excess of capital and a shortage of investment opportunities and the necessity for ever faster growth inherent in monopoly capitalism. We advance the hypothesis that Black labor has a specific role as a basic deflationary factor in controlling these critical effects of inflation. Thus we make two main suggestions: first, Black workers play a critical role since they can be superexploited. This enables employers to pay a proportionately smaller price for the reproduction of the labor force and for increase in the duration and intensity of the labor performed by Black workers. Second, Black workers act as workers and consumers in ways that mitigate the recessionary/inflationary crisis. They are producers in the expansionary phase of the business cycle yet consume relatively little, thus reducing inflationary pressures.

In the recessionary phase of the cycle, they can be excluded from productive employment with relatively little difficulty—"last hired, first fired." Thus, stated metaphorically, we might argue Black workers act as a "cushion," as an economic "buffer" against the dangers of overproduction. Moreover, Black workers depress wage levels for all workers. In short, the manpower of Black workers acts as a "reserve army" on white workers. That is, the very recourse to Black workers causes a relative lowering of wages, thus contributing to keeping the rate of profit as high as possible. Thus, we begin to see the economic meaning of race and racism in the U.S. At the economic level, the superexploitation of Black labor plays a crucial role in keeping reproduction costs low.

The above review of the dimensions of structural differentiation helps to define the substance and character of Afro-American domination. To be of maximum utility, public policy for Blacks must involve an attempt to vitiate basic aspects of structural subordination, including super-exploitation, racial hierarchy, and collectivism. Analysis of structural and historical factors helps situate our discussion of contemporary public policy toward Afro-Americans by suggesting how we can distinguish qualitative change from quantitative change, systemic from nonsystemic alterations; glamour or symbolic policies from policies that can positively alter life chances for large numbers of Afro-Americans. We now turn to a necessarily brief discussion of the historical and political origins of affirmative action policy.

HISTORICAL AND POLITICAL ORIGINS OF AFFIRMATIVE ACTION

Since the political origins of affirmative action are virtually synonymous with the origins of the civil rights movement, we shall begin our discussion in the post-World War II period when changing economic circumstances, and the political and social ramifications that followed, created mounting unrest among masses of Blacks, eventually culminating in a Black struggle against the Southern "Jim Crow" system. By the mid-1960s, national political leaders responded to the rising tide of Black protest and imposed modernizing political reforms on the South. Their success in doing so was a measure of both the underlying economic transformation which had occurred and the force of Black insurgency.

It should be noted as well that the post-World War II era was one of prosperity for the nation as a whole. After World War II, the United States was the only Western nation which had not been physically devastated. While former imperialist powers such as Britain, France, Germany, Japan, and Holland were recovering from substantial destruction, the United States assumed world economic, military, and political leadership. In fact, the United States doubled its industrial capacity domestically while expanding its economic impact internationally by 600 percent between 1945 and 1965.[6] This tremendous economic growth resulted in massive profits for corporations and businessmen and brought about a generally upward trend in all American groups and sectors, including the Black community.

As economic modernization thrust Blacks out of one socio-economic system and into another, their capacity to resist white domination was substantially enlarged. Controls which were readily enforced in a rural society characterized by dispersion and face-to-face interaction could not be well enforced in the urban community, where the ghetto meant concentration and racial separation. Consequently, "behind the walls of segregated isolation, Negroes were better able to build resistance to subordination."[7]

Protest emerged simultaneously with mass migration. Freed from feudal-like controls characteristic of many parts of the rural South, Blacks began to protest the oppression they had always known. Moreover, segregation in the Northern ghettos provided a degree of security, and concentrated numbers provided a sense of strength. Thus, after the first large migratory wave in the World War I period, Marcus Garvey was able to draw a million northern Blacks into his Universal Negro Improvement Association.

Concentration and separation also generated a Black urban wage worker who contributed to that mass base. One significant result was the gradual emergence of a Black occupational sector which was relatively invulnerable to white power and a sector consisting of clergymen, small entrepreneurs, professionals, and labor leaders. In an earlier period, and particularly in Southern rural society, very few Blacks were located in these occupations and those few were usually dependent on whites. The emergence of an independent or at least semi-independent leadership sector was accompanied by institutional expansion and diversification, and by greater institutional independence from the white community. This development, too, was made possible by the economic base which resulted from concentration and segregation. Churches acquired mass memberships, fraternal and other communal associations proliferated, small business could be sustained, segregated union locals were formed, and a Black press could be nourished. These institutions provided the vehicle to forge solidarity, to define common goals, and to mobilize collective action.

In the evolving history of Black protest, these developing occupational and institutional resources were of crucial importance. The March on Washington movement organized by A. Philip Randolph, President of the Brotherhood of Sleeping Car Porters, is an example. Head of a segregated international union, Randolph could act with considerable immunity from white sanctions and his union could provide financial resources and organizing talent. Acting as couriers and organizers in Northern and Midwestern cities where they stopped over, his trainmen instigated rallies and marches to pressure Roosevelt into issuing an executive order establishing a Fair Employment Practices Commission (FEPC) to ensure Blacks access to wartime defense employment. The Black press was also of critical importance for it almost uniformly supported Randolph and continually featured the movement's activities. With this mobilization under way, greater solidarity across class lines was forged. In these ways, economic modernization, coupled with separation and concentration, both freed Blacks from semifeudal constraints and enabled them to construct the occupational and institutional foundation from which to mount resistance to white oppression.

Despite his uneasiness over how an FEPC would affect defense industries in the South and the possibility of alienating the Southern Congressional delegation, Roosevelt was confronted by the prospect of a march on Washington that would cause considerable national and international embarrassment to a country identified with the struggle for "freedom abroad." With the scheduled march only days away, he conceded and signed an executive order which established an FEPC on June 25, 1941.

Truman and Eisenhower followed Roosevelt in issuing executive orders concerning nondiscrimination in employment. In short, as the numbers of Blacks in the cities grew, their protests began to produce concessions from political leaders.

Yet these concessions did little or nothing to affect America's social fabric. *Thus in 1960, the view was developing that "passive nondiscrimination was not enough." Discrimination, it was recognized, could exist and flourish in the simple absence of positive, that is, "affirmative" action.* Black workers could be free to apply for any job—that is what is meant by equality of opportunity—but if they lacked qualifications due to the cumulative effects of generations of past discrimination, they would still be excluded from the better paying jobs and occupations.

Then in 1960, Kennedy came to power with substantial help from the Black vote. In 1956, it had appeared that Blacks were shifting to the Republican Party, but in 1960 Black voters moved back to the Democrats as Kennedy got 68 percent of their vote, up about eight percentage points from 1956. And the Black vote moved back in just the right places. Thus, if any group had reason to expect presidential action on its behalf, it was Blacks following the election of 1960. Without the huge Black majorities in the key industrial centers of the nation, Kennedy could not have been elected. Still, Kennedy had won office by a narrow margin and white Southern defections had been one cause of his near-defeat. A policy of conciliation toward the South appeared to be the expedient course of action.

Moreover, Kennedy, like earlier Democratic presidents, was concerned that a confrontation with Congress over civil rights would cost him support on other domestic legislation. "The reason was arithmetic . . . To solidify the conservative coalition—by presenting an issue on which Southerners had traditionally sought Republican support, in exchange for Southern opposition to other measures—would doom his whole program."[8] Instead of legislative action, therefore, the President opted for a strategy of executive action:

Kennedy's task was to accomplish so much by Executive Action that the demand for immediate legislation could be kept under control. Power to enforce existing Civil Rights law lay in the Department of Justice, and the hand that would wield it was the Attorney General's. . . . If Kennedy's Attorney General won the confidence of those chiefly concerned with Civil Rights and maintained a strong impression of forward motion in this field, the President could stall on supporting new civil rights legislation until after Congress had approved his social and economic program and that required Southern votes.[9]

INSTITUTIONALIZATION AND OPERATIONALIZATION OF THE CONCEPTS OF EQUAL EMPLOYMENT OPPORTUNITY AND AFFIRMATIVE ACTION: PLANS FOR PROGRESS

It was in the context of post-World War II social, political, and economic changes that President Kennedy decided to issue Executive Order 10925, which established the President's Committee on Equal Employment Opportunity (PCEEO), and it was in that Executive Order that the term *affirmative action* was first used. Although the Executive Order was issued under the signature of President Kennedy, it had been drafted by a number of people, including Lyndon Johnson, Arthur Goldberg, and Hobart Taylor, Jr. Taylor, who later became Executive Director of the President's Committee on Economic Employment Opportunity, added the term *affirmative action* to that executive order.

A longtime friend of Lyndon Johnson, Hobart Taylor, had been asked by Johnson to review the Executive Order and make comments and recommendations, as well as to redraft it if necessary. When Taylor penned the words *affirmative action*, he had in mind creating a legal concept which could become the basis of future action. He states:

I wanted to carry out the idea that people should do something, but mostly I had in mind that it would come to be interpreted and come to have conceptual meaning with the passage of time, which is what is taking place. It has been in the courts now, a lot of speeches have been made on the subject, a lot of government departments are defining the actions that people have to take in order to take affirmative action, etc. So it's being clothed with meaning as people proceed to do this, that, and the other thing. But if there were no such phrase as that that was capable of being conceptualized, then these things could not be done.[10]

A more specific indication of the way in which *affirmative action* was conceived and understood emerges as a result of examination of the methods used by the President's Committee on Equal Employment Opportunity to achieve their goals. Established by Kennedy's Executive Order 10925, the President's Committee on Equal Employment Opportunity began operation in March 1961. Much of the initial committee work involved data gathering and development of rules, regulations, and procedures for defining and implementing equal opportunity. The central PCEEO program, however, was *Plans For Progress*, an effort to encourage business to voluntarily implement affirmative action. Plans for Progress was begun by Robert Troutman but was taken over by Hobart Taylor in 1962. Taylor expanded it to include nongovernment contractors. The basic theory behind Plans for Progress was simple, politically pragmatic, and rooted in the economic realities of the time: voluntary private industry programs to increase Black presence in the labor force.

Recall that in the 1960s there was a manpower shortage. However, it was expected that there would be a sharp increase in non-whites in the labor force before 1970 and that non-whites would alleviate the shortage of white workers. President Johnson commented on this in forwarding the PCEEO report to Congress:

> *Negroes presently constitute only 10 percent of the work age population, but they may account for 18 percent of the coming manpower increase* (our emphasis). In the next five years, almost a million and a half non-whites will be added

to the work force; less than 800,000 were added during the last five years. The marked increase in non-whites in the labor force will intensify the need for eliminating discrimination in employment, training, and educational opportunities.[11]

Affirmative action as a route to progress in employment opportunity was envisioned as applying to an expanding, not a contracting, economy and it was envisioned as a way to racially balance new jobs, *not* a method of redistributing representation in existing jobs through replacement. Within the context of an expanding economy, therefore, even a notion as potentially redistributive as *affirmative action* could be conceived and interpreted as distribution of existing benefits under the existing racial hierarchy. President Kennedy specifically defined affirmative action to be a form of distributive policy:

> . . . the progress in equal employment opportunity is not based on replacing a group of people who now have jobs with another group that does not. That would merely be sharing the misery—a concept unworthy of America. What we wish to do instead is to share the benefits of our economy,—and spur it to new heights by adding to it productive workers whose services we have previously denied ourselves.[12]

Affirmative action was "sold" by the PCEEO and its supporters as good business. C. William Miller, President of Textron, Inc. and Chairman of the Plans for Progress Advisory Council, stated in 1965:

> [Discrimination] is a double drain on the American economy. It adds to the cost of every business, in such forms as higher unemployment payments, higher taxes for welfare and social services and greater losses through crime and delinquency. It also reduces the market for goods and services, for those who do not earn, do not spend.

Disadvantaged Negroes, Mexican Americans, and other minorities can be constructive contributors to their communities, or they can remain *as very* expensive dependents (emphasis ours).[13]

At the same seminar where Miller's comments were made, former Governor Leroy Collins pointed out:

. . . tourists shun a town like a plague which is in the throes of racial turmoil and . . . no large business considers seriously opening a branch in a town or city with a reputation for having what is referred to as a high TQ (tension quotient), so as businessmen, you are deeply anxious for understandable reasons to offset these negative factors with positive programs designed to promote good human relations and thus good business.[14]

Affirmative action, therefore, was viewed as a non-conflictive, volunteer route to a social good. In an expanding economy racial peace could be "purchased" through affirmative action without either disturbing or altering the fundamental role of black labor or diminishing the access of white workers to the labor market. This is not to deny that the people who started it were well-intentioned or capable because in many ways Plans for Progress was a remarkably well-conceived and executed program within its own limitations and constraints. It is the nature of those constraints that particularly concern us because they were both diachronically rooted in the history of the black presence and synchronically responsive to the currents of change at the time. They were set by the economic, social, and political context of the times and by the limitations of the people (Kennedy and Johnson, mainly) involved. To win the cooperation of the nation's business leaders, Plans for Progress had to be palatable and legitimized as good for business and good for the country. In order to be politically secure, it had to operate within the (friendly) Department of Labor and not produce hostilities that endangered priority legislation in other areas.

PCEEO studies detailed the achievements of voluntary affirmative action through Plans for Progress. In what was termed "the first census of non-white employment"[15] in 1963, the records of 103 Plans for Progress companies were studied. In the initial 1963 report, 1.5 percent of the salaried workers from these 103 firms were non-white and 8.3 percent of their hourly workers were non-white. By December 1963, less than a year later, 2.1 percent of salaried employees were non-white and 8.9 percent of hourly employees. There was an increase of 47.7 percent in salaried (middle-class!) positions and 15.9 percent increase in hourly positions. In absolute numbers of jobs, almost 50,000 jobs were provided for non-whites by the 103 Plans for Progress companies. Total employment for the 103 firms increased 7.6 percent while non-white employment increased 20.5 percent.

A major political outcome of Plans for Progress was the mobilization of some of the nation's largest industrial corporations (through their Plans for Progress involvement) in support of Title IV of the "Civil Rights Act of 1964"[16] and also in support of the Public Accommodations Section of the Civil Rights Act of 1964. By 1964, however, the days of volunteerism had ended. Under pressure from a strong and vibrant Civil Rights Movement and still reeling from the early urban riots, Congress passed Title VI and Title VII of the Civil Rights Act of 1964.

Surprisingly, there is almost no literature on Plans for Progress and the specific historical origins of affirmative action. Yet examination of that record is very informative. We learn that affirmative action emerged in a time of prosperity and was viewed *as incremental policy in that context*. Blacks were seen as added strength to what was projected as an expanding work force in which labor shortages and particularly shortages of skilled labor constituted an ever-present threat. Secondly, although some thought was given to upper-level positions, affirmative action efforts in the Plans for Progress years were focused on inclusion of Blacks in skilled, semi-skilled, and lower-level white-collar positions. The notion that Blacks should be represented at all levels of major companies only became widespread in the late 1960s and early 1970s and occurred as the Civil Rights Movement became more militant in its demands.

The final point we should keep in mind about Plans for Progress is that the image that the government "forced" major businesses into affirmative action is misleading. Indeed, if anything, there was a government-business partnership in Plans for Progress as well as widespread agreement among top business leaders with the initial affirmative action goals. It is only after the economic prosperity of the 1960s began to wane, labor shortages disappeared, politicization of other disadvantaged groups occurred, and demands for inclusion in affirmative action programs escalated, that backlash erupted which eroded its support from industry.

AFFIRMATIVE ACTION IN ACTION: INSTITUTIONAL POLICIES AND THE POLITICS OF RACIAL "BACKLASH"

We now turn to an examination of the effectiveness of affirmative action programs in the late sixties and seventies. In the mid-1960s affirmative action was expanded beyond Plans for Progress to become a national program aimed at integrating the work force at all levels. Federally encouraged "goals" and "timetables" for incorporating minorities into the work force replaced gentle persuasion and corporate volunteerism. Also, during this period white women and other non-Afro-American minorities began to make demands for consideration in affirmative action programs. In this section, we will examine affirmative action during this period in order to assess how much difference affirmative action made to the employment and economic prospects of Blacks.

PRELIMINARY CONCLUSIONS ABOUT THE GENERAL EFFECTIVENESS OF AFFIRMATIVE ACTION

We shall introduce simple descriptive statistics to get some idea about changes in discriminatory practice since 1947, focusing particularly on the post-affirmative action years. *These measures are only suggestive, of course, given the difficulty of measuring the effectiveness of anti-discrimination policies.*

We know that the effectiveness of affirmative action can be directly measured by the reduction in discrimination or can be indirectly measured by the improvement of relative status. Most attempts to determine the effectiveness of anti-discrimination policies have concentrated on the indirect evidence of change in status, rather than the direct evidence of reduced discrimination, because it has been impossible to devise direct measures of discrimination.

For a number of reasons, the problems involved in drawing inferences about the effectiveness of anti-discrimination policies from the indirect evidence are formidable.

1. There is no one indicator of labor-market status and the various indicators need not all move in the same direction in response to anti-discrimination policies.

2. Other non-discriminatory factors, particularly the functioning of the national economy, may influence the labor market status of Blacks in both directions. Thus, it is difficult to sort out the direct impact of anti-discrimination activities.

3. There are no obvious measures of the level of anti-discrimination activity.

4. There is little or no good theoretical analysis of the impact of anti-discrimination policies on the labor-market status of Blacks.

Unfortunately, empirical work has lent little support either to the hypothesis that anti-discrimination policies have been important or to the hypothesis that they have not been important. In fact economists, including Landes, Vroman, Butler, Heckman, Freeman, Finish, Welch, and Sowell, have not identified any criteria by which to evaluate these types of policies and have not defined measures for the benefits of such policies. Thus, we cannot empirically assess the effectiveness of these policies with any certainty. Similarly, our understanding of what would have occurred in the absence of anti-discrimination policies is limited.

Yet, while continuing racial disparities in job and economic status may stem from many causes, they provide strong evidence of the persistence of discriminatory practices. As the Supreme Court has observed, statistics showing racial or ethnic imbalance are important in legal proceedings "because such imbalance is often a telltale sign of purposeful discrimination."[17] Thus, we will examine several specific mechanisms by which the structure of racial inequality is maintained. These can be summed up in four differentials:

1. *Occupational differential*: the exclusion of racial minority workers from the better paying occupations;
2. *Industrial differential*: the exclusion of racial minority workers from the better paying industries;
3. *Wage differential*: minority workers do the same work as whites, yet the former are paid lower wages; and
4. *Unemployment differential*: perhaps the most important dimension defining the status of Blacks, whereby minority workers are saddled with higher unemployment than whites, meaning that the former are compelled to take whatever jobs are available at whatever wages.[18]

Has affirmative action had any impact on these mechanisms?

Occupation Differentials[19]

Has there been any shift of minority workers into "better" occupations from which they have been historically excluded? Based on employment statistics there was a definite improvement in the share of better jobs held by non-white workers (especially evident in the 1960s). However, Black–white parity, that is, the proportional share of occupations based on participation in the labor force, is still far from a reality. The extent of occupational changes among non-white workers can be traced in Table 2 below. For example, that between 1959 and 1969 the number of Blacks in professional and technical positions increased by 129 percent (to 695,000), while the increase in all occupational structures was only 51 percent (to 10.8 million). During this same period, the number of Black managers, officials, and proprietors (the second highest paying category) rose by almost three-fifths (to 254,000), as compared with an expansion of 15 percent (to eight million) for all employees in this category.

Nevertheless, the accelerated movement of Blacks out of the positions at the bottom of the occupational structure did not flow evenly through the entire occupational structure. For example, in 1969, Blacks still held about 1.5 million of the service jobs outside of private households, most of which required only modest skills. This figure represented about one-fifth of the total, roughly the same proportion as in 1959. Moreover, the number of Blacks holding semi-skilled operative jobs (mainly in factories) rose by 52 percent during the decades as compared with an expansion of only 22 percent for all workers. The result was that Blacks' share of the total climbed from 22 percent to 14 percent. Taken together, these two categories of low skilled jobs (chiefly in factories or in non-household services) accounted for a somewhat larger share (42 percent) of total Black employment in 1969 than they did in 1959 when their share was about 37 percent. In contrast, among all employees the proportion was virtually unchanged: 29 percent at the beginning of the decade and 27 percent at its close.

It is also evident, however, that Blacks have benefited differentially from these improvements. While most Blacks remained concentrated in those positions requiring little skill and offering few opportunities for further advancement (such as operatives and non-household service workers), those who were well prepared to compete for the higher paying positions in the upper reaches of the occupational structure did make measurable gains during the 1960s. In short, in the 1970s well-prepared Blacks showed much more success in integrating into the more prestigious occupations than did less well prepared Blacks who sought jobs in the blue-collar sector. While in 1959 almost 80 percent of Blacks were employed in non-prestigious occupations, by 1980 this number had shrunk to roughly 50 percent. Thus, an occupational split symbolizing a growing class differentiation within the Black community was developing. (see Table 3). While between 1959 and 1980 Blacks increased their representation in

TABLE 2
Occupational Deployment of Blacks
(in percents)

Occupations	1959			1969			1974			1980		
	Total	Black	% of Total	Total	Black	% of Total	Total	Black	% of Total	Total	Black	% of Total
Total	100.0	100.0	10.2	100.0	100.0	10.8	100.0	100.0	10.8	100.0	100.0	9.6
White Color (Total)	42.7	14.4	3.5	47.3	26.2	6.0	48.6	32.0	7.1	53.0	39.3	7.1
Professional	11.1	4.6	4.3	13.8	8.3	6.5	14.4	10.4	7.9	15.4	11.5	7.2
Managers	10.7	2.4	2.4	10.3	3.0	3.2	10.4	4.1	4.2	10.4	5.2	4.8
Sales	6.5	1.3	2.0	6.0	2.0	8.1	6.3	2.3	4.0	10.0	5.0	1.7
Clerical	14.4	6.1	4.3	17.2	12.9	12.7	17.5	15.2	9.4	17.3	17.5	9.7
Blue Collar (Total)	37.1	41.2	11.4	36.2	42.9	12.7	34.7	40.2	12.6	31.2	35.6	10.9
Craftsmen	13.2	5.9	44.5	13.1	8.5	7.0	13.4	9.4	7.6	12.9	9.0	6.6
Operatives	18.2	20.0	11.2	18.4	23.9	13.9	16.2	21.9	14.7	13.8	19.5	13.5
Laborers	5.6	15.3	28.1	4.7	10.5	23.9	5.1	8.9	19.0	4.5	7.2	15.3
Service (Total)	11.9	31.9	27.4	12.2	26.7	23.5	13.2	25.1	20.5	12.9	23.1	17.1
Private	3.0	14.7	49.9	2.1	8.5	43.8	1.4	5.1	38.6	0.6	2.6	41.0
Other	8.9	17.2	19.8	10.1	18.2	19.3	11.8	20.0	18.4	12.3	20.5	15.9
Farm	8.3	12.5	15.5	4.3	4.2	10.8	3.5	2.7	8.3	2.9	2.0	6.5

Source: U.S. Department of Labor, Bureau of Labor Statistics, *Manpower Report of President*, 1975, Table A-15, p. 225 & Table A-16, p. 227; 1980 data calculated from 1980 Census of Population, *General Social & Economic Characteristics*, PC 80-1-C1, p. 45.

prestigious occupations by 140 percent, they decreased their representation in non-prestigious occupations by only 21 percent.

Why do we see the decline in overall employment growth for Blacks as a whole? One reason may be that the 1970s were a period of relative quiescence for mass movements against racial discrimination, which means there was less pressure on employers to hire and upgrade minority workers and less pressure on government to enforce affirmative action guidelines.

The 1970s were also a period of economic stagnation and recession, meaning that unemployment rose for all categories of workers and gains that were made in the late 1960s were undermined in the 1970s.

Thus, although affirmative action may have contributed to advances in the 1960s, it was basically a holding action in the 1970s, *meaning that minority workers may have suffered an even greater decline in occupation gains had there been no affirmative action programs.* Moreover, it clearly appears that in the 1970s those Blacks with higher education levels and skills were able to benefit most from affirmative action.

Industrial Differentiation

Industrial employment shows a more mixed picture. Several conclusions are suggested by the data in Table 4. In general, Blacks tend to have a disproportionate share of the jobs in low-wage industries, and they tend to be underrepresented in high-wage industries. For example, in the low-wage manufacturing industries such as lumber and textiles, Blacks' share of the total jobs in 1980 was above their share of all jobs in the private sector. In contrast, among the high-wage industries, only in primary metals and in transportation equipment did Blacks have an above-average share of the total jobs. Among the high-wage manufacturing industries in which Blacks were noticeably underrepresented are fabricated metals, machinery, instruments, paper, and printing. They are similarly underrepresented in wholesale and retail trades, construction, and mining.

Between 1968 and 1980 Blacks made some progress in

TABLE 3

Black Employment in Prestigious verses Non-Prestigious Occupations

Year	Prestigious Occupations (Professional & Marginal)		Non-Prestigious Occupations (Operative, Non-Farm Laborers & Service Workers)	
	Black	Total	Black	Total
1959	7.0	21.8	76.2	39.4
1969	11.3	24.1	64.3	37.2
1974	14.5	24.8	57.9	36.1
1980	16.8	25.7	49.8	31.2

Source: Calculations based on data from Table 2.

TABLE 4
Blacks' Share of Employment by Industry
1968, 1972 and 1980

Industry	1968 Percentage Distribution Total	Black	Black Share of Employment	1972 Percentage Distribution Total	Black	Black Share of Employment	1980 Percentage Distribution Total	Black	Black Share of Employment
Total: Number (thousands)	79,920	8,169	10.2	81,720	8,628	10.6	97,639	9,334	9.6
Total: Percent	100.0	100.0	10.2	100.0	100.0	10.6	100.0	100.0	9.6
Agriculture	5.0	5.4	11.6	4.2	3.6	8.9	2.8	1.7	5.8
Mining	0.7	0.2	3.0	0.7	0.3	4.5	1.1	0.5	4.1
Construction	5.3	4.9	10.0	5.7	5.0	9.2	5.9	4.3	7.0
Manufacturing	27.2	24.2	9.6	24.1	22.6	9.9	22.4	23.2	9.9
Durable Goods	16.0	14.0	9.4	14.0	12.8	9.6	13.8	13.1	9.1
Lumber & Furniture	1.5	2.4	21.7	1.4	2.1	19.2	1.3	1.6	11.9
Primary Metals	1.7	2.2	14.0	1.5	2.0	13.9	1.3	1.7	12.2
Fabricated Metals	2.2	1.7	8.3	1.7	1.3	8.2	1.5	1.2	7.7
Machinery (exc. elec.)	2.9	1.2	4.4	2.5	1.3	5.6	2.8	1.7	5.7
Electrical Machinery	2.6	1.8	7.7	2.3	1.7	7.7	2.3	1.9	8.1
Transportation Equip.	3.1	3.0	10.4	2.4	2.6	11.6	2.5	3.0	11.4
Nondurable Goods	11.2	10.2	9.8	10.1	9.8	10.3	8.6	10.1	11.2
Food & Kindred	2.5	3.0	12.7	2.2	2.5	12.4	1.6	2.0	12.4
Textiles	3.1	3.3	11.7	2.9	3.6	13.0	2.3	3.7	15.3
Printing, Paper	2.5	1.6	6.7	2.3	1.4	7.1	1.6	1.0	6.3
Chemicals	1.5	1.2	8.1	1.3	1.1	8.8	1.3	1.4	10.1

migrating from low-wage to high-wage industries. For example, the Black share of total jobs declined in lumber and furniture manufacturing, in food processing, and in services—all low-wage industries. Their share eased off somewhat in printing and publishing and wholesale trade, in which wages are also below average. At the same time, they expanded their share of employment in a number of high-wage sectors: electrical machinery, transport equipment, paper, chemicals, and transportation and public utilities. In several cases, on the other hand, they became even more heavily represented in low-wage sectors. For example, Blacks' share of total employment rose in textiles, where wages are below average.

Furthermore, viewing industrial statistics from the EEOC, we also see some indication that anti-discrimination policies have had some favorable results (See Table 5.) Black employment in EEOC-reporting firms rose much faster than employment in the economy as a whole. For example, between 1966 and 1980 Blacks accounted for 23 percent of growth in jobs in EEOC-reporting firms, as compared with 14 percent in all firms. Within the white-collar category, however, only clerical workers and sales workers recorded relatively larger gains on EEOC-reported payrolls (42 percent as compared with 19 percent and 12 percent as compared with 8 percent respectively). In sum, the companies reporting under the EEOC requirements are opening jobs to Blacks at a rate much faster than is true for all employers in this country as a whole. At the same time, it appears that the expansion is slower among job categories in the upper reaches of the occupation scale than it is at the lower end.

There are also some indications that the public sector has done better at eliminating racial bias in employment than has the private sector. In 1980 Blacks accounted for 9.6 percent of the total number of jobs reported. However, they represented 15.2 percent of all government wage and salary workers as compared with 8.9 percent of those in the private sector. Moreover, public sector employment represented 27.1 percent of the total number of jobs held by Blacks, but the corresponding proportion for all workers was only 17.1 percent. These data show that Blacks were much more heavily dependent on public service employment than

TABLE 5

Black Total and EEOC-Reported Employment[1]: 1966, 1974 and 1980[2]

(in percents)[3]

Occupation	1966 Total	1966 EEOC	1974 Total	1974 EEOC	1980 Total	1980 EEOC
Total Employment	9.6	8.2	10.8	11.6	9.6	11.7
White Collar (Total)	5.0	2.5	7.1	5.9	7.1	6.1
Professional	5.9	5.3	7.9	10.5	7.2	10.8
Managers	2.8	0.8	4.2	2.8	4.8	3.4
Sales	3.0	2.4	4.0	5.5	1.7	5.6
Clerical	6.3	3.5	9.4	9.0	9.7	10.1
Blue Collar (Total)	12.2	10.8	12.6	14.1	10.9	14.4
Craftsmen	6.3	3.7	7.6	6.9	6.6	6.9
Operatives	12.9	10.8	14.7	15.7	13.5	15.9
Laborers	26.0	21.1	19.0	20.3	15.3	19.8
Service (Total)	21.1	23.0	18.4	23.7	16.2	24.0

[1]Reported to USEEOC by firms with 100 or more employees.

[2]Excluding private household and farm workers.

[3]Percent blacks comprise of total number of employees in each category.

Source: Research Division, U.S. Equal Employment Opportunity Commission, Bailey's Crossroads, Virginia.

were either white workers or workers of other races. (This also means cuts in public service employment such as those implemented under the Reagan Administration will have a greater and more negative impact on the Black community.)

For Black workers, public sector jobs tend to pay much better than the jobs they hold in the private sector (this is not the case among white workers). Therefore, in public service, the average compensation of Blacks was 78 percent that of whites. In the private sector, Black compensation was only 65 percent that of whites.

We can conclude that there has been some positive shift in the racial composition of industrial employment. However, a shift in the racial composition of certain industries may be the employer's way of holding down wages. In the textile industry, for example, there has been a fourfold increase in the number of Black workers between 1960 and 1970. But the wages for Black textile workers are about one-fifth lower than the wages for white textile workers. What this implies is that an industrial shift brings a relative gain but so long as there is a wage differential between Black and white workers in the industry, then the employer can use this to keep his overall labor costs down. This acts to *limit* the potential income gains to be made when workers shift to new occupations.

Wage Differential

According to a recent EEOC report, the median weekly earnings wage differential between full-time Black and white workers decreased steadily at a rate of about 1.6 percentage points per year between 1967 and 1974, or about double the rate of decrease for the previous decade. This would seem to suggest that anti-discrimination measures are having some effect in closing the wage gap. Black workers who have a college education and are in professional and technical occupations are better off, earning about 95 percent of what whites earn in the same occupations. The wage differential is worse in the lowest educational and occupational categories, showing again that whatever the possible effects of affirmative action, they certainly have been much more positive for the Black middle class than for the Black working class.

However, if we look at family income as opposed to individual wages, the situation is altogether different. In 1959, Black family income was on the average about 52 percent of white family income. By 1969, this ratio had increased to 61 percent of white family income. But between 1970 and 1982, the trend reversed with Black family income dropping to only 55 percent of white family income in 1982 (See Table 6). In sum as with occupational employment, the real improvement was in the decade of the 1960s, while the 1970s and 1980s have shown actual decline.

Another common way to assess inequality in the distribution of income is to calculate the share of total money income before taxes that is received by each fifth of families after the families have first been ranked by the size of their total income. These calculations have been made for families in the United States, by the race of the head of the family for selected years 1947 through 1982. (See Table 7.)

Several conclusions can be drawn from the data. First, over the last quarter century there has been very little variation in the share of aggregate income received by each fifth of the families. However, there has been a slight decline in the fraction of total income received by the top 5 percent (Tables 7). Between 1960 and 1970 the share of total income received by the bottom 20 percent did rise somewhat; between 1970 and 1982, however, the share of the total income received by this group receded slightly.

The figures also enable one to compare the way in which income is distributed among the respective Black and white populations. In each of the years shown, the lowest fifth of Black families have received a smaller fraction of the total income of the Black community than the lowest fifth in the white community received from the total income of the white community.

These figures also indicate that Black family income has historically been less equally distributed than white family income although the differences between the two groups have narrowed slightly over the last decade. However, in recent periods of

TABLE 6
Median Income of Families by Race of Head:
Selected Years, 1947–82
(in current dollars)

Year	Total	White	Black and Other Races	Black	PERCENT OF WHITE Black and Other Races	PERCENT OF WHITE Black	Income Gap (BLACK LESS WHITE) Black and Other Races	Income Gap (BLACK LESS WHITE) Black
1947	$3,031	$3,157	$1,614	NA	51.1	—	$1,543	—
1954	4,173	4,339	2,410	NA	55.5	—	1,929	
1959	5,417	5,893	3,161	3,047	53.6	51.7	2,732	$2,846
1960	5,620	5,835	3,233	NA	55.4		2,722	
1964	6,569	6,868	3,838	3,724	56.0	54.3	3,019	3,134
1969	9,433	9,794	6,191	5,999	63.2	61.3	3,723	3,795
1973	12,051	12,595	7,596	7,269	60.3	57.7	4,999	5,326
1974	12,836	13,356	8,265	8,006	61.9	59.9	5,091	5,350
1975	13,772	14,320	9,321	8,723	65.5	60.9	4,999	5,597
1976	14,958	15,537	9,821	9,242	63.2	59.5	5,716	6,295
1977	16,060	16,782	10,142	9,485	60.4	56.5	6,640	7,297
1978	17,640	18,368	11,754	10,879	64.0	59.2	6,614	7,489
1979	19,587	20,439	12,404	11,574	60.7	56.6	8,035	8,865
1980	21,023	21,904	13,843	12,674	63.2	57.9	8,061	9,230
1981	22,388	23,517	14,598	13,266	62.1	56.4	8,919	10,251
1982	23,433	24,603	15,211	13,598	61.8	55.3	9,392	11,005

Sources: (1) U.S. Department of Commerce, Bureau of the Census, *Consumer Income:* "Money Income in 1974 of Families and Persons in the United States," Current Population Reports, Series P-60, No. 101, January 1976, Table 13, p. 24; (2) *The Social and Economic Status of the Black Population in the United States, 1974,* (3) Current Population Reports, Series P-60, No. 54, July, 1975, Table 9; p. 25; and (4) Current Population Reports, Series P-60, No. 142, February 1984.

TABLE 7
Income and Percentage Share of Aggregate Income
Received by Each Fifth and Top 5 Percent of Families by Race
(Selected Years 1947–1982)

A. Upper Income Limit of Each Fifth

Year	White					Black and Other Race				
	Lowest	Second	Middle	Fourth	Top 5 Percent	Lowest	Second	Middle	Fourth	Top 5 Percent
1947	1,756	2,692	3,589	5,052	8,034	760	1,319	1,905	2,921	5,301
1950	1,836	3,021	3,955	5,419	8,852	723	1,479	2,219	3,143	5,155
1955	2,465	4,004	5,252	7,080	10,866	1,043	2,013	3,109	4,408	6,625
1960	3,025	5,000	6,585	9,000	13,964	1,310	2,502	3,900	6,000	9,892
1965	3,870	6,100	8,123	11,013	17,067	1,927	3,300	4,900	7,300	11,800
1970	5,500	8,727	11,691	15,929	24,941	2,972	5,246	7,900	11,700	18,521
1975	7,430	12,000	16,450	22,614	35,000	4,100	7,364	11,358	17,017	26,600
1980	11,310	18,442	25,481	35,400	55,200	5,928	10,600	17,429	26,800	43,400
1981	11,994	19,782	27,606	38,524	60,050	6,072	11,296	18,523	28,738	45,008
1982	12,428	20,468	28,930	41,090	65,665	6,063	11,500	19,600	30,129	48,860

Source: U.S. Bureau of the Census, Current Population Reports, Series P-60, No. 142 *Money Income of Households, Families and Persons in the United States: 1982*, U.S. Government Printing Office, Washington D.C., 1984.

TABLE 7—Continued
B. Percent Distribution of Aggregate Income

	White							Black and Other Races						
Year	Lowest Fifth	Second Fifth	Middle Fifth	Fourth Fifth	Highest Fifth	Top 5 Percent	Index of Income Concentration	Lowest Fifth	Second Fifth	Middle Fifth	Fourth Fifth	Highest Fifth	Top 5 Percent	Index of Income Concentration
1947	5.5	12.2	17.0	22.9	42.5	17.4	.366	4.3	10.4	16.1	23.8	45.3	16.4	.406
1950	4.8	12.4	17.4	23.2	42.2	17.2	.369	3.5	10.3	17.6	25.2	43.4	16.5	.404
1955	5.2	12.7	17.8	23.5	40.8	16.2	.353	4.0	10.4	17.8	25.6	42.2	14.3	.388
1960	5.2	12.7	17.8	23.7	40.7	15.7	.353	3.7	9.7	16.5	25.2	44.9	16.2	.417
1965	5.6	12.6	17.8	23.7	40.3	15.4	.346	4.7	10.8	16.6	24.7	43.2	15.1	.388
1970	5.8	12.5	17.7	23.6	40.5	15.5	.346	4.5	10.6	16.8	24.8	43.4	15.4	.392
1975	5.7	12.1	17.6	23.9	40.7	15.4	.350	4.7	10.1	16.7	25.1	43.3	15.4	.392
1980	5.6	11.9	17.6	24.0	40.9	15.1	.355	4.1	9.5	16.0	25.2	45.3	16.3	.411
1981	5.4	11.7	17.5	24.2	41.2	15.1	.359	4.0	9.4	16.0	25.5	45.1	16.0	.418
1982	5.2	11.6	17.2	24.1	42.1	15.7	.369	3.8	9.0	15.8	25.3	46.2	17.1	.431

Source: U.S. Bureau of the Census, Current Population Reports, Series P-60, No. 142 *Money Income of Households, Families and Persons in the United States: 1982*, U.S. Government Printing Office, Washington, D.C., 1984.

declining or slow economic growth, the differences in income distribution for Black and white families have increased. These differences were marked during the 1969–70 recession and they became even sharper during the 1975 to 1982 period of shrinking economic activity.

Thus, the observed pattern of income distribution implies that lower-income Black families receive a smaller proportion of total money income than do lower-income white families in periods of reduced economic growth. In addition, averages for Blacks as a whole may disguise a deteriorating situation for lower income Black families.

In the 1970s and 1980s, income has been distributed so as to favor whites as compared with Blacks, and the better off as compared with the poor. In viewing family income data, it appears that affirmative action has been of little or no help in the 1970s and 1980s. Instead, the strong expansion of the nation's economy during the 1960s which opened a wide range of opportunities for Blacks, poor people, and the least skilled to participate more fully in the mainstream of economic activity allowed them a somewhat larger share of total income. In contrast, from about 1974 to 1980, under the combined impact of high inflation rates and slower economic growth, these disadvantaged groups have fallen further behind the more fortunate members of society. The outlook is no better: partly because of long term trends towards higher energy prices and reduced rate of capital formation, but also because of the overall thrust of national economic policy, the growth rate of the American economy up through the 1980s will probably fall far below its potential. Under these circumstances, the drift toward greater inequality will likely continue. Income fluctuations are, of course, related to the unemployment differential.

Unemployment Differential

Unemployment more than any other indicator demonstrates consistent racial inequality. For several decades now the official Black unemployment rate has averaged between one and three-

TABLE 8
Unemployment Rates for Persons 16 Years Old and Over
(Selected Years: 1948–1983)

Year	Black	White	Ratio Black/White
1948	5.9%	3.5%	1.7
1953	4.5	2.7	1.7
1958	12.6	6.1	2.1
1963	10.8	5.0	2.2
1968	6.7	3.2	2.1
1973	8.9	4.3	2.1
1978	13.9	7.8	1.8
1983	20.6	8.6	2.4

Source: U.S. Department of Labor, Bureau of Labor Statistics.

fourths to more than twice as high as the white unemployment rate. (See Table 8.) However, the ratio of Black/white unemployment fluctuates from year to year and can affect average family income. In years when Black unemployment is increasing relative to white unemployment, the average income of Black families tends to decline relative to white families, even if the wage differentials of employed workers are eliminated, simply because relatively more workers are unemployed in the Black community.

Government figures indicate that between 1958 and 1968, Black unemployment fell (corresponding with an increase in the relative income of Black families); between 1968 and 1978, the trend was reversed, and Black unemployment decreased *relative to white unemployment* (corresponding with an increase in Black family income relative to whites). By 1983 Black unemployment had increased again and so inversely Black family income had fallen relative to white family income. Affirmative action had made no appreciable impact on these fluctuations.

It should be emphasized, of course, that we are discussing "relative" unemployment figures; the absolute unemployment rates for both Blacks and whites have increased greatly since

1969. This discussion is also based on government statistics which do not include what the National Urban League refers to as the "hidden unemployment rate"—workers who are discouraged and no longer actively seeking work so that they are not even counted in the official government unemployment figures.

While the picture that emerges is a mosaic of both progress and stagnation, and clearly reveals a continuing lack of equity between Blacks and whites, this brief review of government data does suggest that anti-discrimination and affirmative action policies have had some progressive impact on racial inequality, specifically on occupational and industrial differentials. The view is somewhat more ambiguous with respect to wage differentials, and no positive impact on unemployment differences has been demonstrated, since affirmative action in no way seeks to change the total number of jobs available. Nor does affirmative action alone change the seniority system that helps maintain the unemployment differential.

Even in occupational and industrial terms, however, affirmative action programs have been of greater benefit to those Blacks who are able to qualify for the expanding white-collar positions in the corporate sector, with their higher educational and training requirements, than it has to those Blacks in blue-collar positions (although even here some progress had been made in the skilled crafts in the 1960s). On the other hand, affirmative action programs have had little impact in situations where the labor supply is great, that is, in the less skilled manufacturing jobs. In sum, it is clear that for the first time the national professional-managerial job market is more open to Blacks. Some Blacks have entered the middle class (absorbed into governmental bureaucracies, electoral politics, universities, business, and industry) by taking advantage of the liberal employment policies which the turbulence of the period produced. For most poor Blacks, however, occupational conditions did not improve much. For many of these the major gain was the winning of liberalized welfare practices to ensure their survival despite widespread unemployment and underemployment.

EDUCATION AND AFFIRMATIVE ACTION

Desegregating the available jobs, then, is not enough. Another crucial factor is the need for expansion of employment and of educational opportunities. Of particular importance is the rate of higher education in enhancing employment prospects for Blacks. Affirmative action in institutions of higher learning and democratization of faculties and student bodies is therefore not only intrinsically valuable as an expression of "justice" and "fairness," but it is also central to achievement of a redistribution of status, wealth, and power in the society as a whole. Although it is clear that the number and percent of Black and minority students and faculty increased from the mid-sixties to the mid-seventies, exact data on the dimensions of that increase are impossible to acquire. National racial statistics on higher education are scarce, and even when they do exist, are often unreliable and incompatible for the earlier years. We do know that when the number of affirmative action programs reached their peak in the mid-1970s, about 25 percent of the approximately three thousand American colleges and universities had a special admissions program for minorities. Data on Black faculty are also seriously limited, but apparently in 1972–73, Blacks held about 3 percent of all faculty positions, about half of which were in the historically and predominantly Black colleges and universities. Recruitment of Black faculty seemed to level off in the mid-1970s. Lorenzo Morris concludes:

By 1975 black faculty employment reached 4.4 percent or 19,915 blacks out of more than 450,000 faculty. Only 2.2 percent of associate professors were black. (EEOC) Again, about half of these were at black institutions. Then the vast majority of blacks at white institutions clustered at the bottom of the tenure ladder or in positions with no possibility for tenure. Discouraging as these figures have been to blacks, the 1977 figures had to be more discouraging. In 1977 blacks were still only 4.4 percent of all faculty.[20]

As Table 9 below indicates, however, the numbers of minority students enrolled in two year or four year institutions of higher education continued to increase between 1976 and 1980 and leveled off between 1980 and 1982. Note, however, that the Black percentage of total undergraduate enrollment is consistent between 1976 and 1980, declining only slightly in 1982.

The contrast between the fates of Black faculty and of Black students reflects the exigencies of that period in history. Universities and colleges were just beginning to experience decreases in enrollment and to plan for further anticipated decline. Black students represented a new potential population from which they hoped to draw. One must also keep in mind that Black and Hispanic students were concentrated at low-selectivity institutions, many of which were by this time actively seeking to expand student enrollments. In 1973, for example, it was found that 18.7% of the total Black, Hispanic, and Native American/Indian enrollment was in four-year colleges of low selectivity, as compared with 6.9 and 4.8 percent respectively in institutions of medium and high selectivity. Black students, then, were a new source of consumers of higher education. They could be incorporated into higher education without necessitating a sharp redistribution of access. It was not necessary, in other words, for large, significant numbers of whites to be dislocated in order to include Black and minority students.

Incorporation of Black and minority faculty, in contrast, during a period of a growing oversupply of Ph.D.'s (particularly in the education and social science fields in which minorities are clustered) would have necessitated, and did necessitate, some redistribution of privilege. Even the redistribution of access to education and to high status positions in universities aroused widespread academic opposition. Political opponents of affirmative action were joined by academics in condemning the principle and implementation of affirmative action. The addition of voices from academia to the rising chorus of affirmative action critics gave new force and legitimacy to the arguments for its discontinuation.

Table 9
Trends in Total Enrollment in Institutions of Higher Education, by Level of Institution and Race/Ethnicity: Fall 1976 to Fall 1982

Race/Ethnicity and Citizenship	Number Enrolled				% Enrolled			
	1976	1978	1980	1982	1976	1978	1980	1982
4-year institutions	7,090	7,187	7,548	7,629	100.0	100.0	100.0	100.0
White, non-Hispanic	5,984	6,013	6,259	6,289	84.4	83.7	82.9	82.4
Total Minority	930	973	1,048	1,070	13.1	13.5	13.9	14.0
Black, non-Hispanic	603	611	633	611	8.5	8.5	8.4	8.0
Hispanic	173	190	216	228	2.4	2.6	2.9	3.0
Asian or Pacific Islander	118	137	162	193	1.7	1.9	2.1	2.5
American Indian/ Alaskan Native	35	35	37	38	.5	.	.5	.5
Non-resident alien	176	200	241	269	2.5	2.8	3.2	3.5
2-year institutions	3,880	4,028	4,490	4,699	100.0	100.0	100.0	100.0
White, non-Hispanic	3,077	3,167	3,532	3,657	79.3	78.6	78.7	77.9
Total Minority	761	810	894	981	19.6	20.1	19.9	20.9
Black, non-Hispanic	429	443	468	483	11.1	11.0	10.4	10.3
Hispanic	210	227	255	291	5.4	5.6	5.7	6.2
Asian or Pacific Islander	79	97	124	158	2.0	2.4	2.8	3.4
American Indian/ Alaskan Native	41	43	47	49	1.1	1.1	1.0	1.0
Non-resident alien	42	52	64	61	1.1	1.3	1.4	1.3
Total	10,970	11,215	12,038	12,328	100	100	100	100
White	9,061	9,180	9,791	9,946	82.6	81.9	81.3	80.7
Total Minority	1,691	1,783	1,942	2,051	15.4	15.9	16.1	16.6
Black	1,032	1,054	1,101	1,094	9.4	9.4	9.2	8.9
Hispanic	383	417	471	519	3.5	3.7	3.9	4.2
Asian/Pacific	197	234	286	351	1.8	2.1	2.4	2.8
Native American	76	78	84	87	.7	.7	.7	.7
Non-resident Alien	218	252	305	330	2.0	2.2	2.5	2.7

NOTE: Excludes enrollment in U.S. Service Schools that are included in tabulations presented elsewhere in this publication. Numbers in thousands; percentages may not add to 100 due to rounding.

SOURCE: U.S. Department of Education, Office for Civil Rights, unpublished tabulations (December 1983) and National Center for Education Statistics, Opening Fall Enrollment, Fall 1982, unpublished tabulations (December 1983).

OCR, unpublished tabulations, reported NCES, *Condition of Education, 84* p. 76. Full table attached.

THE AFFIRMATIVE ACTION DEBATE

Many of the academic critics of affirmative action added to the bitterness surrounding the debate by asserting that the very concept challenged notions of individualistic competition that are synonymous with "justice" in American thought. Nathan Glazer, for example, states:

Until the early 1970s, affirmative action meant to seek out and prepare members of minority groups for better jobs and educational opportunities. It still means only this much in the field of residential distribution, but in the early 1970s, affirmative action came to mean much more than advertising opportunities actively, seeking out those who might not know of them, and preparing those who might not yet be qualified. It came to mean the setting of statistical origin for employers and educational institutions. *This new cause threatens the abandonment of our concern for individual claims to consideration on the basis of justice and equity,* (emphasis ours) now to be replaced with a concern for rights for publicly determined and delimited racial and ethnic groups.[21]

The nation would, under the pressure of those recently subordinated to inferior status, be permanently sectioned on the basis of group membership and identification and an experiment in a new way of reconciling a national polity with group distinctiveness would have to be abandoned.[22]

If the individual is the measure, however, our public concern is with the individual's capacity to work out an individual fate by means of education, work, and self-realization in the various spheres of life. . . [23]

Justice, in the view of Glazer and the critics of affirmative action, consists of the freedom of individuals to compete equally in the marketplace. Justice is identified with equality, equality with individualism, and both concepts with a free-market arena. At best justice is distributive in the sense of individuals receiving justice according to their "merit". Supporters of affirmative action normally attack this argument because of its weak empirical foundation, arguing that the free competition of *equal, self-sufficient individuals is more myth than reality. The instance of Afro-Americans and the disabilities resulting from slavery and discrimination simply underscore the more general reality.*

However, affirmative action advocates might also attack the philosophical underpinning of this argument. Is justice for Afro-Americans achieved by achieving equality? If equality is what is being sought, with which individuals or groups should equality be sought? If justice for Afro-Americans requires more than equality what else is required and why?

We might suggest that authentic justice for Afro-Americans must attack, diminish, vitiate, the structural features of group domination. Justice must be redistributive. Justice for the dominated must allow the dominated to authentically represent and redress their condition of domination. Emphasis on equality between individuals as an encompassing value does not address the particularity of the degraded group position of Blacks. Seeming equality between individuals within a hierarchical societal context becomes tokenism, a thinly disguised form of continued domination, if it results in delegitimization of the claims of the still-deprived majority.

By starting with a careful examination of things as they are, we avoid the artificial and theoretically crippling, ahistorical axioms of antecedent autonomous selves, abstract equality, and contract as the most just mode of social relations. To that extent, there is no sleight-of-hand deception, no negating of present oppression by appeals to so-called inviolable standards.

Affirmative action, given the above concept of justice, must be evaluated in terms of its relevance as a framework for addressing the authentic aspects of Afro-American domination and creating the possibility of "justice" for Afro-Americans. We might argue that to the extent affirmative action emphasizes collective goals, attacks hierarchy and stereotypically-rooted collectivism, and moves to end economic superexploitation, it has the capacity to bring about institutional redistributive change.

For conservative political thinkers there is a direct translation from liberal philosophical notions of the *abstract* individual to crude notions of the sacred, inviolable, and autonomous rights of the biological individual. As we have seen above with Nathan Glazer, goals and timetables are anathema because they oppose a focus on the individual as the sole unit to which nondiscrimination measures should be applied. Moreover, Glazer deplores the break with the Civil Rights Act of 1964 whose legislative history and Congressional intent, according to him, was clear and unambiguous: "The question in each case is whether the individual was discriminated against."[24] "It would specifically prohibit the attorney general or any agency of the government from requiring employment to be on the basis of racial or religious quotas. Under (this provision) an employer with only white employees could continue to have only the best qualified people, even if they were all white."[25]

Thus, critics allege that affirmative action and merit are antithetical. It makes jobs go to unqualified or less qualified minorities. It goes against individualism and the merit principle where advances and rewards are provided according to ability and accomplishment rather than criteria such as race or sex. Left unexamined is the reality of discrimination. The hegemony of white males in all segments of American life does not result from employment according to the "merit principle" but the existence of hierarchy and patterns of preference and exclusion.

Similarly, starting from a belief in the pluralist equivalence of groups, critics such as Glazer also conclude that affirmative action is not necessary because substantial progress has already been made and was being made in the upgrading of Black employment and income, a progress that had taken place in the same way as with other ethnic groups, i.e., without the benefit of such "extreme measures as affirmative action." The most outspoken Black critic of affirmative action, Thomas Sowell,[26] says that, in fact, affirmative action stigmatizes Blacks since it amounts to a moratorium on the recognition of the achievements of Blacks. In Sowell's view, giving Blacks advantages to compensate for past discrimination reduces Blacks' chances of achieving genuine equality.

Thus, like true democratic contract theorists, Hook, Sowell, Shils, and Glazer, for widely variant reasons, characterize the concept and implementation of affirmative action as unwarranted government intervention. Shils, a University of Chicago and Cambridge University professor, argues affirmative action "reduces the pressure for intellectual alertness and scrupulousness"[27] and claims that through affirmative action, "government is infringing on the freedom of universities."

In sum, democratic contract theory, as translated into public policy and political practice by the conservative academic critics of affirmative action, plays an important role in reproducing an ideological superstructure based on individualism, which obfuscates group inequality through exclusive focus on the individual.

THE AFFIRMATIVE ACTION BACKLASH

By the mid-1970s, the philosophical criticism melded with political opposition and controversy centered around the very concept of affirmative action. At present, in fact, "reverse discrimination" suits have replaced desegregation suits in visibility. Many such suits have developed, however, the main four cases delineate the dimensions of the attack: *Bakke, Weber, Fullilove 1., Memphis Firefighters.*

Although the Bakke case (*Regents of the University of California* v. *Bakke, 98 S. Ct. 2733 1978*) has been hailed by some Blacks as a "victory," most Blacks realize that the case was a direct and damaging challenge to affirmative action. By a vote of five to four, the Supreme Court decided that the University of California at Davis Medical School's Special Admissions Program was unlawful. Four justices, Burger, Stewart, Rehnquist, and Stevens, thought the program violated Title VII of the 1964 Civil Rights Act and did not reach the constitutional questions involved in the relationship of the affirmative action programs to the equal protection clause of the Fourteenth Amendment. Justice Powell, who wrote the opinion for the Court, thought the program violated the equal protection clause. Four other justices, Marshall, White, Blackmun and Brennan, reached the constitutional issues and thought that the program did not violate the equal protection clause and that race could be taken into account in admissions processes. Particularly stirring was the opinion of Justice Marshall:

> While I applaud the judgment of the Court that a university may consider race in its admissions process, it is more than a little ironic that, after several hundred years of class-based discrimination against Negroes, the court is unwilling to hold that a class-based remedy for that discrimination is permissible. In declining to so hold, *today's judgment ignores the fact that for several hundred years Negroes have been discriminated against, not as individuals but rather solely because of the color of their skins.*

> It is unnecessary in 20th century America to have individual Negroes demonstrate that they have been victims of racial discrimination; the racism of our society has been so pervasive that none, regardless of wealth or position, has managed to escape its impact. The experience of Negroes in America has been different in kind, not just in degree, from that of other ethnic groups. It is not merely the history of slavery alone but also that a whole people were marked as inferior by the law. And that mark has endured. The dream of America as the great melting pot has not been realized for the Negro: because of his skin color he never even made it into the pot.[28]

Marshall, in the above quote, is expressing his understanding of the kind of structural distinction we have argued separated Blacks from white ethnic groups. Unfortunately, the court decisions in this case vary in their understanding of theoretical and structural issues, specifically the question of what makes Blacks "special"; the relationship between individual and group or collectivity rights; and the relationship of the language and interpretation of the Thirteenth, Fourteenth, and Fifteenth Amendments to our understanding of the broader philosophical issues.

Kenneth Tollett, Director of the Institute for the Study of Educational Policy, feels that the court in the Bakke case is returning to the tradition of *Dred Scott*, the Civil Rights Cases, and *Plessy v. Ferguson*. He states:

> It (the court) has interceded in the political and social process to prevent public authorities from affirmatively attempting to deal with the injustices Blacks have experienced in this country. *Dred Scott* thwarted the Missouri Compromise which sought to stem the tide of slavery. The Civil Rights cases thwarted the attempt of Congress in the 1875 Civil Rights Act to insure fair and equal public accommodations for Blacks. *Plessy v. Ferguson* (supra) put the imprimatur of the U.S. Supreme Court on a Louisiana law that required railway passengers to have "equal but separate accommodations for the white and colored races." In the abstract, the "separate but equal" doctrine of *Plessy* had a certain intellectual plausibility, but in actuality, it was profoundly hypocritical. What that decision politically, morally and socially sanctioned did more harm than what the decision legally and technically meant. What is most ominous about the *Bakke* decision is that it may morally, politically, and legally suggest that race may not be considered decisively in voluntarily trying to redress discrimination against certain oppressed minorities.[29]

One reason for Tollett's pessimism about the impact of Bakke is the clear statement of Justice Powell, blatantly denying history, that ". . . it was (is) no longer possible to put the guarantees of the Fourteenth Amendment on the struggle for equality of one racial minority."[30] That line of reasoning, of course, undercuts the existing possibility of providing a strong legal justification for policies that seek to end Black subjugation by recognizing that ultimately the fate of individual Blacks will rest on the fate of the collectivity and that, therefore, only policies rooted in that reality will likely be effective.

The *Weber* case involved a further attack on voluntary efforts at affirmative action. Kaiser Aluminum and U.S. Steel had worked out an agreement of voluntary affirmative action in 1974 to voluntarily increase the proportion of Black employees in skilled craft jobs at one of its plants, since Blacks represented only 2 percent of employment in its crafts job and were 49 percent of the civilian labor force and 16 percent of the available craftsmen in the area.

Thus, they established an on-the-job training program for craft jobs, with a one-white, one-Black entrance ratio until minority representation equaled the minority percentage of the area civilian labor force. Entrance to the program was based on seniority within each racial group. Between April and December 1974, a total of seven Black employees and six white employees were selected for the program in one of their plants. Then, Brian Weber, a white employee of Kaiser, applied for several of the training programs, but never was among the whites selected for training. He had no problem with the whites who were chosen ahead of him. But he contended that several of the Blacks who were chosen had less seniority than he. Therefore, he charged that he was a victim of reverse discrimination and that this violated Title VII of the 1964 Civil Rights Act.

The appellate court ruled in Weber's favor saying that since there had been no discrimination suit brought by any of the particular individuals selected for the program, there was nothing to remedy. And if the 50–50 scheme did not remedy anything, it was simply racially-based preference and hence unlawful. Affirmative action from the appellate court's view must only be concerned with the individual. Thus, Kaiser and U.S. Steel would have to have lost such a suit brought by an individual or voluntarily admitted they were discriminating. Of course, no employer would voluntarily admit discrimination and invite back pay awards to minorities and other mandated relief. In fact, Kaiser officials have admitted that they adopted the voluntary plan to escape such court remedies. "If we did not do something on our own," Kaiser said in court, "then the government is going to do it for us . . . (and) whatever their remedy is . . . it's one heck of a lot worse than something we can work out for ourselves.''[31] So they had adopted the program because they "had no Blacks in the crafts to speak of" and knew that the courts were likely not to agree they had not discriminated. In short, they were trying to get away with the most minimal affirmative action efforts they could.

In the Supreme Court decision, *United Steelworkers* v. *Weber 443 U.S.* 193 (1979) the Court held that Title VII of the Civil Rights Act of 1964 did not prohibit training plans entered into by an employer and a union which assured a certain number of admissions to Blacks.

The Fullilove case (*Fullilove* v. *Klutznick 448 U.S.* 448 (1980)) tested the "set-aside" provision of the Public Works Employment Act of 1977 requiring that minority businessmen get a percentage of the work. Fullilove confirmed the authority of Congress to use race-conscious language, rules, regulations, and devices in lawmaking to assist disadvantaged minorities.

Taken together, the *Bakke*, *Weber*, and *Fullilove* cases seem to answer the critics of affirmative action by upholding the right of *private* organizations, *state* instrumentalities, and the U.S. Congress to take race into account as a positive factor. However, with the 1980 election and 1984 reelection of Ronald Reagan, an avowed opponent of affirmative action, the political and legal future of affirmative action remains in jeopardy.

The current jeopardy of affirmative action is seen clearly in *Memphis Firefighters (Firefighters Local Union No. 1784* v. *Stotts et al, 82-206, 82-229* 9 1984). Two Black Memphis firefighters had filed a petition against the Memphis, Tennessee Fire Department for making hiring and promotion decisions on the basis of race in violation of Title VII of the 1964 Civil Rights Act. A consent decree was entered with the stated purpose of remedying the Department's hiring and promotion practices with respect to Blacks.

Subsequently, when the city announced it would reduce city employees due to budget deficits, the District Court ordered a modified layoff play aimed at protecting Black employees with less seniority than some white employees. The District Court ruling cited the need to protect against the "last hired, first fired" phenomenon which has plagued Blacks in every recession in U.S. history. The Court of Appeals upheld the District Court's ruling.

The Supreme Court, however, reversed the rulings of the lower courts by ruling out class-wide remedies in seniority cases. The ruling also dangerously seeks to void class action rulings by narrowing remedies to only those who can prove they have been *individually* discriminated against. This has been an ongoing goal of the Reagan administration. The Court has shown in this rightward turn that it is providing ammunition to the Administration in its efforts. This action may seriously undermine affirmative action and set a precedent for the denial of class-wide remedies in numerous areas. For example, while civil rights groups such as the Legal Defense Fund and the NAACP have argued that the ruling applies only to civil rights conflicts involving seniority, the Justice Department has declared its unequivocal victory against quotas and "race-conscious" remedies and announced plans to re-examine all anti-discrimination agreements involving government.

Thus numerous questions remain. May public entities initiate voluntary affirmative action programs absent of specific findings of past discrimination? If not, what agencies are competent to make such findings and to design appropriate remedies? At what point does voluntary affirmative action by private employers transgress Title VII? Should strict scrutiny or some lesser standard of constitutional review be applied to benign affirmative action programs? Does Title VI permit voluntary affirmative action outside of the academic context?

Nonetheless, it remains true that in every context in which the Supreme Court has squarely confronted the issue it has affirmed the legitimacy of affirmative action. What remains judicially unsettled are the constitutional and statutory boundaries of that legitimacy.

CONCLUSION: TOWARD A THEORY OF AFFIRMATIVE ACTION

We began by suggesting that affirmative action was a form of *institutional* racial public policy characterized by the distribution of material benefits to individuals rather than to collectivities and by the change, transformation, or alteration of important institutions, systems, or subsystems of the society. Affirmative action did transform the life chances and opportunity structure for large numbers of Blacks and in the process changed the American labor market by ending formal and informal sanctions against all Blacks entering certain professions, colleges and universities, and leadership and managerial roles. For a short period of time (mid-1960s to mid-1970s), affirmative action also involved some small amount of redistribution of access to education and employment. What was in fact accomplished, however, was more symbolic than real. Even the symbolism of redistribution generated a backlash and a resounding attack on the principle of affirmative action.

A theoretical understanding of affirmative action must account for its origins and transformation and suggest the way in which affirmative action is related to larger social, economic, and political issues.

The presence of Blacks in America has always evoked questions of a systemic nature: What is the nature of the regime? Who is a legitimate member of the political community? In the Civil War period the fundamental question was, shall the political system persist? In the colonial period when America was sometimes defined as a "white man's country," the Black man had "no rights a white man was bound to respect." Racial hierarchy and collectivism characterized Black sociological existence in the U.S. and set Blacks apart structurally from white ethnic groups. Economically, Blacks were a superexploited, reserve labor supply. Congruence thus existed between sociological collectivism and hiearchicalization and economic exploitation. Racial public policy in the U.S., therefore, has always reflected the dilemmas of a society attempting to act within an individualistic, egalitarian ideological structure while providing practically for

Blacks whose structural position was a direct, blunt, and flagrant contradiction of those lofty ideals.

In the 1960s, under pressure from the civil rights movement, the structural position of Blacks underwent a change in form. Overt markers of racial hierarchy and collectivism were abolished and a genuine effort was made to create a segment within the Afro-American community whose experiences would approximate those of white ethnic groups. Specifically, this would be a segment for whom the individualism and egalitarianism of American ideology would not be rendered obviously mythical by legal segregation or exclusion of Blacks from any area of American life and, indeed, this middle-class segment of the Black community was used to provide political ammunition to those who wished to quell the urban rebellions and end seeming Black revolt against the regime. This prosperous segment would serve the purpose of obfuscating the continual hierarchical, collective, and economic deprivation plaguing the vast majority of Afro-Americans by being living examples of the possibility of "achievement."

It is important to understand, however, that the struggle for limited advancement of Blacks during the early period coincided with the interests of key elites. Reasons for this congruity of interests reflect the circumstances of that time. In academia an impending shortage of students in higher education meant that new students had to be recruited from different population sources. Blacks filled seats in universities and colleges that otherwise would have remained empty. In the economic sphere, there was economic prosperity, a demand for labor in general, and also the belief among businessmen that Blacks represented a new and untapped potential source of skilled labor.

By the time a few gains were registered, however, the domestic economy had begun to change. Facing strong competition on the world market from other capitalist countries, particularly Germany and Japan; the decline of the dollar; increasing independence of nations like those in the Middle East, Africa, Asia, and Latin America in controlling and setting prices for their own resources; and greater demands for higher wages and lower prices from both organized and unorganized workers at home, the U.S. went into a severe and persistent economic crisis. This resulted in limited availability of and increased competition for jobs, educational opportunities, and so on, as well as a cutback of social services on the one hand and higher prices and taxes on the other. With the decreasing need for labor in general, there was less "space" for Blacks, minorities, and women in the job market. In academia, labor market pressures were reflected in faculty employment. Despite successful efforts to recruit Black students, Black faculty recruitment was stymied by the oversupply of Ph.D.'s, forced retrenchment in higher education, and the direct necessity to replace whites with minorities in order to achieve a fair representation of minority faculty in higher education. At this juncture, Black interests diverged from those of big business and other elites. Affirmative action came under attack when the possibility of redistribution of access, resources, and status became a possibility in an era of economic downturn. Both academic and legal attacks on affirmative action focused on its violation of abstractly defined and understood definitions of individual rights.

In his disappointing dissent in *DeFunis v. Odegaard, 416 U.S.* 312 (1974) Justice W. O. Douglas states the legal arguments for an individualistic approach to the constitution which comes close to denying the special historical circumstances of slavery and legal segregation which created unique, collective barriers for Blacks:

There is no constitutional right for any race to be preferred. The years of slavery did more than retard the progress of Blacks. Even a greater wrong was done to whites by creating arrogance instead of humility and by encouraging the growth of the fiction of a superior race. There is no superior person by constitutional standards. As DeFunis who is white is entitled to no advantage by reason of that fact, nor is he subject to any disability, no matter his race or color. Whatever his race, he had a constitutional right to have his application considered on its *individual merits* (our emphasis) in a racially neutral manner.

That statement could only be made about a society presumed to now be open, free, egalitarian, and just. It says nothing of value about a society plagued by continued racial hierarchy.

We have argued that affirmative action emerged because of the demands of the civil rights movement and was accepted by big business due to the labor shortage in the 1960s. Similarly, more Blacks were educated to fill additional positions in the market place because of the need of universities to tap new sources of tuition revenues; by the late 1970s economic downturn and ideological co-optation of the Black political position undermined the utility of affirmative action for Blacks. By that time affirmative action had already contributed to increases of the middle-class segment within the Black community. Affirmative action then came under strident attack on the ground that it violated individualism and egalitarianism. The attacks, of course, conveniently ignored the collectivism and hierarchy of legal segregation. With the election of Ronald Reagan, the might of the Presidency and of the executive branch were added against affirmative action.

This brief history and theoretical interpretation of affirmative action suggests the difficulty of implementing and sustaining institutional (and by extension structural) policies. Since these policies are crucial if Black subordination is to be altered or ended, our analysis of the fate of affirmative action can only be sobering.

NOTES

1. Richard Burkey, *Racial Discrimination and Public Policy in the United States* (Lexington, Mass.: D.C. Heath, 1971) pp. 38–39.
2. Marguerite Ross Barnett, "A Theoretical Perspective on Racial Public Policy," in Marguerite Ross Barnett and James A. Hefner, *Public Policy for the Black Community: Strategies and Perspectives* (Sherman Oaks, California: Alfred, 1976)
3. Robert Dahl, *Who Governs?* (New Haven: Yale University Press, 1961) p. 52.

4. Barnett, *op cit.*, p. 13.

5. *Ibid.*, p. 14.

6. Barry Bluestone and Bennett Harrison, *The Deindustrialization of America* (New York: Basic Books, 1982), p. 114.

7. Norman V. Bartley, *The Rise of Massive Resistance* (Baton Rouge: Louisiana State University Press, 1969), p. 74.

8. Frances Fox Piven and Richard Cloward, *Poor People's Movements: Why They Succeed, How They Fail* (New York: Pantheon, 1977), p. 227.

9. Ibid., p. 231.

10. Interview with Hobart Taylor, Jr., 1978.

11. "The President's Committee on Equal Employment Opportunity," *The Committee Reporter*, vol. 1, no. 3 (May 1965), p. 18.

12. Ibid., p. 12.

13. Ibid., p. 13.

14. Ibid., p. 13.

15. See, *Plans for Progress: A First Year Report By The Plans For Progress Advisory Council*, August, 1964. pp. 2-3.

16. Interview with Hobart Taylor, Jr., 1978.

17. Terry Eastland and William J. Bennett, *Counting by Race: Equality from the Founding Fathers to Bakke and Weber* (New York: Basic Books, 1979), p. 112.

18. For other analyses of these mechanisms of inequality, see John C. Livingston, *Fair Game? Inequality and Affirmative Action.* (San Francisco: H. H. Freeman and Co., 1974), p. 11. Also see David Swinton, "Problems in Studying Discrimination: A Harking Paper," in *Urban Institute Monograph 17* (Washington, D.C.: The Urban Institute, 1980), p. 4.

19. Summaries of data in the following sections on economic differentials are drawn from the tables. See sources at the bottom of the respective tables.

20. Lorenzo Morris, *Elusive Equality: The Status of Black Americans in Higher Education* (Washington D.C.: Howard University Press, 1979), p. 114.

21. Nathan Glazer, *Affirmative Discrimination: Ethnic Inequality and Public Policy*, (New York: Basic Books, 1975), p. 4.

22. Ibid., p. 43.

23. Ibid., p. 220.

24. Ibid., p. 43.

25. Ibid.

26. Thomas Sowell, "Affirmative Action and Pious Fraud, *Inquiry*, August 21, 1978, p. 12.

27. Edward Shils, "The Case Against Affirmative Action," *The Chronicle of Higher Education*, December 5, 1980, p. 1.

28. *Regents of the University of California v. Bakke*, 98 S. Ct. 2733, 2798–2799.

29. Interview with Kenneth Tollett, 1980.

30. 98 S. Ct. 2733, 2754.

31. DeFunis v. Odegaard, 416 U.S. 312 (1974).

What are the political and economic consequences of the retrenchment and block grant strategies that the Reagan administration has put into effect? Marilyn Gittell and Gary Orfield look at some of these consequences at the state and municipal level in the essays in Part II.

The growth of state services since the New Deal has resulted in expanded bureaucracies and increasingly complex interest-group politics at the state level. Supplanting categorical with block grant aid has devolved additional power from the federal government to the states, shifting important areas of decision-making to the states and greatly increasing the significance of state education. Gittell argues that rather than bringing educational decision-making closer to the people, as the Reagan administration claims, the block grant strategy actually removes decision-making farther from the people, since categorical grants often provided funds directly to local school districts. The reduction in total federal assistance accompanied by the supposedly wider discretion in expending federal funds will heighten competition among rural, suburban, and urban school districts and between rich and poor districts, and sharpen conflict between claimants for funds for education and for other interests. Gittell fears that unless urban community and neighborhood groups, largely minority and poor and historically oriented to local and federal politicking, can quickly re-orient themselves, they will lose out and suffer in the intense competition with well-organized professional education associations and groups who are thoroughly familiar with bureaucratic and legislative politics at the state level.

At the municipal level, the deep and rapid reduction in federal education aid has been an unmitigated disaster. The enactment of the momentous Elementary and Secondary Education Act in 1965 had greatly expanded the dependence of education on federal funding. Moreover, specific legislation which targeted federal assistance to the poverty of students provided important aid to urban school districts. Furthermore, these districts benefited from other non-education federal programs which produced resources for the schools. The increasing growth of inter-governmental grants to cities in general and education in particular to some extent masked the perilous condition into which many cities had fallen since World War II. By the early 1980s, the largest school districts found themselves victims of a three-sided crisis: a sharp and rapid cut in direct federal assistance; reductions in state aid; and close and severe recessions creating high unemployment and accompanied by the highest interest rates in history, driving up the cost of bond financing and retarding the growth of assessed property values taxable for school funding. Support for increased funding has grown since the federal and state cuts of the early 1980s but the underlying situation is still precarious for most large urban systems.

The advent of retrenchment politics severely aggravated the problems, some of which became apparent before the election of President Reagan, of the nation's largest school districts. School systems in New York, Cleveland, and Chicago were virtually bankrupt, and the states suspended accountability of local school officials to the citizenry as the price for fiscal rescue in those cities. Education groups mobilized to exert pressure on Congress to block additional cuts that the administration planned to enact, but the net effect was merely to hold spending at a much lower level. The federal share of public school budgets fell from 9.8% in 1979–1980 to 7.5% in 1981–1982, the lowest level since aid programs were enacted in the mid-1960s. Recent federal policies, moreover, have distributed funds in ways that harm urban districts and favor suburban and private schools. Increased funding by some states between 1983 and 1985 eased the crisis in some large districts but there is no guarantee that additional funds to relieve the underlying problems will be made available in the future.

The key to understanding the politics of retrenchment in education policy, Orfield argues, is the racial composition of these districts. Only 17 of the largest 50 districts enroll majority white student bodies, while five, New York, Chicago, Los Angeles, Philadelphia, and Detroit, accounted in 1970 for more than 20% of the nation's Black and Hispanic students. Rural- and suburban-dominated state legislatures turn deaf ears to entreaties for more aid to urban schools serving predominantly Black and Hispanic students. The cities themselves have little fiscal capacity and/or lack the political will to increase assistance. In Philadelphia, for example, whites comprise 63% of the electorate yet fewer than 11% of white households have students enrolled in public schools. This surely was a factor in the city's willingness to tolerate a long, bitter, and destructive teachers' strike in 1981 rather than to vote the tax increases needed to support the schools.

Orfield's prognosis is grim. Without a change both in the political climate and an upturn in economic fortunes, the big city public school systems upon which minority students, faculty, and administrators rely heavily will continue to be plagued by low morale, shrinkage in curriculum, inability to adapt to economic and technological change, and a range of futile and destructive strategies to cope with retrenchment.

RETRENCHMENT AND STATE INTEREST GROUP POLITICS:
THE IMPACT ON EDUCATION

Marilyn Gittell

President Reagan's expansive plans for a "New Federalism" will influence the course of state and local politics for the next decade. Contrary to widespread common belief and media propaganda, however, the state activities have risen and fallen with the direction of federal policy. The expansion of federal programs and spending under the New Deal simultaneously expanded the states' role—The Great Society programs benefited states and localities, not only in the flow of dollars, but also in the growth of their own services and professional bureaucracies. Federal legislation mandated increased staffs and paid a large share of their costs. As the *Wall Street Journal* correctly pointed out in its editorial of January 12, 1983, the reduction in federal funding for domestic programs will result not in increased state spending, but in reduced state spending and services. We can observe differences in state responses to Federal policies, some following the Federal lead, others struggling to supplement reduced Federal spending. Much depends on the vitality of state economies and the commitments of state leadership.

States as Political Systems

The expansion of state services over the last five decades has, however, produced some changes in state government which significantly shape the politics of retrenchment. Interest-group politics in the states has become more complex, being strongly influenced by migration patterns, and by fundamental economic changes in states and regions as well as in the growth of states' services as active partners in American federalism. Montana can no longer be considered a subsidiary of Anaconda and Maine is no longer solely dependent upon the lumber industry. Colorado has become the Western regional center of the Federal government as well as an energy center of the country. The oil industry's control and dominance in Texas is challenged by the emergence of high technology. The Midwest is no longer dominated by steel and automobile interests. Service industries have replaced manufacturing everywhere. Service bureaucracies and professional government workers and their public service unions are a major force to be contended with at the state and local level. In fact state and local governments have grown at a faster rate than the Federal treasury in its years of expanded programs. Interstate or coalition state politics has been greatly enhanced by the development of such agencies as the Governors' Conference, the Education Council of the States, and myriad cross-state and local professional associations. These are strong pressure groups fostering continued federal and state support for special programs and particular services.

The continuing debate in the professional journals regarding the political character and behavior of state governments centers on whether states are, in fact, independent political systems making policies suited to their own individual needs. Statistical analysis of state programmatic spending as well as studies of innovative legislation suggest strongly that federal policy is an overriding influence on state political behavior. These studies conclude that the states fall in line with federal grant programs, unable to resist the flow of federal dollars. The research shows that selected states are leaders, others followers in different historical periods. California, New York, and Michigan have been regional leaders over a long period of time. They set an example for contiguous states which eventually emulate their policies (Walker 1969). While supporting conclusions that state policy behavior can be explained by this system of policy emulation, other analysis has suggested that who leads and who follows in policy adoption may vary according to the type of policy and the time period examined (Gray, 1973).

Attempts to categorize the policy behavior of states, as reflected in expenditure patterns or social welfare programs, have shown inconsistent results (Sharkansky, 1967). Regionalism continues to be the major independent variable explaining state political behavior. Southern states, in particular, seem to act in a consistent fashion; their governmental structures are all highly centralized. The North Atlantic and Midwestern states tend to be less centralized and the Western states are a mixed breed, combining a populist tradition with strong state development. Changes in population characteristics as a result of migration have, however, produced changes in structure in states like Florida and South Carolina where decentralization is more evident.

The Politics of Retrenchment

The history of the politics of education at the state level can be distinguished from that of other state services in some respects, although in other respects it represents a microcosm of the broader state political arena. Educational decisions are one output of the competing actors in the broader game of retrenchment politics, and educational policy will bear the scars of that battle for decades to come. It is instructive, therefore, to analyze the way in which the political game is likely to develop.

The anti-urban bias of state governments will be a major factor in the character of retrenchment politics. Sharp cuts in aid combined with the devolution of authority over block grants to the states at a time when some of them have serious revenue losses as a result of a declining economy has serious consequences for particular state populations. In a study conducted by the U.S.

Conference of Mayors in October 1982, 70 percent of the cities surveyed (officials from 55 cities responded) reported they were "not fairly represented" in the process by which the state distributed federal money given them in block grants. The cities indicated that they could not influence state decisions (*New York Times*, October 14, 1982). Results of changes in the allocation of block grants in education in Michigan and Pennsylvania as well as other states showed resources to urban centers declining while suburban areas benefited (Gittell, 1984).

Early revenue-sharing experience provides some insight into state behavior at a time when federal funding levels were retained or increased and state discretion replaced federal categorical aid. General revenue sharing, initiated in 1972, allowed state governments to use revenue-sharing funds for any purpose except matching funds for federal grants. Local officials, however, were restricted to specified categories in their use of the money provided for operating and maintenance expenditures; funds could be used for any capital expenditure. Revenue-sharing money is, in effect, unrestricted money in the overall state budget-making process with increased state discretion. Evaluations of the results of state policy direction in the use of those funds indicate a shift in their allocation, from urban to suburban areas. A survey by Technology Management Incorporated reported 72 percent of the 574 communities that responded to the survey ranked capital expenditures in their top three spending choices. The other two were operating and maintenance expenditures and environmental protection. Of the 35 responding state governments, five said they expected to use funds for social development. At the bottom of the state list of priorities were community development and economic development, with none of the responding states having plans for such expenditures. In another finding, Caputo and Cole reported that 44 percent of all units of government felt that the revenue sharing money had been used to help avoid tax increases!

Suburban areas received greater portions of revenue-sharing funds than central cities. In addition, certain states in the Sun Belt benefited from the Federal allocation formulae. When the Treasury Department made its first allocation of revenue sharing funds, it used the final reports of the 1970 population census and had a special survey made by the Census Bureau to update the state and local tax data to 1971. The result of using the later tax information caused the nation's fastest-growing areas to benefit most, while Eastern and Midwestern states suffered losses.

Because of population growth, suburban areas show a greater tax effort even though the tax burden on residents has not changed. Central cities with static or declining population can have a higher tax effort index only by actually increasing the tax burden. Central cities operate at a disadvantage, therefore, with regard to any allocation formula which favors areas showing greater tax effort.

States with higher per-capita incomes are penalized in the allocation of funds. It is the more urbanized states which generally have above-average incomes. In revenue sharing in the intrastate stage of the distribution process, double weight is given to per-capita income, further hurting urban areas within the state. Allocations to some urban areas are curtailed by ceiling provisions in the law.

The Omnibus Crime Control and Safe Streets Act of 1968 provided block grants to states and provided early insights into possible responses. Congress had mandated that at least 40 percent of the planning funds go to local governments. The states were to determine the formulae for distributing the money. Conflicts arose immediately between mayors and state governments. Cities complained that states were using a per-capita distribution formula which totally ignored the concentration of crime in urban areas. There was little the cities could do besides complain, and the programs continued to ignore the special needs of urban areas.

From the first announcements of the block grants in 1981, efforts by state legislatures to wrest control over block grant funds from the governors were evident:

The legislature is going to have to take a hard look at the programs turned over to us and determine which of these the state really needs. . . . Then there are three practical things you have to remember: One is that the poor do not represent an active constituency, second, politically it is easier to cut social service, and third people are embarrassed by Florida's reputation for crime and they want something done about it. (*New York Times*, January 17, 1982, pp. 1, 27).

An Arizona official noted what the new-found state power means in deciding where to make cuts: "It's trading off little kids against handicapped people against retarded." In states where competition between the governor and the legislature exists, the question of control over federal funds will be particularly pronounced.

In some states unearmarked federal funds will be used to supplant declining state funds; in others federal funds may supplant local funds. The politics of retrenchment in the states, as a result of reductions in federal spending, and any decline in revenues resulting from economic changes, will be dominated by competition between urban, suburban, and rural areas. In education, conflict will emerge over the allocation of revenues to higher vs. lower education, to state agencies vs. local districts, to various kinds of programs and special education needs; and over priorities of allocation for salaries, programs, and equipment. The arena will be the state capital: the target will be executive and legislative decision-makers. The participants will include a variety of private sector interests, organized professionals inside and outside the bureaucracy, local officials, and a range of community and issue organizations.

Interest Groups as Political Actors

Theories about state interest-group politics in education are often related to the degree of centralization and the extent of resources of state education agencies. The assumption is that the more developed the state education agency, the less likely it is that interest groups will influence decisions. The more centralized the state control, the more limited the local discretion, the less influence interest groups of all kinds can exert.

Most analysts assume that active interest group politics increases local discretion. In fact, much depends on the character of interest-group balancing. In most states school professionals dominate education policy-making at the state level. They have been successful in maintaining a high level of support for education in competition with other state services (Gold, 1983). If education professionals and teachers are well organized, they may prefer state decision-making on some issues, although their influence is also effective at the local district level. Some states lack diverse or competitive or active interest group politics. This would be particularly true in the South, although that is also changing. Centralized states like Florida and South Carolina in recent years have implemented extensive programs in education to encourage citizen participation through parent councils at the local and state level. These changes are likely to result in real differences in the competition for funds as these newly active groups recognize the power to be wielded over limited funds at the state level.

Those who have a long tradition of lobbying at the state level, with sufficient resources to support political campaigns and maintain offices, are a constant force in state capitals, and they will be in a prime position to influence decisions and guarantee their own rewards. Although there is variation among the states, with some more encouraging to broader representation and access than others, the predominance of professional interests is likely to remain constant. Urban schools districts will face traditional anti-urban attitudes; in some states, like California, this will not be as important as it is in Illinois, Ohio, and Michigan. In New York State the Governor's effort to reallocate school funds on the basis of need was met by angry protests charging him with undue preference for New York City over suburban and upstate interests. Suburban dominance of many state legislatures will almost certainly guarantee that the reduction in federal aid for compensatory education programs (largely beneficial to urban school districts) will result in greater disadvantage to urban districts and urban schools. Poor and minority populations recently organized to pressure for special federal programs and aid have been successful in developing strong ties to federal bureaucrats. These same groups have little access to or familiarity with state officials. A real test of their strength will be their ability to turn their attention to the state arena.

Responses to Retrenchment

The interest in the development of high technology and information systems and economic development is placing new demands on the education establishment and will be reflected in the politics of retrenchment of almost every state. Resources will more likely flow to those programs which respond to these interests. Higher education faces the reality of lower birth rates until the 1990s with state budget cuts to universities easily rationalized by quantitative criteria. The differences in commitment to post-secondary public institutions by region are likely to be reflected in some states' willingness to shift to more qualitative judgments to continue support to their state university systems. Open access to higher education is likely to be a low priority for states facing financial pressures. Already the goals of educational "excellence" are being used to screen out students and lower enrollments further. Within states, conflict among urban, rural, and suburban interests, and rich and poor school districts will become more prominent as the competition for funds heats up. Declining enrollments in urban schools will make them vulnerable to per-capita reductions in funding.

Increased state control over reduced resources will foster some shifts in the roles of the various participants in the struggle for state funding. Two battlegrounds are likely to develop if retrenchment politics moves into higher gear: first, in the raising and allocation of resources among the various governmental functions; second, in competition for funds among the various education interests.

The states' response thus far to the "new federalism"—the conversion of federal aid from categorical to block grants—includes the creation of special task forces and commissions to recommend how adjustments should be made. With state legislatures asserting themselves in the allocation of funds, new processes have been adopted.

The assertion of legislative power in the review of federal grants is a relatively new state phenomenon. Four states enacted strong legislation in 1981: Massachusetts, New York, Oklahoma, and Iowa. At least eleven states have adopted formal roles for themselves in reviewing block grants. About forty states have instituted procedures giving their legislatures some new power with regard to block grants. This increase in legislative oversight theoretically can work to create more open state political systems. The anti-urban bias of state legislatures, especially as compared to governors, is, however, worrisome. Unless urban areas and community organizations become more sensitive to and involved with state electoral politics, they may find themselves suffering at the hands of suburban special interests and provincial legislators. Geography will become an important criterion for the allocation of funds because of the legislative concern about their districts. Cities will be at a distinct disadvantage.

The state response to cuts in federal aid and revenue shortfalls thus far has been to use surpluses and/or reduce expenditures. Some states have increased taxes. All of the states except Vermont are required by their constitutions to balance their budgets. The pressure to cut services and increase taxes generates conflict between governors and legislators, forcing trade-offs on services. Local governments most dependent on federal and state aid are particularly at risk and cities are therefore most vulnerable.

A major concern about state government has been its vulnerability to special interest group politics, particularly private sector pressures. Also part-time legislators, short-term governors, and old-style bureaucracies tend to be less responsive to demonstrated needs.

A more optimistic view suggests that the states have been restructured, reformed, and made more responsive over the last two decades and are responsive to the needs of urban areas and minority populations. An ACIR report states:

Continuing a reform period unparalleled in their history, they (the states) are emerging, for the most part, as competent, vigorous and assertive government. They are more open, more responsible, more accountable than they were in the past. (ACIR, 1982)

Interest group access and system openness depends upon the availability of information, the mechanisms provided for access, and the ability of groups with limited resources to organize. Urban and grass-roots interest groups think access to legislatures would enhance their effectiveness and would encourage greater involvement on their part in the decision process. Historically, governors have, however, served minority and poor populations better than legislatures. In either case it will require strong coalition building and organization on a state-wide basis for these groups to have their voices heard. In many of the states the capitol is located far from the main city making the problem of access even more difficult.

The Politics of Education: Federal Programs

Primary and secondary school education, legally a state function, is administered and controlled at the school-district level. At its peak, federal aid represented only 8 percent of total school-district revenues. The 8 percent, however, was specifically earmarked for compensatory programs, comprising more than half the school system budgets allocated for these purposes. Urban school systems were the primary beneficiaries. The reductions in those funds, therefore, was felt disproportionately by that population. The reduction in federal funds is dramatic because it represents the abandonment of the redistributive function of the central government under a federal system that evolved over four or five decades.

The major categorical program, Title I, provided federal funds to areas with heavy concentrations of economically and educationally deprived children. As defined in the legislation, assistance was to be provided to local educational agencies but was targeted for the education of children of low-income families. The remaining five original titles of the Elementary and Secondary Education Act provided funds to supplement state education resources in all schools.

Specifically, Title II provided aid to develop school libraries and for the acquisition of textbooks and other instructional materials. Title III provided federal funding for the development of supplemental educational centers and services. Title IV provided funding for educational research and training. And Title V set aside money to be used by state departments of education to strengthen their own administrative agencies. Title VI outlined and defined the terms of federal regulations and requirements for receiving grants. Other titles added in the 1960s and 1970s provided funds for handicapped children (Title VII) and bilingual programs (Title VIII) to redress educational inequities caused by unfamiliarity with the English language. Stimulated by court decisions which determined that lower-income and minority children, largely in urban school systems, were deprived of equal treatment, the federal funding was an attempt to counterbalance these inequities.

Although each of these educational titles, further refined in categorical-aid programs, included minimum standards to be met by state and local agencies and guidelines for implementation, they did not give federal agencies direct control over local educational policies. State and local school systems implemented these programs in ways that reflected their own political culture and school politics. In comparison to federal title programs, court-mandated actions are far more coercive in dictating school policies.

Although the Congress reduced the Reagan plan for education block grant funding, the policies of limited reporting, rejection of affirmative action and dispensing with parent participation were adopted.

The first consolidation of education categorical aid, a limited measure, peculiarly included The Emergency School Aid Act which was adopted in 1972 to support local desegregation programs. It amounted to 28 percent ($150 million of $537.5 million in 1981) of the cost of all twenty five programs under the block grant consolidation. A library assistance program represented a slightly larger percentage ($161 million). Under the Emergency School Aid Program states and localities determined the character of their own programs; funds were used to support magnet schools, special equipment, additional teachers and aids. Three hundred and thirty districts received aid under the program in 1981. Large cities like St. Louis, New Orleans, Buffalo, and Cleveland have had their aid cut radically as a result of the consolidation of funding. Desegregation now is one of many functions for which the block grants are allocated and the states have set the standards for the appropriation of these funds.

The total amount of money available for the twenty-five programs has declined from $537 million in 1981 to $480 million in 1983. Most states have distributed funds on a per-capita basis which ignores the special needs of cities (Stanfield, 1983; Gittell, 1984). This first experience of the block grant approach to education suggests a pattern which would probably be followed in future consolidation of categorical programs into block grants.

The categorical aid programs included two important elements in addition to compensatory education or equity. Aid under Titles III, IV, and V went directly to local districts and the private sector (i.e., universities), thus bypassing state governments. In addition, several of the titles included provisions for broadening participation in the decision-making process, for example, by creating parent and community committees. Concerted efforts to undermine direct federal grants to local districts has been a goal of many state governments over the years. As early as 1967, state school professionals expressed their dissatisfaction with this arrangement, and they were successful in restoring their control over Title III monies in a compromise plan worked out with Republican representatives in Congress.

The argument made that the Reagan administration is seeking to return educational decision-making to its rightful place, closer to the people, is not substantiated by the change from categorical to block grants. Since many of the categorical grants now provide federal funds directly to local districts, the shift to state control will undermine local control and is contradictory to Reagan rhetoric.

The major proportion of federal funds for elementary and secondary schools went to programs for the educationally deprived and to economic opportunity programs. In 1979, 60 percent of all federal dollars were earmarked for these purposes. Title I was effectively distributed to meet the needs of deprived student populations. Central cities and rural areas benefited more than suburban areas under Title I. In 1977, central cities received 38.3 percent, non-metropolitan areas 33.8 percent, and suburban areas 27.9 percent of the total allocation of Title I funds. The National Institute of Education has written (1977): "As a funding program, Title I's effects are distinctive. It is more redistributive than any other class of federal and state programs. Though it is not meant to be a device for equalizing per pupil expenditures among school districts, it does equalize to some extent." Berke and Kirst wrote: "ESEA I appears to be the primary source of the sensitivity to urban and rural finance problems" (Berke & Kirst, 1972, 400). School districts with large proportions of nonwhite pupils and districts with low median family income levels receive the highest proportion of Title I funds.

Other federal funding titles clearly favor suburban school districts, especially when state discretionary decision-making is involved. The percent distribution of all federal education funds for fiscal year 1970 shows that suburban areas received more Title I funds than non-metropolitan areas, but central cities still received the largest amount of funds. Under the category of "state discretionary funding," suburban areas fared best, receiving almost half of all the federal dollars involved. This is especially true in the subcategory "all other," including Title II and III of ESEA and parts of the National Defense Education Act. Berke and Kirst point out that in these categories . . . major cities have received even less aid than should have been allotted to them in view of just their proportion of the states' pupil population. When considerations of comparative costs or student need are taken into account, the pattern appears far more discriminatory" (Berke & Kirst, 1972, 3). The authors further state that NDEA and ESEA III "frequently worked to make the rich districts richer" (Berke & Kirst, 1972, 400). According to the Congressional Budget Office (1977), "state discretionary programs slightly favor suburban, middle income, middle wealth districts." In 1970 suburban areas received 45.7 percent of all federal dollars to education, central cities 37.1 percent and non-metropolitan areas only 17.1 percent.

The Politics of Education: The States

Our knowledge of state government and the politics of education allows us to make some predictions. Formerly rural-controlled legislatures are now largely suburban-dominated. State education grant-in-aid formulae, challenged in the courts in several states, continue to reflect either a distinct bias in favor of wealthy suburban school districts or a disinclination to use aid as a redistributive mechanism.

This resistance to change and general stasis at the state level is nowhere more evident than in the area of school finance. A number of states have been under state court order to revise their system of financing public education. Yet even where the state is under explicit order to change the practices, they have been delinquent in acting. The *Serrano* decision was handed down in 1971, yet no change has yet been made in the California financing system. New Jersey has been searcing for a "thorough and efficient" financing plan since 1972. The *Hellerstein* decision in New York was handed down in 1978. In all three cases the states have established study commissions, let contracts for computer models of alternative finance systems, and hired education professionals as consultants; yet no changes in aid formulae have occurred.

Court cases were necessitated by inequities in funding as a result of plans adopted by state governments. Maryland and Colorado have had similar more recent court decisions. The urban school systems have been the major victims of these inequities. Under Reagan's block grants federal funds were distributed to local districts by states in the same way that state education aid is distributed or by the same formulae used under revenue sharing. Cities suffered losses under these practices as need was replaced by geography as a criterion for funding (Gittell, 1984).

Conflicts among urban, suburban, and rural areas were heightened as they competed for limited funds, and suburban areas were the major beneficiaries. Certainly compensatory programs in urban schools will be further threatened if urban districts must compete for state funds and federal guidelines disappear. The lack of state priority for urban education needs is a major factor. Usdan summarized the circumstances which produced federal programs in the 1960s:

> The structural and functional weaknesses of the states have been a salient factor in precipitating the current crisis in interlevel governmental relationships. Many of the states for a variety of reasons have virtually abdicated responsibility for the nation's urban problems. As a result, the states have been bypassed by problem-plagued urban centers, which have been compelled to turn to the federal government for assistance (Usdan, 1972, 64).

In 1976 Thompson confirmed the continuing prejudices of state legislatures:

> Deadlocks have frequently occurred in state legislatures over urban school problems. As a result of rural and suburban control, coupled with an anti-urban bias, states have neither met the challenge of the urban education crisis nor provided for equality of educational opportunity. The urban school crisis has not been met by the states, and the conflict has been pushed to the federal level (Thompson 1976, 155).

Mecanto, in his analysis of state school politics, noted that despite "the relatively greater need of city students, the 37 largest cities were spending, on the average, $124 less per pupil than their respective suburbs . . . state school aid is not allocated to overcome this difference. Instead, it actually flows in greater amounts to suburban schools. This enhances the ability of suburban districts to spend more per pupil than cities and contributes to the growing gap between suburban and city school expenditures." (Mecanto, 1970, p.97).

In a more recent study of the state legislative role in educational politics, Rosenthal and Fuhrman (1981) made some informative findings. Generally state legislators involved in educational policy concentrate their attention on budgets and appropriations. They exercise little discretion, however, over federal funds. Legislators who choose education as an area of special interest tend to continue that concern over a period of time, maintaining their membership on key committees. These legislative leaders rely most heavily on state education agencies and teachers associations for their information about educational issues. Legislative staff also rely on state education agencies for their information.

Rosenthal and Fuhrman consider their most crucial finding regarding educational leadership in the states to be the fact that new legislators are not interested in education as a policy area. The only exceptions are the professional educators who become legislators. This is occurring at a time when the legislative role in education is growing, and senior legislators concerned with education are about to retire. This circumstance could make educational policy-making in the future a totally financial issue with little regard to special needs of special populations. Control over local districts by state education agencies and/or state budget offices is likely to increase as a rational reaction to the need for budget reductions. This is already evidenced in state budgeting for higher education in several states where purchases over $1000 require state approval.

Wirt categorizes the states with regard to their educational governance as centralized and decentralized. The more decentralized states are likely to be competitive, open, and more responsible. The most decentralized are Wyoming, North Dakota, Texas, Mississippi, Nevada, Massachusetts and Connecticut (Wirt, 1977). The more centralized states will provide less access.

Governors in the past have not seen themselves as leaders in the development of educational policy. There have been some notable exceptions as when Governor Rockefeller took on the cause of the advancement of the State University of New York as a personal goal in the 1970s. A recent dramatic exception was the action of Governor William Winter of Mississippi in 1982, who championed extensive changes in primary and secondary education as a major thrust of his new administration. His education program called for state-supported kindergartens, raising the mandatory age for those remaining in school from 12 to 14, salary increases for teachers, and increasing the number of school aides in reading programs. The goal, the governor said, was to make Mississippi competitive with other states in the Sun Belt. Up until 1982 Mississippi spent $1090 per pupil in public schools, one half the national average. The governor joined the issues of appeal to industry and educating the population as a viable labor force to rationalize support for greatly increased expenditures. (*New York Times*, 27 December 1982). Although Mississippi was unique in its total failure to support public education in the past, the governor's role and the rationale for new educational policies may portend a thrust for educational politics in the future. More governors may find themselves assuming more responsibility with regard to educational policies as they are faced with increased pressures from legislative and private interests competing for limited state funds.

The most important government actor taking on new responsibilities in the shift of responsibility to the states will be the state education agencies. These enlarged bureaucracies are not only the most important source of information for governors and legislators, they have a direct vested interest in the competition for funds.

The State Education Agencies

The most recent comparative state research on the professional staff of state education agencies was conducted by Kirby et al., in three states. The authors summarized their findings by noting:

. . . professional personnel in each of the states we studied comprise extremely homogeneous groups. These state departments of education are largely composed of men (95%) who have lived their lives in the rural area of the states they serve; who have gone to a state teachers college . . . who had begun careers as professional educators, generally in rural schools, before entering the department; and who had been invited to join the department by another member of the SDE (State Department of Education). Clearly, this degree of homogeneity is not simply the result of chance. Explicitly and implicitly recruitment policies have produced this result (Kirby *et al.*, 1967, 39).

Kirby also found that over half the professional staff was over 50 years old and that there is little mobility within the state education agency; most hirees remain in their appointed position for their entire careers. Top level staff, rather than being promoted from within, are brought in from the outside. Those in the lower ranks receive salaries below prevailing urban and suburban schedules, limiting the attractiveness of the positions to professionals from those districts. There is a dearth of minority staff members in state departments and limited sensitivity to the problems of the minority school population in urban areas (Kirby, 1967).

State education agencies have been described as supportive of the status quo and loath to take independent initiative. Campbell has noted, "I do not have as much faith in the states as some people, perhaps. In fact, I think there are very few states that are doing anything that shows any initiative today. I think most states are grinding along doing only those things they have to do." (Quoted in Bendiner, 1969, p. 169.)

Major expansions of the state education agencies and an increased emphasis on the professional qualifications of their staff have occurred over the past 10 years. However, the impetus for these changes has not been the result of actions of the states themselves. The expansion in professional staff, to the degree that it has occurred, is primarily the result of federal programs which required reorganization of state administrative structures. Reduced federal support will require state education agencies to make choices about where cuts should be made, including the contraction of their own empires. There will be a great temptation to further centralize state controls in order to maintain their status.

Higher education and primary and secondary education bureaucracies are generally separated at the state level. Each has its own separate constituency and although cooperative efforts have been encouraged, it is more likely that competition will increase. State agencies in higher education, public colleges, and universities throughout the country have already responded to budget cuts by increasing admissions requirements to reduce size. These policy decisions will place a burden on the primary and secondary schools which they will be hard pressed to meet. If education funds continue to be reduced, we are likely to see more state education agency policies which further limit access under the guise of increased standards. In some cases proposals like the one made by the New York State Education Commission will reallocate funds according to how professional and other resources are distributed, e.g., adding a year at the bottom (age 4) and deducting a year from the top (age 17).

Interest Group Politics at the State Level

The federal shift to the block grant approach, relying on state discretion in the allocation of funds, could alter political bargaining at the state level. As compared with federal categorical programs, the block grant could potentially increase interest group participation in the decision-making process at the state level. However, as in any policy area, the bargaining process is not open to all groups equally, and some groups are more experienced, have greater resources, and are able to function at the state level, while other groups lack access and resources.

Professional interest groups, which have local chapters in most, if not all, school districts, have been organized on the state level for a long time and have been a regular part of the state bargaining process. The contacts and leverage they have developed will be a strong base from which to move into bargaining for the allocation of education block grants. Teacher associations are considered the most influential group in the education arena (Rosenthal & Fuhrman, 1981). They are important contributors to political campaigns, and legislators and governors are quite sensitive to that fact. In California, the teachers association is the third largest contributor to legislative races. Teachers also serve in large numbers as volunteers in legislative campaigns. In the 1982 gubernatorial election in New York State teachers were a major source of preelection manpower in local districts throughout the state, and they were not modest in claiming credit for the governor's election. Teachers associations are a strong and unified interest group. If competition among different kinds of school districts (e.g., city vs. suburban districts) develops, their unity will be affected and influence may be diffused. Interestingly, the American Federation of Teachers in New York State did not support the governor's reallocation of education funds according to need. They labeled it a "Robin Hood" program. They recommended added revenues for poor school districts without disrupting current levels of support to other school districts—a protective policy.

On the larger battleground of competition with other governmental services, education interest groups can be expected to maintain a strong united front. Professionals, parents, local school boards, and bureaucrats will work together for common goals. In sharing the education pie, however, the coalition will become a new battleground for different geographic and special interests. The groups which will be least able to influence the bargaining process will be those which have purely local and neighborhood education concerns, particularly community-based organizations. Such groups generally lack statewide networks. Their experience and access is largely at the city or district level, and in more recent years at the federal level.

A 1980 study of sixteen community organizations concerned with education issues in three cities demonstrated the limited contact community and neighborhood organizations had with state education decision-makers (Gittell, 1980). Community-based organizations which represent lower-income and minority populations will be at a disadvantage in competition with highly organized statewide professional lobbying groups in the state political arena. These community organizations have been the major source of support for urban school funds for compensatory programs. And it was the federal government which was most responsive to their pressures. The shift of decision-making to the state, it is to be hoped, will encourage urban school constituencies to take a more active interest in state politics. Activist neighborhood groups in urban communities may adjust their strategies and orientation to lobby their interests at the state level. It is unfamiliar and unfriendly territory and will require reeducation as well as new political organization. Lower-income and minority groups have been neglected by, and they in turn neglect, state politics. This puts them at great disadvantage in this era of stronger state roles.

Certainly all of the evidence thus far points to a stronger role for state education agencies, which are more responsive to professional interest. So long as professional educators' interests are the same as their clients', their access is useful. When conflicts arise, community or client interests might be significantly undermined if they are not organized and manifest at state capitols. Many of the community-based education agencies at the school district level were funded directly by federal grant programs, bypassing the states. Those funds often sustained these organizations and encouraged their participation in educational matters. The cutoff of these funds is likely to reduce the number of such organizations and/or undermine their participation at a time when they could be an important voice at the state level.

Far more energy and effort will have to be expended by local groups to build coalitions to influence state electoral politics, education policies, and programs. One can argue that this major stimulus to state politics is productive. Greater attention will be directed to state legislative elections and the state policy process. Highly organized efforts by coalitions of urban school interest groups potentially can influence a range of state education policies, not only affecting the distribution of federal funds, but also changing general state aid formulae which are heavily weighted in favor of suburban and rural districts. It was the failure of some states to address urban school needs in the past that resulted in the development of federal programs; this in turn changed state agencies and general public perspectives on urban education. It will therefore be more difficult for states to revert to their old practices, but Reagan's "New Federalism" is sending a potentially dangerous message.

REFERENCES

Advisory Commission on Intergovernmental Relations. *The State and Local Role in the Federal System.* Washington, D.C.: ACIR, 1982.

Bailey, Stephen K.; Frost, Richard; March, Paul E.; and Wood, Robert C. *Schoolmen and Politics*, Syracuse: Syracuse University Press, 1962.

Bendiner, Robert. *The Politics of Schools*, New York: Harper & Row, 1969.

Berke, Joel. "The Role of Federal Aid in the Post Rodriguez Period." In *Education and Urban Society*, Vol. V, No. 2. February, 1973.

Berke, Joel and Kirst, Michael. *Federal Aid to Education.* Syracuse University Press, 1972.

Congressional Budget Office. *Elementary, Secondary and Vocational Education: An Examination of Alternative Federal Roles.* 1977.

Dommel, Raul R. *The Politics of Revenue Sharing.* Bloomington: Indiana University Press, 1974.

Eidenberg, Eugene, and Morey, Roy. *An Act of Congress: The Legislative Process and the Making of Education Policy.* New York: W. W. Norton, 1969.

Gittell, Marilyn et. al. *Limits to Citizen Participation: The Decline of Community Organizations.* Beverly Hills, Cal.: Sage Publications, 1980.

___, *The New Federalism: The States Response.* National Urban Coalition, 1984.

Gold, Steven D. "Recent Developments in State Finances," *National Tax Journal*, 36:1 (March, 1983), 1-29.

Gray, Virginia. "Innovation in the States: A Diffusion Study." *American Political Science Review* 67(1973): 1174-1185.

Jones, Charles O., and Thomas, Robert D. *Public Policy Making in a Federal System.* Beverly Hills, Cal.: Sage Publications, 1976.

Kirby, David J., and Taleman, Thomas A. "Background and Career Patterns of State Department Personnel." In *Strengthening State Departments of Education,* edited by Ronald F. Campbell, Gerald E. Stroufe, and Donald H. Layton. Danville, Ill.: Interstate Printers, 1967.

Mecanto, Philip J. *School Politics in the Metropolis.* Columbia Merrill, 1970.

Nathan, Richard P.; Manuel, Allen; and Susannah, E. *Monitoring Revenue Sharing.* Wash. D.C.: Brookings Institute, 1975.

National Institute of Education. *Title I Funds Allocation: The Current Formula.* 1977.

New York Times, 17 January 1982, pp. 1, 27.

New York Times, 27 December 1982.

New York Times, 14 October 1982.

Newitt, Jane, ed. *Future Trends in Education Policy.* Lexington, Mass.: D. C. Heath, 1979.

Rosenthal, Alan, and Fuhrman, Susan. *Legislative Education Leadership in the States.* Wash. D.C.: The Institute for Educational Leadership, 1981.

Sharkansky, Ira. "Government Expenditures and Public Services in the American States." *American Political Science Review* 61 (1967): 1066-1.

Stanfield, Rochelle L. "No Solution," *National Journal,* January 15, 1983, p. 128.

Thompson, John T. *Policymaking in American Public Education.* Englewood Cliffs, N.J.: Prentice-Hall, 1976.

Usdan, Michael D. "Urban-State Relationships." In *Metropolitan School Organization: Basic Problems and Patterns,* Vol. 1, Berkeley, California: McCutchen, 1972.

Walker, Jack, "The Diffusion of Innovations Among the American States." *American Political Science Review* 63(1969): 880-899.

Wall Street Journal, 12 January 1983.

Wirt, Frederick M. "School Policy Culture and State Decentralization." *The Seventy-sixth Yearbook of the National Society for the Study of Education*, Part 2: *The Politics of Education*, edited by Jay D. Scribner. Chicago: National Society for the Study of Education, 1977.

BUDGETS AND BIG CITY EDUCATION

Gary Orfield

American urban public education is facing serious financial problems which were exacerbated as real federal and state aid for many urban systems was reduced in the early eighties. Teacher strikes, cutbacks in staff and educational programs, warnings by educational leaders, parent protests, struggles over raising local taxes, and other signs revealed a sense of alarm in a number of the largest urban districts.

The problems appeared in the most severe form in certain very large cities, where financial stress and declining educational results have been accumulating for years. The fact that these cities have been educating mostly Black and Hispanic children and that their small white enrollments continue to decline rapidly mean that the cuts have particularly critical importance for minority children and very little for white families, who are overwhelmingly suburban in these metropolitan areas. The fact that the cuts primarily affect relatively powerless Black and Hispanic communities in central cities at a time when the balance of power in state and national politics has shifted to white suburbs means that there is shrinking support from higher levels of government for the targeted aid that would be necessary to make a significant difference.

Although support for educational funding has increased substantially since the federal and state cuts of the early eighties, the trends indicate that the underlying financial situation remains threatening to many big-city systems. In some states the multiplication of responsibilities imposed on school districts by the new educational reform laws and the increasingly high graduation standards their students will by forced to meet will only increase the pressure on the big-city districts whose resources are growing far more slowly than their responsibilities.

Since the 1975 financial crisis in New York City, a number of the largest school districts in the U.S. have experienced very serious and disruptive budget pressures. All five of the districts that were the largest in the United States in 1975—New York, Chicago, Los Angeles, Detroit, and Philadelphia—have, for example, faced either severe temporary reverses or chronic fiscal crises year after year. A number of other leading systems, including Cleveland, Boston, San Jose, and other cities in Michigan, Ohio, California, as well as other states, have been hard hit. At best, the resulting disruptions were demoralizing and damaging to school systems, their staffs, and the lengthy organized efforts that are necessary for successful educational reform. At worst, the financial nightmare contributed powerfully to a downward cycle of continuous decay.

The circumstances of the late seventies and early eighties combined to put a terrible financial squeeze on big-city districts. Raging inflation and soaring energy bills, a national tax limitation movement beginning with the 1978 passage of California's Proposition 13, a series of severe recessions that led to the shutdown of many central city businesses, and an unprecedented level of interest charges on school bond issues all combined to force educational cutbacks.

Given the negative trends it was inevitable that the budget cuts and policy changes in federal education policy in the early Reagan Administration were seen as grave threats. The cuts were sharp and rapid in 1981 and more were asked by the President in each of the next two years. The 1981–82 recession deepened the threat by drastically reducing state revenues and triggering midyear cuts in funds already built into local school budgets. The fiscal vise closing on a number of the largest school districts was very tight. Even though both Congress and many state legistures became more supportive of education by the mid-eighties, the situation of many big city school districts remained precarious.

This essay will explore the fiscal trends affecting big-city districts, and their growing dependence on state and federal aid in the past generation. It will look at the changes in federal aid in the recent past and discuss the basic role of the states in educational finance, the present fiscal crisis, and the multiple demands state governments face from the interaction of recessions, Reagan budget and program cuts in many areas, state tax ceilings in some states, and the education reform movements. The changing population of central cities and the changing enrollment of their public schools will be discussed, and the reasons for the weakening political position of the central cities will be explored. Finally, this paper will consider the kinds of questions that should be addressed when assessing the ultimate implications of these sweeping changes for the students in the schools and for the teachers and principals who make the schools function. The problems are serious, and the trends suggest that they will continue. They will have a heavy and disproportionate impact on Blacks, Hispanics and poor whites, and we have very little idea of their impact on children and schools beyond simple economic data.

CITY DEPENDENCE ON STATE AND FEDERAL AID

Many older cities have been in decline since World War II, but some of the negative consequences of the departure of the industrial and commercial job base as well as of much of the middle class, were masked by the prosperity of the sixties and the expansion of governmental employment and intergovernmental grants during that period and through much of the seventies. These mitigating factors meant that central city schools in many severely declining cities with shrinking tax bases experienced buoyant growth in budgets and staff through the early years of the seventies. Budgets rose and staff grew even as enrollment fell. With the new resources came the new and large responsibilities of

Table I
REVENUES OF SELECTED
URBAN SCHOOL DISTRICTS FROM LOCAL PROPERTY
TAXES AND FEDERAL AID, FISCAL YEAR 1980*

City School District	District Federal Aid Revenue	Property Tax	*Percent of Revenues from: 1979–1980* Increase/Decrease Revenue in Property Tax Revenue
Chicago	11.9	23.2	+ 5.9%
Los Angeles	11.4	11.9	− 39.3%
Altanta	16.8	36.9	− 6.8%
Houston	9.6	46.4	+ 13.3%
Philadelphia	18.1	22.6	+ 2.5%
Detroit	14.5	28.9	+ 7.0%
Cleveland	32.1	35.8	+ 15.4%
St. Louis	18.1	36.5	+ 1.5%
Denver	9.4	59.0	+ 2.6%
San Antonio	19.3	22.8	− 4.0%
El Paso	19.8	23.4	− 4.4%
Corpus Christi	15.7	30.1	+ 1.9%

*1979–1980 school year
Source: U.S. Bureau of the Census, *Finances of Public School Systems in 1978-79*, Series GF 79, No. 10, (Washington, D.C., U.S. Government Printing Office, 1980). *Finances of Public School Systems in 1979-80*, GF80, No. 10, (Washington, D.C.: U.S. Government Printing Office), pp. 18–40.

providing for compensatory education, training for the handicapped, bilingual education, desegregation, and other functions. Although the schools were never content, they did have real increases in resources to deal with their massive responsibilities.

The other side of increasing generosity of other levels of government was the creation of school institutions, staff, and expectations that could not possibly be met without a continuing expansions of grants. Local revenues, based overwhelmingly on property taxes, did not come close to keeping up with inflation.There was little or no prospect of replacing lost revenue from other levels of government with local resources. If there was a serious sequence squeeze on school aid at either the state or federal levels, the consequences would be immediately felt. A hard simultaneous squeeze from both levels in 1981 occurred during the worst economic period central cities had faced since the Great Depression; the impact on urban schools was staggering. The preceding table shows the level of federal and local funding and the stagnant property tax income in 12 cities at that period.

Each of the school systems listed in the foregoing table is a predominantly minority system and is cut off from most if not all of the economic growth of its area. Chicago, Atlanta, Philadelphia, Detroit, Cleveland, and St. Louis have substantial Black majorities. San Antonio, El Paso, and Corpus Christi are Hispanic majority districts, and Los Angeles is, too. Denver and Houston have a combined Black and Hispanic majority. Although the City of Houston has exercised annexation powers in a sweeping fashion, the school district has not been able to expand since the fifties. In Denver, where the city could easily annex and the school district would automatically expand with it, a state constitutional amendment in 1972 fixed Denver's boundaries in the rapidly growing metropolitan area.

What is abundantly clear from the table is that with few exceptions such cities depended more on federal aid than average U.S. districts and experienced little growth in property tax revenue. On the average these twelve districts were receiving federal aid that was equal to more than half of their local property tax revenues. To replace a cutback of 50 percent in federal aid in terms of real dollars, such districts would have had to raise local property taxes by more than a fourth, an extremely difficult task in central cities simultaneously afflicted by many other cuts and increasingly occupied by the poor and families without children.

WHAT HAS THE FEDERAL GOVERNMENT DONE?

Federal aid to schools became an important source of funding for urban school budgets following the enactment of the Elementary and Secondary Education Act of 1965. A variety of federal legislation including the Bilingual Education Act and Emergency School Aid Act, and non-education programs ranging from the "War on Poverty" to the now discontinued CETA public employment program and the community development block grant legislation have produced resources for urban schools. The fact that a number of federal aid programs targeted aid according to poverty of students, concentration of students needing English language instruction, compliance with desegregation orders, and other conditions much more likely to affect central cities than suburbs meant that a good many central cities received a substantially greater fraction than average of their local school budget from federal programs than suburban districts. (See Table 1.)

The basic strategy of the Reagan fiscal changes in 1981 was to drastically lower federal revenues, expand the defense sector of the budget, increase payments for interest on a growing federal debt, and continue very expensive transfer payments, including Social Security and Medicare. This meant that the whole burden of reduced expenditures had to be focused on the "discretionary" programs, mostly grants to state and local government. This entire category of the federal budget was subjected to three successive reductions during 1981 and was targeted for additional large reductions in the budget submitted by the President in 1982 and 1983, and in the budgets projected for the President's second term of office. The reductions during 1981 took the following form—first, reductions to the already enacted budget for Fiscal Year 1981 through the recision process, then a general round of large reductions and program changes included in the Omnibus Budget Reconciliation Act; and, finally, further cuts embodied in the Conte continuing resolution enacted late in the year. The net impact of these cuts was large.

The immediate impact on public education was not great in the first year of the Reagan Administration, because education programs are forward-funded for a year in advance. Except for the CETA workers, who were terminated in the summer of 1981, and the recision in the budget for Fiscal Year 1981, the schools would not really feel the impact until September, 1982, almost two years after the beginning of the Administration. The Reagan agenda, however, affected the budget process and the long-term battles for elimination or continuation of programs and staff in school districts across the nation.

The Council for the Great City Schools, representing 28 of the largest urban school districts, serving slightly more than a tenth of all U.S. students, calculated the impact of the Reagan cuts on their districts. The total aid to these systems from the Department of Education fell from $968 million to $827 million during the 1981 school year and would have dropped again by an additional $234 million if Congress had adopted cuts requested by President Reagan in Fiscal Year 1982 and 1983 budget proposals and recisions. Although the districts had about 10 percent of the students, the Council estimated that they received 22 percent of the first year cuts, 17 percent of the proposed fiscal 1982 recision, and 12 percent of the cuts in the President's new budget for Fiscal Year 1983. While all school programs were expected to suffer from the Administration's policy of eliminating targeted programs and combining them into smaller block grants, the new policies worked to the special disadvantage of the big systems (Council of the Great City Schools, 1982, 1–2). There was a particularly dramatic impact on the big school districts which had been receiving substantial grants to assist desegregration under the Nixon Administration's Emergency School Aid Act, since under the Omnibus Budget Reconciliation Act this program was ended. The money for desegregation aid was subsumed under block grants to the states, which sharply reduced funds to a number of large districts: Cleveland, for instance, exchanged $4.7 million in special purpose aid for $701,000 under the Block Grant; Buffalo exchanged $7.7 million for about $446,000; St. Louis exchanged $5.1 million for $522,000; and Seattle exchanged $4.2 million for $394,000 (Council of the Great City Schools, 1982, p. 3).

Aid to the schools from other federal agencies also plummeted. The CETA employment program, which provided $178 million during academic 1980-1981, dropped to $7 million in 1982 and fell to zero in 1983. Bilingual education fell from $30 million to $20.8 million during 1981. Refugee aid was "zeroed out" in David Stockman's phrase, as were grants from the Energy Department.

The cut is considerably sharper if one considers the real rather than the nominal value of the grants. The President's budget for Fiscal Year 1983 assumes a 27 percent inflation rate between Fiscal Years 1980 and 1983. Thus, the true value of the 1983 federal aid money to these districts according to Reagan's plan, would have been $.74 billion, a decline of 55 percent in the real federal aid in a three year period. (The Administration's assumptions can be calculated from the *Budget of the United States Government, Fiscal Year 1983*, U.S. Office of Management and Budget, 1983, pp. 9-61.) Fortunately, the President's plan was changed in Congress and inflation was less than expected.

The following tables show the detailed impact of the actual and planned changes in federal aid on the public schools in Cleveland, one of the most financially troubled cities. The table shows a decline in total aid to Cleveland in constant value dollars of 61 percent in three years. The Philadelphia projected decline was also 61 percent in constant value dollars.

Education groups, of course, mobilized to prevent additional major cuts from being written into appropriations bills and Congressional budget resolutions. They did defeat or substantially alter some of the President's major proposals. It is important to remember, however, that the battle was fundamentally over holding the line at a much lower base than that which existed in 1980 and one that would be further eroded by the silent "budget cutting" caused by inflation. Long-term appropriations ceilings for a number of programs were written into law in the Administrations's massive 1981 budget bill. Of even greater importance, since the revenue base of the federal government has been so severely reduced by the 1981 tax bill while so many long-term commitments to weapons systems have been made in the Defense budget, it is difficult to conceive of significant increases in federal educational funding unless there is a far-

TABLE 2
ACTUAL AND PROJECTED AID TO CLEVELAND SCHOOLS, FY 80- FY 83

	(1) FY80 1980-81	(2) FY81 1981-82	(3) FY82 Cont. Res. 1982-83	(4) FY82 Revised 1982-83	(5) FY83 Programs 1983-84
Title I (ESEA)	$12,565,783	$12,093,546	$10,838,014	$9,417,150	$7,755,023
PL 94-142	1,439,548	1,775,561	1,890,262	1,365,147	1,365,000*
Impact Aid	774,000	126,128	—	0	0
Vocational Ed.	1,996,812	1,432,078	1,374,795	1,091,587	1,312,130*
Adult Ed.	648,385	676,927	584,865	571,998	
Bilingual Ed.	375,511	291,748	233,690	212,424	−179,436
Indian Ed.	75,000	70,205	66,239	60,721	42,745
Title IV-B	509,617	508,275			
Title IV-C	270,000	132,301			
ESAA	7,085,000	3,798,615	−701,536*	680,665*	625,125*
Ethnic Heritage	0	59,380			
Teacher Corp.	20,000	148,688			
Career Ed.	0	75,867	72,832	0	0
Law Ed.	0	132,194	126,906	0	0
Follow Through	125,743	125,743	93,121	0	0
CETA	8,666,107	4,500,000	0	0	0
Child Nutrition	10,586,727	11,276,727	12,212,565	12,280,000	12,833,000
Refugee Aid	15,000	26,574	26,574	0	0
TOTALS	$45,153,113	$37,250,438	$28,347,347	$25,679,692	$24,111,459

*Monies supplied under Block Grants
Source: The Council of the Great City Schools, February 1982

reaching political change and large federal tax increases. The huge tax cut built into the governmental system a chronic revenue crisis and a great barrier to any kind of expansion of domestic expenditures.

The Effect of the Reagan Revolution. The Reagan agenda in education policy held sway on Capitol Hill only in 1981 but the measures adopted that year did make a significant difference in the long-term role of the federal government. The National Center for Education Statistics estimated that the federal share of public school budgets fell from 9.8% in the 1979–80 school year to 7.5% in the first full school year of the Reagan period. The share was the lowest since federal aid programs were enacted in the mid-sixties (*Education Week*, August 29, 1984). The sharpest reduction came in the 28 programs consolidated in the new block grant, which received 56% less in constant value dollars according to a 1984 Congressional Research Service study (*Education Week*, September 19, 1984). Those funds were also distributed by the states in a way that hurt central city school districts and aided suburbs and private schools (*Ibid.*, September 19, 1984 and October 26, 1983).

After the initial cuts, Congress not only rejected the major subsequent proposals for reductions, but even voted additional funds for some programs, such as compensatory education, and for the restoration of a small desegregation aid program. Between the 1982 and 1984 school years federal aid actually increased 1–3 percent in constant value dollars (National Governor's Association study, cited in *Education Week*, January 11, 1984). The increases, however, were not enough to prevent the federal share of school spending from continuing to decline.

The Diminishing Search for Equity. The federal government had not only expanded its role in school finance in the sixties but had also targeted that aid in ways that forced attention onto the schooling of the most disadvantaged. The block grant experience showed that that role would not be taken up by state education agencies. Other developments showed shrinking hope for state court action.

Urban school districts have been on a fiscal roller-coaster since the beginning of the eighties in terms of state aid for public schools. The decade began with the states dealing with severe fiscal crises by cutting state aid at the same time that the federal cuts were hitting the urban systems. It was also a discouraging time for those hoping for judicial reform to help the big city fiscal crisis. The most dramatic defeat came in New York State where the state's highest court threw out a challenge to the state's school finance system supported by the largest urban districts. Even where the courts have attempted to produce more equitable funding through judicially imposed reforms there have been many barriers to change and only limited success. In New Jersey, for example, the courts attempted to respond to a particularly severe form of educational inequality. New Jersey is a very highly urbanized state but it is dominated by an almost continuous suburb that extends from New York to Philadelphia, punctuated by a series of shells of rapidly decaying and predominantly minority central cities and old industrial suburbs. The contrast between conditions in the affluent suburban areas and the nearby central cities, such as Newark and Camden, may be as stark as any in the United States. After a sweeping state supreme court decision in 1973 finding the New Jersey school finance system unconstitutional a massive confrontation between the courts and the state legislature, threating state-wide school closings, had produced some temporary improvements. By 1984, however, things were clearly becoming worse again. The spending gap between rich and poor New Jersey districts grew from $600 per pupil in 1980 to $1100 in 1984 (*Education Week*, May 23, 1984).

Experts on school finance noted in 1985 that the movement toward equalization of funds was in bad condition nationally. Professor Robert Berne of New York University noted: "The national mood has been away from equity kinds of concerns. The problem hasn't been solved, but other concerns have superseded it." (Friendly, 1985.) Even at the height of the school finance movement there had been much more a pattern of state aid expanding in a way that provided substantial new funds to affluent as well as poor or highly burdened districts. Although 28 states had adopted school finance reforms since the movement began in the 1970s most had not succeeded in ending the disadvantaged position of poorer districts.

Allen Odden, the former Education Commission of the States specialist long known for his studies of school finance trends, reported that there was a tendency for states to adopt new school finance policies that redistributed funds to poor districts for two to three years. That impact, however, tended to erode under the year-by-year pressure of inadequate state budgets and suburban political power. (*Ibid.*)

There have been surprisingly few studies documenting either the educational effects of cutbacks in financing central city education or on the more recent increases in requirements and state funding. A 1985 study of changes in high school course offerings in the eight large urban districts in California that educate a quarter of the students in the nation's largest state is a notable exception. The authors discussed the direct link between dollars and programs:

> Resources in the form of people, materials and facilities are the very stuff of curriculum . . . . Finance influences both what is offered to pupils and how offerings are organized and conducted. And finance change guarantees curriculum change . . . . (Catterall & Brizendine, 1985; p. 330.)

The study found that the impact of the 1978 state Proposition 13 cutbacks were slow in being felt in much of the school program but that the schools faced major constraints by the early 1980s. Overall between 1978 and 1983, per-pupil expenditures rose 33 percent, but the cost of living was up more than sixty percent. The real dollars going into public schools dropped by about a fourth during this period (Ibid., p. 334). The declines were largest proportionately in the largest urban systems, Los Angeles and San Francisco, (Ibid., p. 337).

The possible responses of the schools were rigidly constrained by union contracts and other stipulations restricting firing of teachers, by increased federal and state requirements for education of the handicapped and the non-English speaking, and by increasingly rigid state requirements for minimum skills proficiency, requiring strong focus on this educational task. At the same time high school graduation requirements and college admission standards were raised (Ibid., pp. 339–41).

The fiscal pressures immediately eliminated summer schools, which had served about a fourth of the state's students. Half of the cities reduced the number of hours of instruction. Hiring freezes increased the chronic shortage of math and science teachers with necessary qualifications. Laboratories and vocational equipment were not kept up. School districts reported widespread reductions in programs including: "honors courses, advanced placement courses, social science electives . . . English electives" and a variety of vocational courses. At the same time, in large part in response to regulations and requirements, resources were transferred from regular programs into bilingual education, special education, remedial training, and computer courses (Ibid., pp 342–44). In Los Angeles the school day was shortened in 11th and 12th grades, the credits required for graduation were cut 10%, summer school ended, and there were 1500 fewer teachers (Ibid., p. 345).

The authors reported that the new California state funding approved in 1983 came with an extensive set of new requirements for graduation from high school. It was too early, they suggested, to know whether the damage to the urban schools curriculum could be repaired and whether the increase in state aid would be a long-term trend (Ibid., p. 349).

Recent School Budgets in Eight Large Cities. The nation's largest school districts are extremely important for Black and Hispanic students in the U.S. Although only a tiny fraction of white students are enrolled in the largest systems, most Blacks and Hispanics attend a few dozen central city school districts and millions are concentrated in the very largest. A recent comparative study of expenditure trends in the 1979–84 period examined the six largest central city systems—New York, Los Angeles, Chicago, Philadelphia, Detroit and Houston—and two major second-level systems, Cleveland and Denver. The study found wide variation in recent trends, variation that was primarily related to the extent to which additional state aid offset a difficult local revenue situation. Fairly consistent Congressional defeat of President Reagan's cutback proposals since 1981 meant that there were not serious recent federal reductions in most cases.

Although this was a period of the enactment of major educational reforms, spurred by the *Nation at Risk* report and very active school reform movements, five of these cities were spending less per capita in constant-value (adjusted for inflation) dollars in 1984 than they had been five years earlier. Denver dropped 16 percent, Chicago 12%, Philadelphia and Detroit, 7%, and New York City, 5%. The largest increase, 23%, came in Los Angeles, and was largely a response by state government to the major cuts following enactment of the 1978 Proposition 13 tax reduction initiative that made public education in California largely a state responsibility by drastically curtailing local property taxes. Houston expenditures grew 12% during a period of enormous local economic boom. Cleveland, which had faced a continual fiscal crisis in a state with low state school expenditures, showed an 8% growth in real dollars. The state education reform law increased the state share of the city's expenditures from 38% in 1982 to 54% the next year. Local revenues were not keeping up with inflation in most districts (Houston was a notable exception), meaning that there was less and less ability to fund education locally. In Philadelphia, in 1984, local funds accounted for only about a fourth of expenditures. New York City's local increase was well under inflation and far less than the increase in state and federal aid during the 1976–84 period. The city's share of school costs dropped from 57% in 1976 to 37% four years later, before rising again to 46% in 1984 as real external aid dropped. Total state revenues to the Philadelphia schools during this period peaked in 1981 and fell substantially during the next three fiscal years (Greer & Hess, CPPS: 83-97).

One fundamental difficulty that school officials confronted was the fact that their costs soared throughout the mid-seventies to early eighties period. Between 1975 and 1982 the cost of purchasing the same educational services increased 82%, according to a School Price Index developed by the National Institute of Education. The average annual rate of compound inflation was almost 9% (*Educational Week*, November 23, 1983). Even before a school district could begin to think about adding anything to its program, in other words, on average it had to increase revenues 82% per pupil. A part of the problem could sometimes be dealt with through a decline in enrollments, which fell nationally by 10% during this period. (Ibid.) The real difficuly, however, was that neither local nor state tax systems tended to increase revenues as rapidly as costs rose. The problem was particularly acute in older central cities whose property was simply not increasing in value at anything close to the national inflation rate, even if there were no political problem in raising assessments. (It was very high but accurate increases in property assessments in California that triggered the Proposition 13 tax revolt.) (Kuttner, 1980.)

Often these trends were disguised by inflation. In other words, the educational reductions would come at times when nominal expenditures were rising but inflation was rising faster. For example, between the 1970–71 school year and the 1979–80 year, total national expenditures for elementary and secondary education grew from $46 billion to $96 billion. When inflation was taken into account, however, the actual increase was only 4%. Average teachers salaries grew from $9,269 to $19,157 from fall 1970 to fall 1981, but the real value of the typical teacher's income had actually declined $2,809 in 1981 dollars (NCES, *The Condition of Education*, 1984 Ed., pp. 48–51). In many central cities the trends were much worse, particularly since the mid-seventies.

THE STATE FISCAL SITUATION

State governments had to face reduced revenues from two successive recessions in the early 1980s, self-imposed fiscal limits in a number of the more prosperous states, new burdens and diminished federal aid from the block grant provisions of the Reagan budget, and rising welfare and unemployment costs. The states of the East and Midwest, traditionally supportive of public expenditures, were wracked by severe erosion of their industrial base and increasingly effective competition from low-tax, anti-union states and other nations for relocation of their remaining large employers. These trends, in addition to a conservative political mood parallel to the mood in Washington, meant that the chances for increased state aid or even state aid that rose as fast as inflation were minimal to nonexistent in many states in the early eighties.

Although there was considerable support among state officials for the block grant provisions of the President's first budget, enthusiasm had cooled, and the second round of changes were greeted with statements about the impoverished condition of the states and their inability to assume any additional financial burdens. Organizations representing the governors and legislatures sounded the alarm about the financial conditions of the states.

As local school officials responded to the federal cuts by turning to the states for help, they found the states struggling to cope with the effects of very drastic cuts in a wide variety of federal aid programs and revenues falling well below projections. States had to face these issues at a time when very tough competition for businesses prevented them from raising broad-based taxes and when a rapid-fire series of recisions, sweeping budget cuts, tax changes, and sudden program changes came so fast and on so many fronts that the situation became virtually incomprehensible.

A study by the National Conference of State Legislatures in January 1982, reported that the states were in bad financial straits. Forty-two percent of the states said that their revenues were running behind the projections on which their state budgets were based. Almost half were already eliminating jobs in state governments. Many were facing the politician's ultimate nightmare—simultaneous tax increases and visible cuts in services. Eight states had particularly serious problems, including California, Ohio, Michigan, and Massachusetts. The states, like the federal government, had not foreseen the 1981 recision and "at least 19 states reduced spending during fiscal year 1981 to below the levels appropriated when the budget for the year was first passed." (Gold and Benker, 1–3.)

Congress cut the states' budget by $284 million in late 1981 and had to make another cut in 1982. In January, 1982, the Minnesota legislature cut over $500 million and raised taxes by

$225 million. Ohio raised taxes substantially in late 1981 and confronted an additional $1 billion deficit for the next fiscal year. California and Colorado imposed across-the-board cuts in late 1981 (Gold & Benker, pp. 5-9).

> The dismal fiscal situation of the majority of states results from the national economic malaise. A recession implies slow growth of personal income, which leads directly to slow growth of tax revenue and increased demand for social services. The cutbacks of federal aid are not the primary cause of state fiscal distress, but they exacerbate it. In fact, those cutbacks could hardly have come at a worse time in view of the anemic character of state budgets (Gold & Benker, p. 12).

The broad scale of the Reagan cuts in state aid meant that state policymakers were faced with demands not only from the school districts, but from many sectors of the society—all in a climate of intense opposition to tax increases. Governor George Busbee of Georgia told a Senate hearing in late 1981 that the sudden changes meant that "the budgets of the states are in disarray and chaos" (*Chicago Tribune*, 7 November, 1981). Maryland state legislator Lucille Maurer described the tension in Annapolis: "I've talked to the blind. I've talked to the elderly. They all have the same problem: They say they already aren't getting the services they need, and this is before the really big cuts have hit" (*Washington Post*, 20 January, 1982).

A survey of state school officials by the Education Commission of the States showed that they were most worried about a state fiscal crisis that was so serious that it made the large federal cuts a secondary consideration. Florida and Michigan, for example, cut money out of their aid budgets for the current year in late 1981 as South Carolina had done earlier in the year. Missouri was unable to make its aid payments on time, and school officials were worried about getting less money in 1982 because revenues were dropping (*State Education Leader*, Winter 1982: 1, 8-9).

Increasing evidence of state budget troubles appeared in 1982. When the state surplus that had cushioned the impact of Proposition 13 in California was gone, a $350 million shortfall was projected in the 1982 fiscal year, and the problem was far more serious when the new fiscal year began.

The block grant for education created by the first Reagan budget consolidated a number of programs, turned over discretion in spending to the state governments, and cut the total amount of money. Some of the individual grants had been favorable to big cities. The state governments in most cases simply distributed the diminished funds on a per-student basis. In Arkansas, for instance, the state Department of Education pointed out that "there will be less money to spend and it can be spent feasibly in only a limited number of ways." The funds would be "allotted on an enrollment basis with adjustments for high cost students" (*Arkansas Education Update*, 1981). Participants on the Education Commission of the States Steering Committee noted that funds would generally be distributed according to population, not need. A Colorado official concluded that "innovative school district and inner-city districts would be hit hardest," with the sharpest losses in those districts which had been receiving federal desegregation aid. Enrollment would be the key to distribution, with rich suburban districts getting as much per child as inner city systems and there would be "very few rules" (*State Education Leader* 1982, p. 12).

National studies of the way in which the states actually spent the funds received under the block grant confirmed the early projections. The biggest of the programs combined into the grant was the desegregation aid program and the largest losers under state control were big-city districts under desegregation orders. By early 1983, according to a report of the Council of Great City Schools, the 30 large urban districts represented by this organization enrolled a tenth of the public school students in the United States but had absorbed one quarter of the education budget cuts in the first two years of the Reagan administration (Council of Great City Schools, 1983, p. 2). In late 1984 another Council report showed a substantial transfer of federal aid from central

TABLE 3
GROWTH OF STATE TAX REVENUE
FISCAL YEAR 1981

STATE	*PERCENT GROWTH*	*MAJOR CITIES**
Colorado	– 3.4	Denver
Nebraska	– 1.8	Omaha
New Hampshire	.5	
Michigan	1.9	Detroit, Flint, Grand Rapids, Lansing
Missouri	2.3	St. Louis, Kansas City
Arizona	2.4	Phoenix, Tucson
Arkansas	2.7	Little Rock
Tennessee	3.2	Memphis, Nashville, Knoxville, Chattanooga, Johnson City
Indiana	3.3	Indianapolis, Gary-Hammond
Illinois	3.3	Chicago
West Virginia	4.7	
Montana	4.8	
Pennsylvania	4.9	Philadelphia, Pittsburgh, Harrisburg, Allentown
Iowa	5.3	Des Moines
Minnesota	5.4	Minneapolis-St. Paul
Delaware	5.4	Wilmington
California	5.9	Los Angeles, San Francisco-Oakland, San Diego, San Jose, Oxnard, Fresno, Bakersfield, Sacramento, Riverside, Anaheim

*Cities in 100 largest metropolitan areas
Source: U.S. Census Bureau, "Quarterly Summary of State and Local Revenue", October 1981, in *State Education Leader*, Winter 1982, and metropolitan data in *American Demographics*, December 1981.

cities to suburbs under the new laws (*Education Week*, November 7, 1984).

The Economic Recovery, the Education Reform Movement, and State Policy. After two years of very difficult times for school leaders, both in Washington and the state capitals, both the national mood and the state financial situation took a turn for the better in 1983. With their heavy reliance on sales taxes and the importance of state income taxes, state revenues are very directly connected to changes in the economy. During 1983 a rapid expansion began to brighten the prospects of state treasuries after the sudden and often drastic downturns of the previous years. At the same time a number of national reports showing a serious crisis in American public education helped to generate a widespread reform mood and a willingness to raise taxes for schooling in a number of state legislatures. In state after state sweeping reforms were enacted, putting substantial new burdens on schools. In some states these changes were accompanied by substantial increases in state funding. By early 1985 the great majority of states had raised requirements and mandated state-wide testing and dozens were raising teacher training requirements and providing increased incentives and higher salaries for teachers. Governors across the U.S. were campaigning for major school reform packages. A number of states enacted new taxes to pay for the education programs, most commonly through sales tax increases. In some states, particularly in the Sun Belt, the state expenditures for education increased by 25 percent or more in just two years, from the school year beginning in September 1983 to the proposed budget for the 1985–86 school year (*Education Week*, February 6, 1985).

A study by the National Council of State Legislatures reported that education had been the leading budget question in 31 states in 1984. A number of states long lagging in school funding made large changes. In the South, Alabama, Arkansas, North and South Carolina, and Tennessee all raised their spending for schools more than a sixth. Two states that had adopted tax restrictions that hurt education, California and Massachusetts, repaired some of the damage with large 1984 increases. Michigan and Maryland voted for more funds, but some of the other large older states showed little change (*Education Week*, October 19, 1984, p. 11).

Another sign that the era of severe state retrenchment might be at an end came in the record or public referenda in the 1984 election. Tax limitation and tax rollback measures with strong support were defeated in all four states where they were on the ballot, including California and Michigan, while voters in five of the six states considering tax increases for education gave their assent (*Education Week*, November 14, 1984 p. 7). It was by no means clear, however, that funds were increasing fast enough to keep up with new duties in many states, and the new laws seldom recognized the heavy burden of educating up to a much higher standard in the central cities. Educational Testing Service expert Margaret Goertz noted, for example, that there had been no financial provision for many of the new science, math, language, and computer requirements that were suddenly imposed on schools without the necessary teachers of materials (*The New York Times*, February 19, 1985).

THE STATES AND THE FISCAL COLLAPSE OF URBAN SCHOOL DISTRICTS

When major city school districts or the city governments that finance them face fiscal collapse, the state government becomes a key actor in the process, given the broad state control over school programs, the powerful state role in school finance, and the inability to obtain a Congressional response to any individual city's problem. When one of the largest governmental institutions faces bankruptcy, there is both a spillover impact on the credit ratings of other institutions and an immediate political crisis as officials consider the implications of closing public education for hundreds of thousands of children or facing a bitter strike. Often, during the sixties and seventies, the big city districts were able to forestall crises by obtaining additional state aid or benefiting from an infusion of federal dollars. In the late 1970s as state governments faced severe fiscal pressures of their own and the big cities faced erosion of their political power, the reaction was very different. The states responded by taking control of key fiscal decisions of the city school board, by imposing major budget cuts, and by protecting bondholders.

The definition of the issue of central city school financing has changed with the political tide against public spending and against additional spending to help people from minority groups who dominate the enrollment of the big-city districts. A poll during the 1980 election showed, for example, that only 26 percent of the public favored additional spending for improving conditions of Blacks (Ladd, 1980, p. 55). The issue that was once viewed as a vital social concern was in 1980 viewed primarily as a financial and political problem to be solved by imposing cuts on wasteful urban bureaucracies.

Direct state fiscal controls have been imposed upon school budgets in Chicago, Cleveland, and New York. All the major cities of California have become almost totally dependent upon state school funds in the aftermath of Proposition 13. The fate of the Detroit and Philadelphia school systems has revolved around negotiations with the state government in which local cutbacks are part of the state requirements. In Boston, state tax law forced drastic cuts on the public schools and produced an intense struggle between the schools and other major local services such as police and fire protection. A number of Ohio school districts continued operations with loans from the state government which impose conditions on local district operations. A report in mid-1981 described the nature of the state control in Cleveland:

> The Cleveland schools are now in a financial receivership imposed by the Controlling Board of the Ohio General Assembly as a condition of receiving the $19 million loan. The State Superintendent of Schools . . . has financial control of the system. He has appointed an advisory committee to assist him and with his approval the Cleveland school board has named a new financial administrator. This receivership . . . has the authority to make the necessary changes to improve financial planning, personnel policies, and budgetary control in the system (Hoffman with Parham & Edlefson, 1981, p. 1).

After the Chicago schools went bankrupt in the fall of 1979, the state legislature rapidly enacted a law that gave operating control of the finances and all related aspects of the Chicago public schools to a new government agency, the Chicago School Finance Authority. The law also required the resignation of the existing school board and the appointment of a new board in Chicago. The Authority, headed by a white suburban business-man appointed by the Governor, was given sweeping power over the schools. After the Chicago Board lost its credit rating and could not borrow funds to pay its teachers and supplies in November, 1979, the state took drastic action to keep the schools open by forcing Chicago to cut expenditures and raise taxes sufficiently to guarantee repayment to bondholders and by requiring the city school board to give up any control over the money needed for this repayment. The basic policy problem from the state perspective was regaining a credit rating high enough to borrow money without having the state assume any more of the burden of financing education in its largest city. The result was a new and superior level of school government whose mission was totally defined in fiscal terms and whose goal was to guarantee that investments in Chicago school bonds would be safe. The new agency had no duty to assure either that the schools operated or that they met any kind of educational standards.

Among the powers of the Chicago School Finance Authority was the right to veto the school budget and thus close the schools. In fact the Authority was required to do this if the budget was not balanced. The Authority would exercise internal administrative control over the district by possession of veto and removal power over the district's chief financial officer, the "duty to prescribe an accounting system" for the district, the right to veto any contracts it wishes, the authority to "direct the Board to reorganize its . . . management and budget systems in whatever manner the Authority deems appropriate to achieve greater financial responsibility," and a wide range of other financial and management powers (Chicago School Finance Authority, 1980, p. 11). Since virtually all school policy issues have budgetary implications, the Chicago agency had vast power while the Chicago school board had only a fraction of its former discretion.

The New York City schools, serving almost a million children, came under rigid outside budget control after the city's 1975 budget collapse. To keep the city from bankruptcy, local self-government was in good measure repealed. The city now "must satisfy the federal and state governments, on which it depends for aid, that it is making fiscal progress . . . ." The new Emergency Financial Control Board was granted "powers over the city's budgetary, borrowing and management decisions that before 1975 would have been unimaginable" (Sinnreich, 1980, p. 110). This state-created board gave only two city officials among its seven members "powers to police the city's budget, to approve or reject city contracts, and to order the preparation of a three-year city fiscal plan" (Auletta 1980, p. 90). Through the efforts of the Emergency Financial Control Board, the state-created Municipal Assistance Corporation, and the requirements of federal officials, city workers and city agencies, in exchange for a temporary $2.3 billion loan from Congress, were forced to accept a wage freeze and mass firings of city employees, firings that cut particularly deeply in the schools (Newfield & DuBrul 1978, pp. 182–186).

Under orders from the Emergency Financial Control Board and the Mayor, the school budget was suddenly cut by $262 million. As the 1976 school year began, the district's Deputy Chancellor, Bernard Gifford, estimated that there had been a "cumulative cut in teachers since June 1975, of 22.9 percent" and a shortening of the school day by 90 minutes. Many school programs were cut by as much as half. According to Gifford, "no municipal agency providing basic public services" since 1900 had "been forced to absorb cuts of the magnitude or at the rate experienced by the public schools of New York City" even during the Depression (Gifford, 1976, 33). "Of all the areas of city life," concluded another study, "the schools have been among the hardest hit in the layoffs" for reasons which included the perception that "the schools became yet another minority service that elicits little consideration from New York's new decision-makers" (Newfield & Du Brul 1978, 235).

The direct assertion of state fiscal control and denial of local power of school officials to spend anything that would imperil bond repayment were the most dramatic signs of erosion of local discretion, and they usually came after spectacular problems. Less blatant but very important examples came in other cities as the state and federal governments refused to provide new funds needed to resolve crises. In the fall of 1981, for example, both Philadelphia and Boston school districts faced strikes over their inability to pay the cost of contracts negotiated by teachers in good faith. With the Reagan Administration in office and the prospect of declining federal aid, officials in those cities and elsewhere turned to equally hard-pressed city councils and state government for help. Neither district received any significant help. Detroit obtained help in the form of state authorization to raise the city's own taxes, but only in exchange for agreement of the city's public employee unions to reduce agreed compensation and other benefits. Facing possible bankruptcy, Detroit's Mayor Coleman Young pushed this agreement through with the threat of mass firings as the only alternative.

In contrast to the movement of the seventies toward increased state funding of education with no major expansion of state control, the trend in the big cities facing fiscal crises from the mid-1970s to the early 1980s was toward loss of local control in key decisions, increased state authority but no new state resources, and continued necessity for cutbacks. For the time being, school authorities in big cities face more controls, less discretion, little ability to start anything new, and clear signs that the new power will be exercised most vigorously to protect bondholders, not the educational process.

With the expansion of state funding in the 1983–85 period, fiscal crises eased, at least for a time, in California, New York, Michigan and Ohio as the city schools received substantially increased state aid. These policies, however, did not either end the local dependence or provide any assurance that there would be the additional funds available each year in the future to prevent recurrence of the crisis. Those cities that did receive some relief were also faced with the pent-up pressure of teacher union demands for higher wages after a period in which their real income had shrunk. The nature of the underlying problems was painfully apparent in Chicago, which had not received any increased state aid by mid–1985.

The Chicago Situation. After the Chicago public schools went bankrupt in 1979, thousands of teachers were fired, new local taxes imposed, and a major reduction of curriculum and educational services took place. There was no money for adequate salary increases for city teachers. A massive 1984 study of school finances showed that neither the state nor the federal government were expanding aid to assist the city's severe educational and fiscal crisis. The state's share of Chicago's school costs actually declined from 54% in 1980 to 45% in 1984, while the local share climbed from 32% to 40%.

When considered in constant value dollars, Chicago's local revenues per student peaked in 1972 and had declined 41% by 1983. State aid for the city peaked in 1980 and declined 20% in the next three years. Federal revenues fell 23 percent in the first two years of the Reagan Administration. In real terms, Chicago's per student school spending in 1983 was the lowest it had been since 1971. Between 1978 and 1983 the city's real buying power per student fell by a fifth (Greer & Hess, 1984, pp. i-viii). In spite of evidence that between 40 and 50 percent of the students were dropping out of high school and very few schools were operating near national norms, and in spite of a strong increase in mandatory state requirements, the schools had far fewer real resources at their disposal than in the past (Designs for Change, 1985). The trends in the state suggested that the disparities between Chicago and its suburbs would only continue to widen. One result was the bitter and continuous conflict between school board and teachers which produced mid-school year strikes in both 1983 and 1984.

CAN THE CITIES HELP THE SCHOOLS?

If the federal government won't help, some states won't help, and local school district revenues in the large districts are not rising significantly, there is only one other source of new funding on a large scale—the city governments. In a number of large cities the school systems are directly financed by the city governments, and in others cities may provide assistance. Some cities, such as Boston and Philadelphia, were the foci for heated battles over school funding during the early 1980s.

The possibility of aid from the city governments depends, of course, both on the availability of money and on the decision of city authorities to spend the money for the schools rather than other services or tax relief. Unfortunately, the data strongly suggest both that the cities with the most troubled school districts are themselves experiencing grave financial difficulties and that city governments in general have been subjected to the same kind of double shock as the states from the combined effect of the Reagan cuts and the successive recessions of 1980 and 1981–82. Large cities faced not only very serious budget problems of their own, but real threats of drastic cuts in such basic services as police and fire, transportation, sanitation, and many other services. Chicago, for example, faced not only a possible inability to open schools in the fall of 1982 but also the distinct possibility that the buses and subways which make it possible for the city to operate might not be running due to lack of funds. All of these problems are exacerbated by the fact that the interest rates on tax-exempt municipal bonds, the basic instruments for both capital financing and for remaining solvent during periods of low cash flow, reached historic highs which greatly increased local government costs.

There is also evidence that in the competition for scarce local dollars the schools may not do very well. People believe in education, but at the same time, for instance, they are terrified of crime. Since most central-city residents do not have school age children, the first commitment can be more abstract than the second. The schools are often far more important to the minority community than to the white community that still dominates politics in all but a handful of cities, even those with virtually all-minority school districts.

Like central-city school districts, city governments themselves became more dependent upon aid from state and federal governments during the sixties and seventies, particularly the poorer central cities. Between 1967 and 1977 the percentage of the city budgets coming from the states rose from 21 to 26 percent, and federal aid went from 5 to 12 percent. Among those cities with the greatest need, federal aid per resident increased more than 300 percent between 1970 and 1976 (*President's National Urban Policy Report* 1980, 6-3, 6-6). The Carter Administration worked to target the federal aid money more firmly to poor cities and to poor neighborhoods within those cities but provided only a temporary boost in aid.

Three studies of urban fiscal problems during 1980 and 1981 disclosed very difficult conditions in many big cities and serious harm from the first round of budget cuts by the Reagan Administration. When the Congressional Joint Economic Committee surveyed cities shortly before the beginning of the Reagan Administration, it reported that most cities had had operating deficits in both of the last two years and that revenues were shrinking in terms of constant value dollars. Large central cities with more than a quarter million people were in the worst shape. These cities received about a third of their revenue from state and federal governments and reported that they expected a decline in federal aid (even under the Carter budget) and no new state aid.

Cities had already begun job freezes or layoffs. In 1979–80, the largest cities were cutting fire, police, and sanitation services. The cities said that they did not have money to put those (7.2 percent) city workers paid by the federal public employment program onto city payrolls (*President's National Urban Policy Report* 1980, 7, 65, 67). A committee staff report analyzed the problems of the big cities *before* the Reagan cuts:

> In many of the largest cities retrenchment has already occurred and to maintain existing service levels will require further increases in local taxes, user chargers, and fees. It is these cities . . . which . . . have suffered as high tax rates have combined with other factors to encourage the flight of population and business to suburban locations. A sharp and sudden reduction in inter-governmental assistance can mean a further deterioration of services and/or a new round of tax increases. Either can generate a new wave of out-migration and a further decline in the fiscal viability of many cities (*President's National Urban Policy Report* 1980, 33–34).

A November 1981 survey of 100 cities by the U.S. Conference of Mayors found that city governments were faced with "immense burdens" including "major cutbacks in employment and training programs, crippled housing efforts," and "reduced transit service at a higher fee."

The American Public Transit Association reported on a crisis in mass transit developing in major cities that would be intensified by the Reagan plan to eliminate operating subsidies. A survey showed that 66 percent expected regular fare increases and declining ridership. Fare hikes and deteriorating transit efficiency seriously threatened the viability of an essential service in some of the largest cities. In 1981, New York City fares rose 25 percent, and Los Angeles fares increased by 31 percent, while in Boston and Cleveland fares escalated by 50 percent (American Public Transit Association, 1981, p. 43).

After the first Reagan budget was approved, the Joint Economic Committee surveyed 50 cities. Most large cities were cutting "virtually every service they offer" and the cities with the worst unemployment were cutting the deepest: Chicago, Newark, Detroit, Cleveland, Baltimore, Miami, New York, Los Angeles, and Oakland. Cities in this category expected to lose the most federal aid, with most predicting at least 18 percent fewer federal dollars. Only one city in nine expected state aid to rise as fast as inflation. Every major urban service was scheduled to be cut in a majority of high unemployment cities (Matz, 1982, pp. 5, 8, 21–22, 43–54).

Given the difficulties facing the central cities, it is easy to understand their inability or unwillingness to provide substantial new money for the schools. Maintaining basic public services traditionally financed through the city budget was difficult enough, and the threats to the financial viability of the city itself were so serious that new efforts to help other institutions were viewed in a very dim light.

Boston school revenues were cut sharply in 1981 as a result of a state property tax limit referendum. After appeals to the state and the city proved futile, the school board fired 1,000 teachers, including 750 who were tenured, thus violating its contract to lay off no one with tenure. Public reaction was stronger, however, to layoffs of police and firemen, and the available city funds were used to restore part of those cuts, much as they had been in New York City at the time of its 1975 fiscal crisis (*Boston Globe*, 3 September, 1981; *New York Times*, 7 September, 1981).

The Philadelphia school board had settled one of the longest teachers' strikes in U.S. history in 1980 with a two-year contract promising no dismissal of tenured teachers. The district had been unable to get more state or city funds, however, and had a deficit of $71 million the first year. A $152 million deficit loomed for the second year. In spring of 1981 the board voted to "lay off 3,500 teachers, enlarge classes, reduce teacher planning time and rescind a promised salary increase of 10 percent," all in violation of the contract. In an unsuccessful effort to solve the pending crisis, Mayor Green went on television to tell the city about the "enormous crisis" the schools faced because of fiscal pressures that had brought the schools "to the brink of complete chaos and absolute bankruptcy." He offered to support a 10 percent tax increase if the teachers gave up their raises and other provisions and permitted firings. Raising enough local money to fulfill the contract, he said, would mean a 62 percent tax increase which would "destroy the city's economic climate." The compromise proposal failed, and for the second consecutive fall the schools did not open (*Philadelphia Inquirer* 24, 31 August, 1981; 1, 3, 10 September, 1981). The *Philadelphia Inquirer*, noting the seemingly intractable nature of the problem, pointed out that "no significant additional money is going to come from federal or state sources" and that it would be very difficult to obtain local funds:

> There is no constituency for such tax increases, in the City Council or on the streets and in the neighborhoods . . . No more than 20 percent of the population of Philadelphia has children in public schools. Even many among that minority feel overtaxed and underserved (*Philadelphia Inquirer*, 11 September 1981).

After fifty days of strike a state court ordered the school board to honor its contract though it lacked the money, running school until the money ran out. No long-term settlement was in sight (*Philadelphia Inquirer*, 22 January 1982). By tolerating a long strike once again and rejecting a more modest long-term proposal drafted in late 1981, the city authorities were sending the message that the matter was not especially urgent and, in any case, there was not much they could afford.

The state school reforms of 1983 and 1984 diminished the fiscal crisis in some big-city school districts and permitted partial rebuilding of educational programs. The congressional rejections of Reagan budget proposals stopped the further shrinkage of federal aid and provided some small additional aid to some cities. It was important to remember, however, that the state aid depended on state revenues that were highly sensitive to recessions and that there was no prospect of any substantial increase in federal assistance under the Reagan government's continuing deficit crisis. There was nowhere to turn at the local level because the central cities were being hit by many of the same negative trends in the economy and in public policy. Changes approved in the 1985 congressional budget process to reduce federal aid to cities would only increase their problems. (Congressional Budget Office, February 1985).

AN EXPENSIVE INSTITUTION WITH A POWERLESS CONSTITUENCY

Urban public schools are expensive institutions built up on a long consensus about the importance of education. However, they now serve communities with shrinking resources and declining power in the overall society, communities in which school operations have often become irrelevant to those with the most resources and influence. Large urban central city school districts are already predominantly Black and Hispanic institutions in most parts of the country. More and more, a number of the most important are coming to be not only minority institutions but institutions which primarily serve poor minority children. They are located in cities where far less than half the voters have school-age children and where a large fraction of the middle-class voters (who vote at much higher levels) who do have children do not use the public schools. They are often school districts with a negative and deteriorating public image.

Urban schools are terribly important to minority children but of only marginal importance to the white community. Perhaps a sixth of the Black and Hispanic students in the United States are in the five largest urban central city districts. The most recent available calculation (1976 enrollments) showed that almost half of Blacks and about 60 percent of Hispanics went to school in the fifty large school systems that enrolled the largest number of children from their respective groups (Taeuber & Wilson 1979).

About two-thirds of American students attended school in metropolitan areas in 1979–80. Eighty-nine percent of students within metropolitan areas went to public schools (94 percent of Blacks, 91 percent of Hispanics, and 86 percent of whites). Eighteen percent of the metropolitan enrollment was Black and 8 percent was Hispanic.

Less than a fourth of whites but more than half of the Black and Hispanic students in the nation attended central city schools. Among central city students, 1 white in 6 was in a private school, compared with 1 Hispanic in 10 and 1 Black in 14. Among students in metropolitan areas, almost one third of whites were in the central cities as were 72 percent of Black and 62 percent of Hispanic metropolitan-area children. (Chicanos were somewhat less likely than other Hispanics to attend central city schools but still far more likely than whites.)

Central city elementary public schools enrolled 4.5 million students in 1979–80; 2.7 million (60 percent) were white, 1.7 million (38 percent) were Black, and .7 million (16 percent) were Hispanic. When Hispanics who are white are counted as minority students, it is clear that a majority of central city school students in the elementary grades were from minority backgrounds (U.S. Bureau of the Census 1981, 11–18). The elementary enrollments forecasted the overall enrollments of the future. Central city public schools were rapidly becoming predominantly Black and Hispanic institutions.

Enrollment data from 1980 for the nation's 50 largest central city public school districts show that only one-third (17) were majority white. Eighteen of the districts had mostly black students; three were predominantly Hispanic. Hispanics were the largest group in two other school systems while Asians were largest in one system. Among the white majority districts, seven had less than 60 percent non-Hispanic white children, and most of those had trends that suggested that they would have a minority of whites in a few years. The decline in white enrollment in the largest districts from 1968 to 1980 was massive. Atlanta had 86 percent fewer white students; Detroit, 78 percent; New Orleans, 71 percent; Cleveland, 66 percent; Chicago, 62 percent; and Los Angeles, 63 percent fewer (1980 U.S. Department of Education Office for Civil Rights data). Even in areas with relatively healthy central cities and a good racial climate such as Denver, there were as few as one-eighth of the metropolitan-area's white public school students in a central city system that educated mostly Blacks and Hispanics (Orfield & Fischer, 1981).

The implications of these trends for future public support for central city education are examined in Sandra Featherman's 1981 report, *The Future of Public Education in Philadelphia*. With only 28 percent white students enrolled in public schools, and almost a third of the city's children in private and parochial schools, the school district's need for sharp increases in local taxation (if far-reaching cuts and bitter labor disputes are to be avoided) do not produce much local support. Local research shows that about two-thirds of the city's households have no school-age children, and only about one household in five has a child in public schools (Featherman, 1981, p. 4-5). "Whites constitute 63 percent of the voters, but fewer than 11 percent of white households have children in public school." (Featherman, 1981.)

The problem in Philadelphia, as in Chicago, Houston, New Orleans, Atlanta, and a number of other cities showing this trend, was not white flight from busing. There was no busing plan in any of these cities, except for a very small-scale program in Atlanta. The problem was expanding residential segregation, the aging of the city's white population, and the settlement of young white families in outlying suburbs. One reason was the extremely negative middle-class perception of the public schools. These trends continue to operate in spite of small islands of urban renovation, and the problems will grow worse in years to come.

The demographic trends help to explain what happens to public schools during fiscal crises. After the New York crisis in 1975, the schools took more than their share of cuts. In the early 1980s, the Philadelphia and Boston city governments were not willing to make significant resources available to the schools when they confronted strikes and massive financial problems. The first black mayor of Chicago, Harold Washington, rejected a request for city funds for the schools. The great numbers of children that depend upon the public schools are not the children of the people who control the economy and politics of the city.

As time passes, more and more big city school districts will become minority institutions. The school crises that are normally described as fiscal problems will become, to an even greater extent, racial problems. These crises threaten the viability of the nation's most important institution for children from the two largest minority groups.

BROADENING THE RESEARCH AGENDA

Proposition 13 and the collapse of the New York City government in 1975 attracted the attention of the research community to the questions of fiscal decline and crisis. Now, the recovery of state funding has distracted attention from the underlying problems, at least for a time. There is, nonetheless, a good deal of research on the financial, political, and administrative aspects leading to fiscal crisis and on the nature of the problem when it arrives.

Much of this research has been highly informative and has provided a much better and more accurate view of the nature of the crisis and possible ways out. A number of the studies of declining school districts show, for example, that the decline is by no means due exclusively to declining resources. In fact, the research shows that troubled school districts such as Philadelphia and Cleveland and New York in the first half of the seventies had per-student expenditure levels that were rising far more rapidly than inflation (Hoffman, 1981, p. 6; Featherman, 1981, pp. 21–22). The problems were caused in part by overstaffed systems which failed to decrease employees or close buildings as enrollments dropped very fast. In some cities, such as Boston and Philadelphia, old-fashioned patronage continued to inflict unnecessary hacks on the school staffs, diminishing their ability to manage decline or to hold community confidence. One study shows that districts only reduce administrators when the fiscal pressure becomes severe. Others show the nature of the political struggles created by retrenchment (Levine, Rubin, & Wolohojian, 1981).

When central city districts face fiscal crises the seniority provisions of their teacher contracts force them to compound the difficulty by retaining all of their highest cost older teachers and to fire many much less expensive young teachers, including a disproportionate share of minority educators. This raises per-student costs for a given class size and decreases flexibility.

The issues which have dominated the research to date are important and significant. There are a number of very serious questions raised by the contraction and collapse of large central-city school systems that deserve more attention from the research community. If researchers follow the present mode of analysis and concentrate most attention on the fiscal aspects, they will be accepting the current definition of the central-city school problem as a fiscal and management problem—which it undeniably is. But it is also a great deal more. It is a set of serious problems about the nature of our urban societies and the future of their most important public institutions. It raises a set of questions about the fate of the educators who have committed their careers to those large institutions. It raises a set of questions about the capacity of the reduced and maimed urban districts to adapt to providing the training necessary in an urban economy where the nature of work is already very rapidly changing. Finally, it raises questions about our racial future. The big city school systems are the largest and most important minority public institutions in many states. Minority families still see them as the key to possible mobility of their children. We should expand the research agenda to address these issues more adequately.

MORALE

Anyone who has worked in an American university or college facing rapid fiscal decline in recent years knows from personal experience some of the impacts of severe budgetary problems on a complex organization and the individuals and programs that operate within it. Because universities, like school systems, have the vast bulk of their budget in staff salaries which cannot usually be lowered much in the short run, the administrators must rigidly clamp down on those things that can be controlled—new hiring, promotions, travel, office support, materials, maintenance and repairs, new equipment, library acquisitions, and related matters. The cuts embitter ambitious staff members with plans for new initiatives, make employment prospects much less attractive both for those inside and for those looking for jobs, encourage those who can to transfer, and produce endless small signs to deterioration and cutbacks of a seemingly petty and trivial nature which produce an atmosphere of discouragement and resignation. The long-term consequences, as employees experience continuing declines in their standard of living, as new projects and new staff become impossible, and as increasing burdens are placed on fewer and fewer people in a deteriorating physical setting, are deeply pessimistic.

Professors who have observed this process in the colleges should try to imagine the greater difficulties of life in a declining big-city school system where many of the problems are magnified by distinct political, social, and institutional features. We must think about working in a crumbling school in a ghetto or barrio in a highly bureaucratized setting, trying to serve students desperately needing education in communities with pervasive problems of poverty, discrimination, crime, transiency, and social and economic collapse. Often there might not even be enough books and paper—but there would be no shortage of forms to fill out. One would not know whether the school was going to open until just before the beginning of the school year. Sometimes there would be the emotional, professional, and financial trauma of a city-wide strike. When there were cutbacks, seniority and "bumping" provisions in the contract would produce chaotic and massive reassignments of staff, and a teacher could easily end up in a school s/he didn't want and even in a subject s/he had never taught. When school started up there would be resentment over the fact that the cuts had eliminated many of the young, low-seniority, Black and Hispanic teachers and administrators so important to the minority communities. And then there would be the prospect that the same thing would happen each year into the future.

Much of the existing research on cutbacks is economic, and it does not touch on the questions of decline in organizational and personal morale. Researchers interested in the fate of the public schools as institutions serving a very complex and important function and in teachers and principals as the central actors in the educational process must define more appropriate variables and measures.

THE TEACHER'S PREDICAMENT: THE STRIKE AS THE ONLY WEAPON

When urban school districts with powerful teachers' unions face severe retrenchment, they must come to terms with teachers' organizations that have succeeded (since the sixties) in winning substantial benefits for teachers in many big cities. Most of these unions had been told in the past that no money was available, only to see money provided from some source when the only alternative was closing the schools. When federal and state funds are reduced, local funds are inadequate, and both the possibility of borrowing and the cost of borrowing offer little hope, school officials can only cut costs in the short run by a freeze on hiring, firing teachers and administrators, or reducing compensation. School closings, another incredibly difficult political process, can account for more modest savings. Steep local tax increases are another possibility, but these often require approval of an increasingly poor big-city electorate with a diminishing number of families with school age children.

Needless to say, teachers' organizations do not willingly accept firings and pay cuts for their membership with nothing but the prospect of similar additional demands in the future years. Because of prolonged inflation, many teachers have experienced recent declines in their real standard of living even before these demands are made. This means that bitter strikes become almost inevitable when times are hard. In cirmcumstances where the local officials have little discretion to respond and the state officials deny additional state aid, it means that the strikes are also likely to be futile. Even when teachers win a contract, as the Philadelphia teachers did after a long strike in the fall of 1980, they cannot have any assurance that the school authorities will have the money to honor its provisions next year.

Often when there is a school financial crisis, the local newspapers and local critics will highlight the high salaries paid to teachers. The teachers' unions have often been unpopular with liberal critics of school policy as well as the business establishment. The new financial control agencies normally suggest cutbacks or freezes in wages or benefits as key elements in solutions. The head of the Chicago agency, for example, suggested a month before school opened in the city in 1981 that the teachers should have no salary increase for the coming year (*Chicago Tribune*, 7 August, 1981). A union wishing to retain the support of its membership could hardly accept such a proposal. Yet a strike not only may fail to get money but may further undermine already weak public support for the schools and encourage parents to transfer their children elsewhere. Whatever the situation is with staffing levels and pay when the fiscal crisis begins, the union usually faces a no-win situation and its predictable actions tend only to feed the cycle of decline.

We need research that better describes the dilemmas of urban teachers and their organizations in a period of decline. Recent reformers have tended to stereotype and blame teachers without understanding the situation in which they work. Since few decision makers have any direct contact with teachers' experience and many are hostile to their organization, better descriptive work and organizational analysis could be invaluable. Policy research on better planning and conflict management could also make a contribution.

CURRICULUM

One of the most obvious effects of a substantial cutback in funds and staffing for schools is a shrinkage of the range of curriculum offered. This is most obvious in the upper grades where a quasi-market system for electives can interact with staff reductions to rapidly diminish educational choices. Because most evaluation focuses on a very small number of educational outcomes—such as reading and math achievement levels—and since the cuts are generally in other areas, little data on these effects are normally produced, and virtually none come into the policy debate.

The effects on the future lives of students can be suggested with a simple example. At a time when most students are entering college, it is reasonable to propose as a basic standard for secondary education that no student be assigned to a school where he or she cannot prepare for college. Yet in many big-city high schools the distribution of students and the background of students mean that the standard subject classes operate far below grade level on a national scale, and adequate college preparation in both basic subjects and electives such as physics, advanced algebra, calculus, or basic computer training appeal to only a small fraction of the students. A handful of teachers can be decisive in keeping pre-college training intact. With cutbacks it is easy either to lose key teachers who cannot be replaced or to lose classes because of standards that raise the number of students who must enroll in an elective in order to keep it in the curriculum. Even before cutbacks many students in ghetto or barrio areas found themselves in public high schools where it was all but impossible to prepare adequately for college. Cuts only accelerate this process, sometimes drastically (Orfield, Mitzel & Associates, 1984, chapters 7–10).

Educators should closely monitor the educational budget changes. While there are many complex and perhaps unanswerable questions, there are also some that are simple. A student cannot possibly succeed in a field he is denied the opportunity to study in and cannot prepare for college in a school which lacks either courses required for college admission or courses that are essential in preparing for college-level work. It should not be difficult to find out the number of city high-school students who are, in fact, receiving a comprehensive education in a meaningful sense and how many are receiving adequate training only for low-skill, low-paying jobs requiring no college.

ABILITY TO ADAPT TO ECONOMIC AND TECHNOLOGICAL CHANGE

Cutbacks produce a bias against change in school systems for many reasons. Money for new staff, often carriers of new ideas and approaches, and for new equipment essential for the proposed program, are usually the first things to go in a fiscal squeeze. A system cannot hire outsiders while firing loyal employees who have met the district's standards. When there is no money to buy the basic necessities of supplies and equipment for existing curriculum, money for new starts rapidly vanishes. Money for staff retraining essential to any broad implementation of a new approach is another common target for budget slashers.

The problem is that there is very strong evidence that central city economies are changing in ways that require some major changes in central city schools if children are to have a reasonable chance at the jobs that will dominate the city economy.

Cities have been struggling since World War II in a highly unsuccessful effort to maintain the manufacturing base of their economies. In spite of urban renewal, tax abatements, subsidized job training, and numerous other incentives, manufacturing facilities have moved to the suburbs or beyond or even to other countries. Those cities that have retained significant activity and job creation in their core are rebuilding their economies not around manufacturing and other relatively low-skill jobs, but around white-collar jobs requiring high levels of skill. Thus the relatively healthy urban centers such as Manhattan, the Chicago Loop, and central Washington, D.C. face a difficult situation in which massive joblessness and a strong demand for white-collar workers exist side by side.

A study of trends in the Chicago economy illustrates the problem. During the seventies, it concluded, "many manufacturing jobs were lost in the Chicago area; however, there were large gains in trade, business services, finance, insurance and real estate." Future projections showed "relatively more white-collar jobs, and fewer low-skilled positions for operatives, laborers, and personal service workers, especially in the city of Chicago where most of the region's unemployed are located" (Stone & Steele 1981, p. ii). In Philadelphia more than a fourth of the jobs were in manufacturing in 1970, but were down to a sixth in 1980, and plants continued to close in the 1981 recession. As industrial jobs were replaced by service jobs, city residents tended to lose and suburbanities to gain. Blacks and Hispanics in the city were hit especially hard since they often had the lowest seniority with the firms. According to a Rutgers University survey, "roughly 70 percent of the manufacturing jobs are held by people who live in the city while only 30 percent of the office workers are city dwellers" (Robbins, 1981). With more than a fifth of the Black adults and far more of the teenagers without jobs, students were obviously in need of training for the kinds of jobs that would be available in the future.

A recent study by the Education Commission of the States suggests that the National Assessment of Educational Progress shows an actual decline in the types of skills now most in demand in the economy and a need for major revisions in school programs (Forbes & Gisi, 1982). If this is true, it is a need that will be exceedingly difficult to meet in large school districts under severe fiscal pressures. If it cannot be met, however, the largely non-white students they serve are apt to face even more drastic problems finding work in the future.

The draft report by the Education Commission points to the National Bureau of Labor Statistics job projections for the 1980s, projections which point to a predominantly white-collar work force by 1990, with 12.1 million new white-collar openings during the decade (Forbes & Gisi, 1982, pp. 15–35). Among blue-collar workers the prospects are grim, except in the skilled trades. Even in manufacturing higher levels of skills will be needed by many workers in increasingly automated plants.

The National Assessment showed that higher-level literacy skills, mathematical application ability, and physical science scores had all dropped nationwide during the seventies. The analysts pointed out that perhaps in response to criticism of the past generation, the schools had become so fixated on teaching the basic skills that they had lost the ability to provide the kind of training needed for a robot- and computer-age economy (Forbes & Gisi, 1982, pp. 15–35).

The problems are particularly acute in the central cities, which are feeling the effects of deindustrialization and conversion to a service economy in the most dramatic ways. The industrial facilities in the older cities tend to be the most obsolete and noncompetitive. New industrial investment is overwhelmingly concentrated in outer suburbs or small towns, much of it in regions with low labor costs and little unionization. This means that not only has there been sharp overall decline in the number of relatively low-skill, high-wage factory jobs in many metropolitan areas but also that those that remain are increasingly inaccessible to central city residents. The growth sectors are primarily white collar, which provides some entry-level clerical jobs for central city women but tends to require more educational background for many positions, particularly the good entry-level jobs that are typically male. When one considers the traditional strong concentration of male minority workers in industry, their extremely high dropout rates in central city public schools, and the change in the occupational opportunities being created by the economic shifts, the implications are highly disturbing.

If the need was for a different approach to education and the initiating of better technical training, obviously the school district that had funds to hire newly trained teachers familiar with the latest approaches and to buy the machines and supplies for good programs would have a decisive advantage. So would the students who had the good fortune to live in those school districts. The Council of Chief State School Officers expressed the worry "that a new disadvantaged class may emerge: those who do not have access to technology in their schooling" (Forbes & Gisi, 1982, p. 35).

RACIAL IMPACT

Because of the very large minority populations enrolled in central city schools and the very small fraction of white students in the older and poorer districts, a fiscal policy change that affects these school systems is also a policy with a powerful racial impact. In 1970 more than one-fifth of the nation's Black and Hispanic students were enrolled in just five school districts—New York, Chicago, Los Angeles, Philadelphia, and Detroit. All of these systems have since experienced grave financial problems and related serious educational difficulties. When Chicago public schools reduce services, it means a reduction of educational opportunity for seven of every ten Black and Hispanic students in Illinois but for only a very small fraction of the white children. When Governor Jerry Brown of California froze school construction funds in response to a threatened state deficit, it had a direct and immediate impact on the Los Angeles public schools. At a time when most school districts are worrying only about which schools to close, the enormous Hispanic migration to Los Angeles has produced more than 200 overcrowded Hispanic schools. Thus the freeze had a racial impact.

As our central city school districts increasingly become minority institutions, budget decisions become racial decisions. At a time of shrinking opportunity in the central city economies, the public schools become even more important as a possible route to a decent job and a decent life for Black and Hispanic children.

Typically, minority faculty and administrators are also very largely dependent upon big-city school districts. Few are employed in the more prosperous suburbs in most metropolitan areas. Black and Hispanic teachers and administrators play a very important role in minority communities where respect for education is high and mobility depends far more on public employment than it does for whites. Cutbacks often hurt minority employees even more than their white counterparts, since they have less seniority. Thus, cutbacks in large city school districts are really cutbacks in the role of Black and Hispanic educators in a metropolitan area or sometimes in an entire state. They are also a direct threat to the social and economic mobility of many minority families. At a lower level in the educational hierarchy, cuts in part-time jobs for parent aides, and the elimination of CETA jobs in the schools, have eliminated what for many minority parents had been the first step out of the welfare-dependency syndrome. There has been little research on these important racial consequences of budget changes.

SUMMARY

After a period of substantial growth in federal and state investment in big city education in the late sixties and early seventies, the largest urban districts have in recent years faced wild fluctuations. There was a severe fiscal crisis in the early Reagan years in many cities and, in spite of growing state aid in some regions recently, there are serious negative long-term trends in the cities' ability to pay for even the existing inadequate levels of public education. Both federal and state governments have increased the difficulties by loading major added responsibilities on the city school systems without providing the needed funds. With little prospect of added funds from Washington and increasing suburban domination of state legislatures, the prospects for the cities when the state revenues fall during the coming recessions will be grim.

Big city districts face even heavier burdens as changes in the economy make education an increasingly urgent need for the low income Black and Hispanic students that increasingly dominate their enrollment. City officials are faced with brutal decisions about further increasing local taxes and increasing their disadvantage in competition with the suburbs or weakening local education, which may be the key to any kind of economic future as the job market evolves. There are no choices without serious costs.

Although a long history of mistakes and misjudgments usually comes to light when there is a serious financial collapse and the process commonly exposes excessive payments and unnecessary expenditures in some areas of the district, the research on fiscal cutbacks should reflect the fact that it is not the officials of years gone by who bear the cost of the cuts, but the students, the young teachers, and the schools as institutions. The people who are hurt are often disorganized and voiceless. It is very important that researchers learn their stories and give them voice. In a society where the education of the poor and minority children is so thoroughly separated from those who shape opinions and make decisions, research is one of the last avenues by which this vitally important social information can be communicated.

REFERENCES

"1980 Guide to Metropolitan Areas," *American Demographics*, Vol. 3, no. 11 (December 1981), pp. 25-42.

American Public Transit Association, "Testimony before the Subcommittee on Investigations and Oversight, Committee on Public Works and Transportation," *New York Times*, October 21, 1981.

Arkansas Education Update, 1981. Little Rock: Arkansas Department of Education.

Auletta, Ken, *The Streets Were Paved With Gold*. New York: Vintage Books, 1980.

Boston Globe, 3 September, 1981.

California State Controller, *The Potential Impact on California of Administration Fiscal Plans and 'New Federalism'*, Feb. 3, 1982.

Catterall, J. & Brizendine, E., "Proposition 13: Effects on High School Curricula, 1978-1983." *American Journal of Education* Vol. 93, No. 3, May 1985, pp. 327-351.

Chicago School Finance Authority, Official Statement of the Chicago School Finance Authority Relating to $83,000,000 General Obligation School Assistance Bonds, 1980 Series D, Chicago: Dec. 9, 1980.

Chicago Tribune, 7 November 1981.

Chicago Tribune, 4 March, 1982.

Chicago Tribune, 4 January, 1982.

Council of Great City Schools, *Analysis of the Effect of the FY82 and FY83 Reagan Budget Proposals on Urban Schools*, February 1983.

Design for Change, *The Bottom Line*. Chicago: Design for Change, 1985.

Education Week: 26 October 1983; 11 January, 1984; 29 August, 1984; 19 September, 1984; 19 October, 1984; 14 November, 1984; 6 February, 1985.

Farris, Gerald, "L.A. Schools Face Loss of $26.6 million," *Los Angeles Times*, 9 March, 1982.

Featherman, Sandra, *The Future of Public Education in Philadelphia*, Philadelphia: University of Pennsylvania Center for Philadelphia Studies, 1981.

Forbes, Roy H. and Lynn Grover Gisi, "Information Society: Will Our High School Graduates Be Ready?" Draft Paper. National Assessment of Educational Progress, Education Commission of the States, March 1982.

Friendly, Jonathan. "The Disparity of Resources," *New York Times*, February 19, 1985.

Freeman, John and Michael T. Hannon, *Effects of Resources and Enrollments on Growth and Decline in School Districts: Evidence from California and New York*. Program Rept. No. 81-B1. Stanford University, Institute for Research on Educational Finance and Governance, April, 1981.

Gifford, Bernard, "New York City's Schools Are Being Bludgeoned," *New York Times*, 20 September, 1986.

Gold, S. D., and Benker, K. M., *State Fiscal Conditions as States Entered 1982*. Paper presented at the National Conference of State Legislators, January 1982.

Greer, James L. and G. Alfred Hess, *Revenue Shortfalls at the Chicago Board of Education, 1970-1984*. Chicago: Chicago Panel on Public School Finances, 1985.

Hartman, James M., "Expenditures and Services." In Raymond D. Horton and Charles Brecher (eds.), *Setting Municipal Priorities 1980*. New York: Allanheld, Osmun & Co., 1979.

Herbers, John, "Legislatures and Governors Battle for Control of U.S. Block Grants," *New York Times*, 17 January, 1982.

Hoffman, Michael J., with David L. Parham & Carla J. Edlefson. *A School System in Distress: A Financial Crisis Repeated—The Cleveland City Schools in 1981*. Citizens' Council for Ohio Schools, 10 June, 1981.

Kuttner, R. *Revolt of the Haves: Tax Rebellions and Hard Times*, New York: Simon & Schuster, 1980.

Ladd, E. C. "More than a Dime's Worth of Difference," *Common Sense*, Summer 1980, pp. 51–58.

Lehne, R. *The Quest for Justice: The Politics of School Finance Reform*, New York: Longman, 1978.

Levine, Charles H., Irene S. Rubin, and George G. Wolohojian. *The Politics of Retrenchment: How Local Governments Manage Fiscal Stress.* Beverly Hills: Sage Publications, 1981.

Lyons, Arthur and Charles J. Orlebeke. *Chicago Area Public Finances, 1970–1990: Trends and Prospects.* Report to Metropolitan Housing and Planning Council, Chicago, October 1981.

Matz, Deborah, *Emergency Interim Survey: Fiscal Condition of 48 Large Cities*, Staff Study, Joint Economic Committee, 97th Congress, 2nd Session, Washington, D.C., 1982.

Matz, Deborah, *Trends in the Fiscal Condition of Cities: 1979–81.* Staff Study, Joint Economic Committee, 97th Congress, 1st Session, 1981.

National Center for Education Statistics, *The Condition of Education*, Washington, D.C.: U.S. Department of Education, 1984.

Newfield, Jack and Paul Du Brul, *The Abuse of Power: The Permanent Government and the Fall of New York*, New York: Penguin Books, 1978.

New York Times, 7 September, 1981.

Office of Civil Rights data 1980.

Printout supplied to the House Committee on the Judiciary, Subcommittee on Civil and Constitutional Rights.

Orfield G., Mitzel, H. and Associates. *The Chicago Study of Access and Choice in Higher Education*, Report to Senate Committee on Higher Education, Illinois General Assembly, 1984, Chicago, Ill.: University of Chicago, Committee on Public Policy Studies Research Project, September, 1984.

Orfield, G. and Fischer, P. *Housing and School Integration in 3 Metropolitan Areas: A Policy Analysis of Denver, Columbus, and Phoenix.* Report to U.S. Dept. of Housing and Urban Development, 1981.

Philadelphia Inquirer, 22 January, 1981; 24 August, 1981; 31 August, 1981; 1 September, 1981; 3 September, 1981; 10 September, 1981; 11 September 1981.

Robbins, William, "Philadelphia Losing Blue-Collar Jobs and Workers," *The New York Times*, 15 August, 1981.

Sinnreich, Masha, "Background Paper." Twentieth Century Fund Task Force on the Future of New York City. New York, World City, 1980.

Standard and Poor's Creditweek, Chicago, January 11, 1982.

Stetson, Damon. "Labor Study Finds Economy of City Now 'More White-Collar than Ever' ", *The New York Times*, March 13, 1982, p. 29.

Stone, Debbie and Eric H. Steele. *Employment in the Chicago Metropolitan Region*, Draft Report for Metropolitan Housing and Planning Council, August 1981.

Taeuber, K. and Wilson, F. *Analysis and Trends in School Segregation*. Paper presented at the Institute for Research on Poverty, University of Wisconsin, 1979.

U.S. Bureau of the Census, Current Population Reports. "School Enrollment—Social and Economic Characteristics of Students." Series P-20, No. 360, Washington, D.C., April 1981.

U.S. Bureau of the Census, "Quarterly Summary of State and Local Revenue," [October 1981], *State Education Leader*, Denver, Colorado: Education Commission of the State). Winter 1982: 1, pp. 5-9, [vol. 16, no. 1].

U.S. Conference of Mayors. *The FY82 Budget and the Cities: A Hundred City Survey*. Nov. 20, 1981.

U.S. Congressional Budget Office. *An Analysis of the President's Budgetary Proposals for Fiscal Year 1983*, Washington, D.C., February 1982.

U.S. Congressional Budget Office. *An Analysis of the President's Budgetary Proposals for Fiscal Year 1986*, Washington, D.C., February 1985.

U.S. Department of Housing and Urban Development, *President's National Urban Policy Report 1980*, Washington, D.C., 1980.

U.S. Office of Management and Budget. *Budget of the United States Government, Fiscal Year 1983*, Washington, D.C., 1982.

Washington Post, 4 November, 1981.

INTRODUCTION TO PART III

The essays in Part III address two questions. By what criteria are we to judge block grants as a mechanism to achieve public policy goals? How does the effectiveness of block grants compare with the alternative of greater federal involvement in the implementation of public policy?

Paul Ylvisaker finds block grants, as implemented by the Reagan administration, wanting in two crucial areas: their effect on our capacity to govern and their effect on the values of the nation. Block grants are a mechanism for evading rather than confronting structural problems in the political economy and ignoring regional disparities. Nor do they enhance our capacity to respond to global problems. He, with many other observers, finds that block grants enhance state discretion without corresponding increase in responsibility. Judging the Reagan program as a whole, Ylvisaker finds particularly disturbing the over- emphasis on reductions and cutbacks without a corresponding concern for equity.

The implementation of public policy can be approached from either a liberal or a conservative point of view. From the liberal point of view, implementation becomes a matter of closing the gaps between the articulation and the achievement of social welfare objectives. From the conservative point of view, implementation helps us understand and explain the limits of governmental action. Michael Lipsky places the execution of policy through block grants at the intersection of liberal concern with distributional consequences and the conservative despair over the government's ability to achieve public purposes. Arguing that the concerns that prompted federal aid to education in the first instance are not addressed through establishing block-grant assistance, he underscores the political consequences of block grants that Marilyn Gittell brought out earlier: the struggles over distribution that block grants encourage (especially when the grants are accompanied by a reduction in the total amount of assistance) brings to the fore the redistributive nature of human-service programs and highlights for the middle class the tax consequences of supporting those programs; and block grants dilute the power of human-service interest groups by moving decision-making out of Washington and into fifty state capitols.

Among the contributors to this volume, Thomas Minter enjoys the unique perspective of having served both as a high-level federal education official and a top administrator in the nation's largest school system. He understands both the pressures that compel federal officials occasionally to "overstep the boundaries into areas constitutionally mandated as state responsibilities" in closely monitoring categorical programs, and the frustrations that local officials often experience in dealing with and trying to impose some order on conflicting federal programmatic rules and regulations. But he emphatically insists on the worthiness of the motives that impelled federal intervention in education through passage of the Elementary and Secondary Education Act and the effectiveness of that intervention in creating greater access, educational opportunity, and exemplary programs. Minter buttresses his assertions by examining recent data which show that children have made significant educational gains under Title 1 programs, and by looking at the experience of New York City in developing Title IV–C programs. It is clear that the replacement of ESEA by the Educational Consolidation and Improvement Act will slow, if not reverse, the progress in access and opportunity that federal involvement in education has made possible.

THE LARGER ISSUES INVOLVED IN BLOCK GRANTS AND RETRENCHMENT

Paul N. Ylvisaker

Block grants and retrenchment are essentially means, not ends; my unrelenting question throughout this essay has to do with the ends these devices are intended to serve, and with the values that motivate their use.

Still, in themselves, the mechanisms have lives and consequences of their own. To that degree they must be judged independently.

I first heard of block grants as a graduate student at Harvard University nearly forty years ago, where Professor Morris Lambie, steeped in the municipal reform tradition of Charles Beard, kept extolling the virtues of their uses in Britain (we then spelled them "bloc" grants) and their likely usefulness in the United States. I mention this to introduce not only some historical perspective but also the proposition that block grants are a recurrent notion, part of a cycle our political system is prone, if not destined, to repeat: First the formulation of categorical grants, each pinpointing a specific need; then the gradual, sometimes (as in the 1960s) explosive proliferation of categorical grants; next a widening perception of the confusing and frustrating nature of this multitude of prescriptions and regulations; then the urge to simplify and consolidate, delegate, and deregulate; subsequently the discovery and exposure of misuse of such discretion or slothfulness, in serving the original purpose of such aid; and finally the reimposition of detailed directives and restrictions; and so on back to the categorical grant.

We are at the point in the cycle when a move toward block grants was almost inevitable—a federal scene cluttered by hundreds of categorical grants, each encrusted with the multiplying barnacles of guidelines and regulations.

Retrenchment is also a cyclical affair: spurts in governmental expenditures responding to general affluence and/or recognized public needs, followed by cutbacks and "breathers" as resources wane, revenues fall, and political reaction sets in. I'm reminded of the "Great Sabbath" in the ancient Jewish tradition, probably the supreme expression of society's cyclical urge to return to "square one."

The current race toward retrenchment was also inevitable. With the world's population doubling inside a generation, with our values of equality and equity spreading apace and confronting the widening gap between rich and poor, and with the productive capacity of the industrial order stalled and constrained, a more or less zero-sum game of global redistribution was bound to occur, requiring cutbacks in national budgets and ambitions everywhere. Again, the haunting reminders of biblical precedent: Joseph's translation of the Pharoah's dream into forecasts of lean years to follow the fat.

Granted their predictability, how does one assess the implications and consequences of block grants and retrenchment? Let me start by noting a paradox and a personal prejudice. First the paradox: I have stressed the importance of motive in the resort to means—sooner or later that motive becomes apparent, and the medium becomes the message. On the other hand, as the means become reality, they take on a life of their own; original intent fades in subsequent practice and is ultimately washed out altogether. One therefore has to distinguish between immediate implications and long-run consequences.

Fair warning: you'll have to distinguish, too, my own personal outlook on the long and short run. I fully appreciate

President Reagan's "point in time"—the inevitability of his moves toward block grants and retrenchment. And I resonate with more than a bit of his rhetoric: his call for hard choices, his appeal to private initiative and self-help. But I do not share his perspective (his retro-romance with an American past that probably never was), or his confidence that in aiding the rich he will best help the poor. I distrust much of his rhetoric; I cannot avoid judging his block grant and retrenchment strategies in the context of all his proposals, programs, and actions—including his tax package, defense budget, and so on.

Within that broader frame, let me pose, discuss—and leave you with—two major questions.

First, *What impact will block grants and retrenchment, as currently proposed, have on America's capacity to govern (or cope)?* Take first the capacity of individuals. Agreed, the poorer are adversely affected—unless you really believe that making life harder for the poor is good for their souls. On the other hand, the wealthier are in a better position to fend for themselves when freed from governmental restrictions and with more disposable income. But that expansiveness may be short-lived. Given cutbacks in governmental spending, more of what were public goods will have to be bought on private account: home, neighborhood, and worksite security; education; recreation; and so on. In fairness, necessity may become the mother of social efficiency and invention, thus easing the transitional burdens. It's worth keeping an eye, for example, on the innovative alternatives to bureaucratic delivery of public goods of the kind proposed by Ted Kalderie of the Hubert H. Humphrey Institute. Note also the creative efforts of the Fund for the City of New York in increasing the efficiency and imagination with which that community does its public business.

Second, look at the capacity of the non-profit sector. Even before the advent of Reaganomics, there were warnings this was the endangered sector of American life. Under the new regime, it is estimated that non-profits will be left each year with $18 billion less to do $22 billion more, given current cutbacks in federal support. Again, one could argue and anticipate that such shrinkage could breed inventiveness and greater efficiency. But the environment of triage that it will bring on will also be enervating and dispiriting.

Third, consider the impact on the social capacity and contribution of business. Regulatory and tax relief will be seen as favorable, enhancing what profits there are to be made in a depressed economy. Presumably, they may also increase the incentive and discretion to handle more of the community's needs. But it's far from certain that business can or will do more. Proposals to increase corporate giving from its current rate of 1 percent of pretax profits to 2 percent (let alone the long-advocated 5 percent and the new statutory allowance of 10 percent) are meeting with quiet and sometimes explicit resistance. The temptation to hunker down in a climate of retrenchment and recession is almost irresistible.

Finally, consider the impact on the capacity of government. The Administration's presumption is that its programs will "free up" the capacity of the federal government (but for what?), and will fully utilize the potential of state and local units. My own historical reading of the federal system is that this country's capacity to govern and to cope is at its peak when all three levels are fully active and vigorously contending. The prospect of one— and the chief—of those levels going quiescent is not a happy one. Further, the abrupt termination of federal involvement interrupts the learning curve in our national capacity to deal with social concerns. Criticize what you will in the parade of past efforts to cope—the New Deal, the Great Society, the War on Poverty, Model Cities—they have left a residual of social capability that cannot be dissipated without considerable damage.

Note, too, that current programs and proposals do nothing in themselves; in fact, they actually harm the nation's capacity to deal with some basic and emerging problems we can't avoid. Let me cite those I regard as most critical.

First are the transitional and structural issues posed by the shift to a service economy, and the social and sector disparities that shift is producing. Evidence is mounting that the service economy, as now developing, is dividing into sectors of growth and stasis/decline (e.g., "producer services" associated with high-tech vs. personal and social services); into better jobs and worse jobs (professional vs. sub-professional; highly paid, full-time and sheltered vs. lower-paid, part-time and uncertain). Filters of income, education, race, and sex are sorting out the cohorts who enter or are excluded from these separating sectors and career opportunities.

Second are regional disparities. A recent analysis of 1980 Census data by the Harvard-MIT Joint Center for Urban Studies shows the current accentuation of those disparities; it does not support a serene belief in the inevitability of equalization, of progression to the mean. Granted, in recent years state governments individually have gained in fiscal and administrative capacity, a number of them accumulating more potential than they have politically seen fit to exercise. But collectively, as a system, the states reveal unsettling disparities. With block grants and cutbacks as presently formulated, I believe those disparities will grow.

Third is our capacity to respond to global concerns. The problem at this level goes far beyond the idiosyncrasies of any one administration; my own premonition is that the system of nation-states is inherently incompetent to do globally what has to be done. Most contemporary national leaders know in their hearts that what they are led to domestically flows only into autarchy and insulation. This nation's dilemmas over what to do about immigration, or trade tariffs, are simply two of a geometrically accelerating number of cases in point. I can see happening to our own national government what has long been a chronic and enervating predicament of the states; they are stuck in the middle, between the realities of the local and the powerful attractiveness of a level above (in this instance, an international order that is, or should be, emerging).

Admitting the vastness of the domestic and global problems referred to, and the eternal gap between human capacity and predicament, I still miss in what is being done and proposed any real suggestion of a noble try—only a shifting of burden, and withal a diminution of capacity. *What will be the effect on the unity, strength, and spirit of the nation?* There are two alternative scenarios implicit in the process of devolution (block grants). The first, which is positive, suggests the releasing of power. The second, negative, makes an art of "passing the buck."

Retrenchment also has its plus and minus sides. The literal meaning of the word suggests a continuing struggle for the same ideals in a more sustainable position. On the other hand, retrenchment easily becomes an invitation to the lifeboat psychology: "I've got mine, now you get yours."

My own judgment? Again, focusing on the totality of program and motive rather than narrowly on cutbacks and block grants, I do not see these moves as constituting the same fight for the same ideals in a more defensible trench. One contradiction is the emphasis on force as a strategy of coping: two examples are the overriding commitment to spending on defense and the response to Haitian immigration. Another countersign is the reliance on wealth as a surrogate for legitimacy in laying claim to resource allocation; to those who have, more is to be given. Disparities in the distribution of privilege and wealth—a chronic threat to a stable society and one which the United States has struggled for generations to stave off—are likely to grow in the encouraging climate of tax breaks for the more advantaged and diminished aid and services for the poor and unemployed.

Nor do I find reassuring the subordination of value considerations to the raw and short-term calculus of the market—whether that be political or economic. The public school system and the values it represents are being subordinated; less than a quarter of American taxpayers have children in the schools. Minorities and immigrants are rapidly becoming the schools' principal clientele; public education in America has become a "sitting duck" for politicans cutting budgets and counting votes. They see no short-term "Return on Investment;" the long run battle for long-range values is being abandoned. And, the equivalent is taking place in the business sector; cost-accounting has failed to reflect inflationary erosions, investment decisions reflect the short-term indices of quarterly profit statements, and shareholders behave as speculators rather than owners.

I have conceded throughout that block grants, devolution, and deregulation give greater elbow-room and discretion; but there are disturbing evidences that freedom has been given without responsibility: grants without strings attached (and Bob Jones University immediately gets one); the retreat of affirmative action; and state allocations without performance requirements. Also, this has been delegation without commitment. What is to happen after 1987, the final year in the New Federalism's bargain with the states? Until then, and only then, is federal aid assured in return for state assumption of responsibility.

More than anything I am dismayed by the all-out dedication to retrenchment and belt-tightening without a matching commitment to equity. "Fair shares of hardship" is the missing motto— a motto far more in harmony with the traditional and constitutional values of this democracy. Instead, we will witness an exacerbation of disparities among regions, among sectors of the economy, among social functions and areas of public need, among classes, and among cultures and values.

This is no time for either majorities or minorities to encourage greater disparities. Diversity, yes; disparities, no.

CONCLUDING COMMENTS

Especially as educators, often so preoccupied with things intellectual, we need reminding that we are engaged in a battle for the public's spirit, not simply for its mind. To engage fully in the battle is a major challenge to conventional academics. The revolution in communications is bypassing our favorite weapons— lectures and books—and by new devices and languages is forcing us out into the unfamiliar idiom of mass communication and public feelings.

I will also challenge conventional liberalism with its historic links to affluence. "Fair shares of hardship" does not come as easily to the tongue as "fair shares of growth and prosperity."

Notwithstanding the ominous and the odds, I'm convinced there's a receptive spark in the voting public. One can discern a political expression of Newton's Second Law—put mischievously in the reverse: for every reaction, an equal and positive initiative. Counter-statements and counter-moves, reflecting an abhorrence of inequality, affirm again that there is a solid phalanx of Americans who have internalized the most basic of human and constitutional values. What is fundamentally offensive to those values will sooner or later be sanded down to what this nation can fairly, and politically, live with.

EIGHT IMPLEMENTATION ISSUES PRESENTED BY BLOCK GRANTS IN EDUCATION

Michael Lipsky

The study of public policy implementation is no more or less than an effort to understand the problems of transforming into practice decisions made by people in authority. As such, implementation analysis is concerned with the critical question of how reliable are political and particularly bureaucratic structures and processes.

Analysis of the Reagan Administration's block-grant approach to education is especially interesting because in a sense this approach is designed and intended to do away with problems of implementation and to overcome the burdens and responsibilities of implementation. This, of course, is impossible. It is possible to reduce the *federal* role in education policy, but to the extent that education policy is *systemic*, comprising contributions from national, state, local, and special district sources as well as from private interests, a reduction of the federal role simply signals an intention to allow the dominant influence of the other contributors in the federal compact to prevail. This observation is familiar to students of federalism who have often observed that lack of federal policy (failure to have an anti-lynching law, or to require minimum welfare benefits) constitutes a *decision* to allow state preferences (in these cases, regarding racial and welfare policies) to prevail (Riker, 1964; Steiner, 1966).

In what follows, I will explain why block-grants have been, in a sense, "anti-implementation," why nevertheless it is impossible to avoid implementation issues, and which implementation issues seem paramount at this point.

Let us first identify the meaning of block grant policy more directly. Generally, block grant policy involves the following features:

1. Authorizing federal aid in broadly defined functional areas rather than more narrow categorical programs;
2. Authorizing considerable discretion in problem identification and program design;
3. Minimizing reporting requirements;
4. Distributing aid by formula rather than by discretionary criteria;
5. Targeting general purpose governments as recipients.

In short, block grants promise to devolve onto the states the responsibility for administration, priority-setting, and the achievement of objectives. Implementation issues seem mostly to disappear if distributing money to states is the task at hand. Block grants create the expectation that there no longer will be federal policy objectives. Policy objectives will be set by the states, which will be responsible for realizing them. If anything, the federal purpose will be achieved in the structure of the legislation itself— according to the conservative rhetoric, restoring the correct balance between state and federal governments.

The study of public policy implementation, in its latest phase, began in the early 1970s, following a decade of expansion of federal government fiscal and programmatic responsibility, and at the beginning of a period of considerable concern about government capacity. Analysts sought to better understand why great expectations of public officials tended to be dashed when incorporated into legislation or executive directives. If implementation was "what happened after a bill became law," some of those who studied implementation wanted to better understand the impediments that were in the way of realizing the law's objectives. (Early studies included Bardach, 1977; Derthick, 1972; Murphy, 1971; Pressman & Wildavsky, 1973; For a good review, see Hargrove, 1975.)

These implementation studies had unusual resonance in the working of public affairs because they seemed to address critical issues affecting a broad spectrum of concerns. For example, liberals were interested in trying to close the gap between articulating and achieving social welfare objectives. On the other hand, conservatives were primarily interested in better understanding and explaining the limits of government action.

The result of combining these two interests in a single research approach has been that it also serves two different masters. For example, implementation research gained considerable attention from education reformers who called upon implementation research to tighten up gaps in Title 1 expenditures, while conservative critics referred to implementation research to support their views that government was trying to do too much, was too costly, and was unlikely to achieve changes in areas such as education and health care, where transformation of citizens' behavior is often the policy objective (Wildavsky, 1979).

These two perspectives on implementation provide a useful background for approaching the issue of block grants. On the one hand, the conservative despair over the ability of government to accomplish public purposes is a primary motivating factor in the development and appeal of block-grant policy. On the other hand, the concern that implementation analysis shows for the distributional consequences of policy provides a useful framework for developing a critique of block grant policy to radically change the balance between federal and state control of public policy.

The tension between the reformers and conservatives can be illustrated by referring to the two ways, generally speaking, in which one can hypothetically close the implementation "gap" (i.e., the differences between expectations and performance). First, one can work on the "input" side to provide resources more adequate to the task and to try to hold those responsible for implementation more accountable. This direction leads to increased funding. It also leads to improved monitoring, deploying of effective sanctions for implementation failures, and increasing the commitment of implementors to the objectives of policy makers.

Second, one can alter the objectives of policy so that implementors are asked to do only that which it is believed they can achieve. To illustrate, one can reduce the number of parking violation scofflaws by more effective policing or by liberalizing parking laws so that fewer drivers are in violation. (One can also reduce the "known" gap by undermining information collection about parking violations—this is a tactic the Reagan Administration has attempted to deploy in several areas.)

The block-grant strategy leans heavily toward reducing the implementation "gap" by the second method—reducing expectations of performance, or, as Aaron Wildavsky (1979) has phrased it, executing a "strategic retreat on objectives." Indeed, the block-grant approach implies that the federal government will attempt to minimize its expectations. The political liability of this stance was revealed when the Congress refused to accept the President's proposals to place education for the handicapped and other categorical programs into block grants, because its members wanted to insure the primacy of the purposes of aid to the handicapped. The logical bankruptcy of this notion is apparent in the formulation that if the federal government is to provide aid without strings, the federal government simply adopts the varied priorities of the states and localities. This approach may or may not be desirable but surely it is not one without purposes or, indeed, federal objectives.

Assessing the implementation issues of the Reagan approach to block grants in education is somewhat hazardous for several reasons. First, to an important extent the Administration failed to achieve its block-grant strategy in education. The block that would have combined programs for special needs, such as aid to the disadvantaged and to the handicapped, was not enacted. Nor were many of the forty-four smaller programs slated for the second education block included in the final legislation. Second, the impact of legislation would only be felt in schools in the 1982–83 school year, so that actual impact observations are not yet available. (Generally, see O'Neill & Simms, 1982, pp. 335–338.)

Nonetheless, it should be possible to comment in an informal way about the implementation issues raised by the block grant approach:

1. The most important observation one can make about all of the Reagan Administration's experiments with block grants, including those for education, is that as experiments they were fatally conceived and irretrievably ruined in execution. This is because the block-grant strategy was inextricably linked with significant budget reductions (which are justified by a corresponding increase in local autonomy). Like virtually every other major proposal for structural change in federal relations made by the Reagan Administration (notably the proposals to take over fiscal responsibility for Medicaid in exchange for states' takeover of Aid to Families with Dependent Children and Food Stamps), the block-grant proposals have simultaneously been strategies for federal budgetary reductions. While states have been welcome, indeed virtually invited, to make up the gap in federal aid, their ability to do so in a period of economic recession has been severely constrained, and their willingness in general to provide state funds to replace federal dollars has been "low," although not non-existent (Peterson, 1982, pp. 178–183; Palmer & Sawhill, 1984, p. 365).

Whatever one may think about block grants devolving responsibility on the states and deregulation in social programs, one cannot learn about the potential of block grants for structural change when the primary question state officials are asking is not, "How can we use our new-found flexibility most effectively?" but instead, "How can we minimize the cost and disruption with which we are suddenly confronted?" Admittedly, some reduction in expenditures might fairly accompany block grants on the theory that states could always identify some low priority issue or area in which savings could be achieved. But the vast reduction of the Reagan budgets, visited in a period of particular financial stringency on the states, fully negates the ambitions of those who seek to learn about the potential for a reconstituted federalism.

2. Implementation studies began with questions about the disposition of events after some authoritative decision was made:

to build a project, to enrich social programs, or to require some actions on the part of public officials or private citizens. For students of implementation the problem of fiscal cutbacks raises some relatively unexplored questions concerning what we may call "negative implementation"—the taking away of program authority and capacity. The following are some of the issues that need to be addressed here.

What kinds of programs and policy initiatives are the first to be abandoned or cut back when states no longer have to provide them, or are no longer motivated by the availability of federal funds (Levine, 1978)? Answers to this question could reveal a great deal about ways in which interest groups have developed around, and in response to, the existence of federal programs.

To what extent does unplanned resistance to cutbacks result in continuing unplanned expenditures because entitlement loopholes continue to exist, or because clients of services are transferred to programs with continued funding? Is it continuation of the federal-income-maximizing game that state and local governments have been playing for the last decade or so? To what extent are program cuts resisted by policy delivery agents who themselves absorb the cost of funding cuts by working harder, handling more tasks, and generally filling in where program gaps exist (Lipsky, 1980)?

To what extent does the "legal density" of state, local, and federal regulations, previously at times considered an impediment to innovation in periods of cutbacks, contribute to difficulties in achieving negative implementation? Does the much-lamented complexity of rules and regulations, with the aid of the courts, protect programs and clients in times of cutbacks?

3. Federal purposes are not solely substantive and programmatic. They are also procedural and constitutional. Some issues of equity, and certainly constitutional anti-discrimination guarantees, will continue to apply to distributing federal monies, even under a block grant system. These objectives constitute ongoing "meta-policy" concerns that do not disappear with program consolidation. The experience with the first round of debate over block grants in education clearly suggests that Congressional resistance to giving up control over federal programs will persist.

To the extent it is expressed in the law, achievement of federal objectives remains an issue in federal program implementations.

Moreover, it is at least arguable that the federal government cannot abdicate historic commitments and purposes that explain the development of federal expenditures for education in the first place. The federal role in education grew, among other things, in response to national concerns over the impact on local communities of federal installations; over national performance in science and engineering for defense purposes; over the life chances of children in low-income families; and over the costs of higher education. These commitments and concerns, which account for a federal education budget in the first place, will not expire with federal block grants.

Both strategically and analytically, I would argue, the federal government cannot be released from implementation responsibilities simply because it blurs its objectives through block grants. For example, there will continue to be a need to monitor the proportion of funds that flow to disadvantaged populations, which at least in this century have been the special constituencies of federal programming and federal influence.

If we turn to the stated structure of block grants additional implementation issues present themselves.

4. Most obviously, we are interested in the mix of programs sustained by the states and localities within the block grant structure. Over time, states and localities will drift toward different kinds of service mixes; we will want to see what different "optimal" solutions to program mixes emerge. We should be particularly attentive to the extent to which states invest in compensatory education of one sort or another, and in program development—two functions that students of federalism have tended to argue might best be played by government at the national level. (See *Education Block Grants Alters State Role and Provides Greater Local Discretion,* 1984; McLaughlin, 1982.)

This suggests attention to several issues that are implicit in the block grant initiatives as major experiments with the federal structure.

5. One advantage of decentralization of authority to the state level is said to be that American federalism encourages experi-

mentation, innovation, and responsiveness to local needs. Yet many analysts are skeptical, based on experience, that states and localities have such specialized needs that only a decentralized structure can accommodate them. They are also skeptical about whether these decentralized units tend to have the resources and institutional capability on which innovations often depend. Thus we should seek to discover the extent to which greater local authority facilitates experimentation and innovation.

6. These last points imply a continuing need at the federal level for data collection and analysis, to permit the assessment of the program implementation we are discussing.

The Reagan Administration has regarded as relatively trivial the administrative and political costs of setting priorities in federal aid programs, while it has emphasized the benefits it says states and localities will realize because of reduced reporting requirements. However, the reduction in federal requirements does not eliminate the need for monitoring, auditing, and cost control that are the hallmark of modern public administration. Nor does it eliminate the costs of developing improved program performance in the absence of a guiding federal influence. How much of the onerous paperwork against which conservative politicians have railed comes from the heavy federal presence, and how much from modern requirements for accountability, remains undetermined. If the states have indeed matured so that they may now be trusted to run programs effectively, they are also likely to burden administrations with the saddle of reporting requirements.

The implementation issues arising from these concerns are to examine the costs of block grant administration—both the additional costs to the states and the reduced costs at the federal level—and the capacity of state governments to administer these funds effectively and responsibly.

7. Students of implementation are vitally concerned with the political process. They ask to what extent implementation outcomes can be explained by particular political processes. Block grants may be expected to alter political processes in at least two

fundamental ways. First, block grants, with the ensuing local struggles over their distribution, bring to the surface the redistributive nature of human services programs so that an increasingly resentful middle class can clearly perceive the tax consequences of supporting these services. Thus the block grant process should be studied to learn to what extent previously hidden redistributive policies become the basis for conflict. Such developments would already be underway in many states because of fiscal strains in the state and various tax limitation plans.

Second, block grants to the state for human services dilute the strength of human service interest groups by placing decision-making responsibility in fifty state capitols instead of in Washington, and by separating responsibility for distributing funds from responsibility for appropriating them. While interest groups in some states may benefit from this approach because they are already strong, the net result is likely to produce unevenness in program advocacy across the nation. It remains to be seen whether the development and nurturing of interest groups over the decade or so in response to national programs such as Title 1 and P.L. 94–142 in special education have resulted in the development of adequate support networks at the state level. It remains to be seen as well whether these groups will remain vigorous if program responsibility is shifted to the states.

8. A final set of implementation concerns 1 list to remind us of what block grants are *not* about. Block grants would affect funding formulas and reduce funding levels, but they are not concerned with the direct delivery of educational services from teacher to children. Block grants, particularly with spending reductions, may affect the resource base from which teachers operate, but they will not affect actual teaching operations.

We may hypothesize with confidence that block grants by themselves, would have little affect on achievement levels, and if anything will affect them adversely because of their association with funding reductions. By themselves they will not affect school leadership or climate, classroom resources, pupil heterogeneity, or general public expectations on which real educational improvements more reliably depend.

REFERENCES

Bardach, Eugene, *The Implementation Game*, Cambridge, Mass.: MIT Press, 1977.

Derthick, Martha, *New Towns In-Town*, Washington, D.C.: Urban Institute, 1972.

Educational Block Grants Alters State Role and Provides Greater Local Discretion, Washington, D.C.: General Accounting Office, November 19, 1984.

Hargrove, Erwin, *The Missing Link*, Washington, D.C.: Urban Institute, 1975.

Levine, Charles, "Organizational Decline and Cutback Management," *Public Administration Review* 38 (1978); pp. 316–325.

Lipsky, Michael, *Street-Level Bureaucracy*. New York: Russell Sage, 1980.

McLaughin, Milbrey Wallen, " *States and the New Federalism,*" *Harvard Educational Review*, 52 (1982); pp. 564–583.

Murphy, Jerome. "Title 1 of ESEA." *Harvard Educational Review*, 41 (1971): pp. 35–63.

O'Neill, June, and Simms, Margaret, "Education," in *The Reagan Experiment*, edited by John Palmer and Isabel Sawhill, Washington, D.C.: Urban Institute, 1982.

Palmer, John, and Sawhill, Isabel V. (Eds.), *The Reagan Record*, Cambridge. Mass.: Bellinger, 1984.

Peterson, George, "The State and Local Sector," in *The Reagan Experiment*, edited by John Palmer and Isabel Sawhill, Washington, D.C.: Urban Institute, 1982.

Pressman, Jeffrey, and Wildavsky, Aaron, *Implementation*, Berkeley: University of California Press, 1973.

Riker, William, *Federalism*, Boston: Little, Brown, 1964.

Steiner, Gilbert, *Social Insecurity*, Chicago: Rand McNally, 1966.

Wildavsky, Aaron, *Speaking Truth to Poser*, Boston: Little, Brown, 1979.

THE IMPORTANCE OF THE FEDERAL ROLE IN IMPROVING EDUCATIONAL: PRACTICE: LESSONS FROM A BIG-CITY SCHOOL SYSTEM

Thomas K. Minter

I bring to this essay a dual perspective: that of the federal education official and that of the local school district administrator. As a practitioner in urban schools I have been employed as a teacher, principal, district superintendent, superintendent of schools, and as deputy chancellor for instruction in the New York City public schools. As a federal education official, I worked in the Carter administration as Assistant Secretary for Elementary and Secondary Education. Through these roles, I developed strong beliefs that federal involvement in elementary and secondary education has resulted in increased access to education for all individuals and groups in our society; in the improvement of teaching and learning at the local level; in increased capacity to support and provide leadership at the state and local levels; and in developing, identifying, evaluating, and disseminating exemplary, research-based educational practices nationwide.

In this essay I will discuss the federal role in the improvement of educational practice nationally and at the local level, the role and influence of federal or other national program evaluations on local curriculum decisions, and the differences in role perceptions between federal and local school district officials. I will illustrate my discussion with examples of several federally funded New York City public school projects that have improved educational practice in the city's schools and classrooms.

The projects I have selected for illustration have been funded fully or partially by Titles I and IV–C of the Elementary and Secondary Education Act of 1965. These projects reveal the positive effects of combining federal programs to reduce instructional fragmentation, improve instruction, and raise achievement levels. Although Title I is an entitlement program aimed primarily at remediation and Title IV–C is a discretionary competitive grant program, both are administered at the state level and have a mandate to improve educational practice at the local level. In addition, each has been the subject of national and local evaluations. Their individual and combined effects in the New York City public schools suggests that federal programs often have a greater positive effect at the local school district level than national program evaluations might indicate.

The Federal Role Since 1965

Throughout much of the 1960s and 1970s the federal government was substantially involved in the development and implementation of policies across a wide range of social areas, including welfare, health, environment, and education. Most of the programmatic efforts were attempts to narrow the economic discrepancies between blacks and whites, ethnic groups, men and women, the able and the handicapped, and the old and the young. Initiatives for this activism came from all three branches of government. The civil rights movement of the 1960s brought many of these issues to public attention—policy-making was a response to citizen needs that were either unmet or insufficiently met by states and localities and that seemed to be the responsibility of the federal government by virtue of the Constitution's general welfare and equal protection clauses.

The Supreme Court's 1954 decision in *Brown v. Board of Education, Topeka* is rightly regarded as the first unequivocal application to education of the Constitution's equal protection clause. Historically, education in the United States has been regarded as the primary vehicle for the upward mobility of its citizens, preparation to meet employment needs, for facilitating assimilation into the social and economic mainstream, and for creating an enlightened, responsible citizenry. Because of these roles, education since 1954 has assumed a greater federal priority than it had in any previous period. Provisions for education were included in antipoverty, labor, and civil rights legislation. The passage of the landmark Elementary and Secondary Education Act legislation in 1965 established a new role for the federal government in elementary and secondary education and represented the nation's hope for overcoming poverty through education.

Although the federal role in education has remained supplementary to state and local roles, with federal contributions never exceeding 8.78 percent of the total funds spent on elementary and secondary schooling in the United States (Birman & Ginsburg, 1982, p.3), this involvement provided a new direction in education. Despite differences in purpose among the five original Elementary and Secondary Education Act titles, most educators and legislators agree that, overall, the Elementary and Secondary Education Act defined the federal role in education in terms of four basic objectives: (1) to provide equal educational opportunity for economically and educationally disadvantaged students in public and nonpublic schools; (2) to provide access to education for populations previously unserved or underserved, including minorities, the aged, students for whom English is a second language, and Native Americans; (3) to improve the quality of education through the initiation and support of educational research and the dissemination of exemplary research findings; and (4) to address national concerns and priorities (Timpane, 1976; Turnbull & McCann, 1979; Vogel, 1979, p. 98; Ward & Gaeta, 1979; Boyer, 1977; Brandon, 1976).

Prior to the passage of the Elementary and Secondary Education Act, state and local education agencies had little incentive for or experience in developing, implementing, and evaluating innovative demonstration programs in compensatory education. The act carried the federal interest in education beyond its traditional role and reflected congressional concern for providing equal access to education and disseminating research-based improvements in school practice. To the extent that the new federal goals were accepted, federal programs funded under Elementary and Secondary Education Act became models for state and local education agencies throughout the country.

The Reagan Administration: A New Federal Role

In its efforts to reduce federal activity in social and economic programs, the Reagan administration is re-examining the federal role in elementary and secondary education. During his presidential campaign, Ronald Reagan pledged to get the federal government out of the classroom, proposed to disband the Department of Education, and voiced his opposition to busing as a means of achieving school integration. Late in 1981 the President promised to submit legislation to Congress establishing tuition tax credits that would offer substantial benefits to parents who send their children to private schools.

Although it is too soon to know which Reagan proposals will eventually be effected, these declarations by the President, along with the enactment of the Educational Consolidation and Improvement Act of 1981, signaled a significantly altered and, potentially, a sharply curtailed federal role. The Educational Consolidation and Improvement Act took effect in July 1982 and repeals the Elementary and Secondary Education Act. The former Title I of the Elementary and Secondary Education Act is designated as Chapter I of the Educational Consolidation and Improvement Act and retains its categorical status. Chapter II of the Educational Consolidation and Improvement Act consolidates thirty federal education programs into a single block grant. Critics predict that program consolidation and the block grant process will weaken the targeting of services and activities to specific categories of grantees (Turnbull & McCann, 1979, pp. 73–76; Ward & Gaeta, 1979, p. 88). I would argue also, that grants consolidation will increase competition and dissolve former coalitions as members fight funding battles for their individual constituencies. Consolidation will also increase the prospect that certain programs will be eliminated and priorities redirected.

Further, the accompanying reduction in overall funding for compensatory programs raises the suspicion that Chapter II of the Educational Consolidation and Improvement Act will eventually be eliminated. Although this consolidation accounts for only about 10 percent of federal elementary and secondary school authorizations, it has already noticeably altered the federal role by removing from the Department of Education the function of awarding discretionary contracts and grants to state and local education agencies (Elbers, 1982). Responsibility for determining how block grant monies will be spent has been transferred to the states, most of which will, in turn, transfer final decisions to local school districts. In addition, the current administration has indicated that it hopes to consolidate even more federal education programs (Berke & Moore, 1982).

This new federal direction undermines national policies that have functioned over the past two decades to increase equal educational opportunity and is consistent with the current administration's political philosophy, which Wirt (1981) describes as neoconservative. According to Wirt, neoconservatives assume "there is only one valid model of democracy. In this model, citizens directly make public policy, appropriate for the ends of their local areas" (1981, p. 15). Neoconservatives argue that the federal government is inefficient whenever it deviates from this role; that in its efforts to create national policies, the federal government "creates unreal expectations of what people are entitled to," which will ultimately lead to group conflict sufficient to tear apart "the basic unity of the nation" (1981, p. 13).

Differences in Role Perspective

A frequent complaint against federal involvement in elementary and secondary education is that federal officials, through regulatory and auditing practices, overstep their bounds and encroach on prerogatives that were left to the states by the Constitution (Hughes & Hughes, 1972). While there is some truth to this general charge, I believe that there are legitimate differences in philosophy, arising, in part, from varying role perceptions of officials at the federal, state, and local levels of government.

The perspective of federal education officials frequently differs from that of local school district officials, even when they share similar educational goals. Federal officials view programs in terms of congressional and legislative intent. Pressured in the early days of Title I by congressional inquiry and by advocacy groups, federal officials were forced to give their primary attention to state and local compliance with federal regulations and guidelines. Provision of services to children were to be provided solely within the context of legislative and regulatory intent (see Hughes & Hughes, 1972, pp. 124–131). I can illustrate this point from my experience as a former federal education official. When testifying before congressional subcommittees at oversight, legislative, or budgetary hearings, I would inevitably be asked about the efficiency with which a program was being targeted on its intended recipients. If a program was not being successfully targeted I was advised by the subcommittee that the Office of Education should monitor states and school districts more closely, develop stricter guidelines, or develop more tightly drawn regulations. This response was given more often for the administration of categorical programs. As program administration became more restrictive, however, the program became less responsive to state or local interests, needs, and priorities. This was a major reason why categorical programs drew hostility from state and local officials.

Studies and predictions of state behavior in distributing federal monies when categorical aid is replaced by block grants show that the concern of federal officials is legitimate. Research literature indicates that the manner in which federal education policies are implemented depends on the extent to which a state agrees with federal policy goals (McConnell, 1979, p. 114). If the federal officials are uncertain of a state's political orientation, or have evidence of prior attempts to circumvent regulations, they tend to assume a "worst case" scenario (Birman & Ginsburg, 1982, p. 12). In such a situation federal officials would emphasize a compliance and enforcement approach to state and local program monitoring. They would operate as if a state or local school district were deliberately attempting to circumvent federal legislation for its own purposes. Thus, federal, state, and local tensions over regulations and enforcement procedures often have been a serious and substantive cause of intergovernmental friction.

Local school district officials, on the other hand, have expressed the need to provide coordinated and coherent classroom services to children who have multiple federal and state program eligibilities. They often feel frustration with the fragmentation caused by federal programs, with their excessive paperwork, and with the inflexibility involved in that appropriations process (Turnbull & McCann, 1979, pp. 69–72). Local officials want to obtain maximum services from every dollar and serve as many eligible children as possible with minimum restrictions. This means seeking flexible interpretation of guidelines, reconciling contradictory regulations, and serving eligible children in regular classrooms when it is educationally correct to do so. A recent study by Kimbrough and Hill (1981) has provided evidence substantiating the observations of local officials that multiple federal programs in a school often cause unintended problems in providing a coherent, coordinated instructional program. The authors argue that although most federal education programs are intended to supplement state and local efforts and are directed to specific target groups, multiple categorical programs, each following distinct and separate regulations and guidelines, often interfere and conflict with the "core local programs" at the individual school. When a state or local school district proposes a plan or procedure to avoid duplication of services or to provide services to additional children by meshing an education program of its own with a similar federal program, the federal review officer must first be certain that the state is supplementing rather than supplanting federal funds. This official must then ensure that the children for whom the services are intended are receiving optimum benefits and that the proposed additional population to be served will not cause the funding or the services to be vitiated, thereby lessening the effectiveness of the program.

A basic dilemma in the delivery of services remains problematic. Neither program consolidation, which practically eliminates targeting, nor unrestricted service to those who have multiple eligibilities, seems to provide an adequate answer. The best resolution would appear to be in the development of comprehensive state, local, and individual school planning which details how services will be provided to eligible students. In New York City, the public school system's Office of Funded Programs, through an Elementary and Secondary Education Act Title IV–C project, coordinates state compensatory education programs with Elementary and Secondary Education Act Title I programs. The regulations and guidelines of both funding sources are dutifully observed, including the concomitant detractions of each.

The Federal Role and the Evaluation Process

A second charge often heard from those who are opposed to the present extent or purpose of the federal involvement in elementary and secondary education is the assertion that federal programs do not work, that they are not successful in attaining their goals. The innovative requirement for an evaluation component was attached to the original Title I of the Elementary and Secondary Education Act legislation by then New York State Senator Robert Kennedy to ensure that the monies were being spent on the public for whom the program was designed. Although this stipulation was only attached to Title I, federal education officials and research soon applied an evaluation component to almost all federally funded programs. The practice was adopted by the education community and applied to other state and local education programs whether or not they were federally funded.

The early, conspicuously self-conscious evaluation efforts gave rise in the late 1960s and early 1970s to charges that federally funded programs had failed to accomplish their goals. Early evaluation of Title I and Head Start were examples of these negative findings (see Datta, 1975; NAACP Legal Defense and Education Fund & Washington Research Project, 1969). On the other hand, these charges have been mitigated by counter-assertions that the early evaluations may have been unduly rigid and inappropriately focused. Aaron (1978), for example, has noted that the Department of Defense was less rigorous in its evaluations than were civilian departments, such as the Office of Economic Opportunity and the Department of Health, Education and Welfare, which administered many of the social and educational programs of the War on Poverty. Aaron indicates that many of these civilian departments were staffed by liberal economists who were anxious to employ their methodological skills to support their ideological perspectives, and were convinced that through their evaluations they could systematically identify programs which were working while ignoring the political considerations of program implementation.

Aaron's analysis is incisive. In my view, perhaps the most fundamental problem with the early evaluations is that they failed to take into account the political determinants of policy development and implementation. Policy decisions in the public arena are not based solely on their utility. Whether or not social programs are developed depends in large part on whether the political and economic environment at a given time is conducive to certain kinds of policies. It is nearly impossible to imagine, for instance, that Title I could win congressional approval in the current political climate, given the preoccupation with controlling costs and an administration and Senate majority philosophically opposed to policies that redistribute income to the less affluent. (Indeed, those policies which were developed during the 1960s are now being thwarted at the implementation level.) Second, an overreliance on the methodological tools of economics frequently leads analysts to exclude variables which do not lend themselves to strict quantification. Thus, for example, in analyzing the influences which determine the successful implementation of an urban renewal project, an economic analyst might not focus on "strong municipal leadership," because it is not a variable that is easily quantifiable. Elaborating on this point in terms of the complexities of education research, Smith (1975) suggests that "research should be aimed at identifying or developing manageable educational programs and investigating their relationship to child outcomes under varying conditions. . . . Research on programs should offer a rationale for a particular set of elements combining to produce a particular set of outcomes for the students'' (p. 129).

The National Follow Through Program, which was first implemented in 1968, provides perhaps the best example of the difficulties encountered in attempting to evaluate experimental programs in education. Although a five year study by Abt Associates (Stebbins, St. Pierre, Proper, Anderson, & Cerva, 1977) of the seventeen Follow Through models then in operation found no conclusive evidence that any of the models worked best in all sites, the Direct Instruction model, developed by Engleman and Becker at the University of Oregon, has been found by other evaluators to be more successful than others at raising achievement across sites (Wisler, Burns, and Iwamoto, 1978, p. 180). In general, those models that had highly structured classroom techniques and that focused chiefly on cognitive development— Behavior Analysis, High/Scope, and Direct Instruction—tended to produce higher scores in many sites. Smith, however, points out it is easier to evaluate these three models because their classroom treatments "meet the conditions of explicit purpose, prior testing and development and promise substantial, measurable effects in laboratory and small-scale experiments" (1975, pp. 144–145). On the other hand, Follow Through models that employ an open classroom curriculum, as do the EDC Open Education Program or the Bank Street College of Education approach, are more difficult to measure on the basis of standardized tests. These latter models, which are designed to instill greater self-confidence in children and motivate the child's self-application to learning tasks, required evaluation measures that are not so easily quantifiable and are not given to short-term results. I am not suggesting that all evaluations have been overly harsh or that all have underestimated successes in federal programs. I firmly believe, however, that federal program models may be more successful in their local school district applications than national evaluations indicate.

Evaluations of programs that are designed to bring about educational change—through new organizational designs, the introduction of new curricula, or new classroom techniques and procedures—present similar difficulties. The multi-volume Rand study (Berman, McLaughlin, Greenwood, Pincus, Pascal, Sumner, Wirt, Mann & Pauly, 1974–78), examined four federally funded programs that were designed to create educational change: Title III of the Elementary and Secondary Education Act, the present Title IV–C of the Elementary and Secondary Education Act, was one of the programs studied. In Volume I of the Rand study, Berman and McLaughlin (1974) reported that one of the difficulties encountered in determining whether or not a program was successful at the local level was that the rate of proliferation of change might be occurring more slowly than had been anticipated by the federal evaluating agency. The authors suggested that concepts of change then available to researchers might not be sufficiently "discriminating" (Berman & McLaughlin, 1974, p. v). The accumulated findings and recommendations of the Rand study provided the educational research community with valuable theoretical and practical information about the processes and effects of educational change. Those who cite early evaluations of federal programs to support their charges against the effectiveness of federal education programs are either not aware of, or are ignoring, more recent studies.

An Overview of Elementary and Secondary Education Act Titles I and IV–C

Title I

The purposes of Title I of the Elementary and Secondary Education Act were clearly stated if not always clearly executed. Congress formulated three major objectives in this Title: to provide financial assistance to school districts in relation to their numbers of low-income children and within those districts, to schools with the greatest number of low-income students; to fund special services for low-achieving children in the poorest schools; to contribute to the cognitive emotional, social, and physical development of participating students (National Institute of Education, 1976, p. xiii). The first two purposes are concerned with providing equal educational opportunity, while the third objective is couched in achievement language, linking it to the improvement of instructional practice in classrooms.

Title I was funded at $2.8 billion in fiscal 1980 and served approximately 5 million children in 14,000 of the nation's nearly 16,000 school districts. As the largest federally funded educational program established by Congress, the failure of this program to meet its service and achievement goals would have constituted a serious setback to continued large-scale federal funding efforts. An interim study by the National Institute of Education (1976) found, however, that Title I was generally effective in meeting its objectives and that the program does fulfill congressional intent.

Most recent evaluations of Title I programs, nationally, have indicated gains of 12 to 15 percent in first-grade reading and mathematics scores on fall-to-spring testing; third-grade students achieved gains of 7 to 15 percent (Rotberg, 1980, p. 7). Studies showing the successes of Title I continue to mount. The preliminary findings of a $15 million federal study of Title I children in grades one through six, drawn from a national sample of representative schools, reveal that Title I students showed higher average educational gains than would be expected in the absence of compensatory education services (Wang, 1980).

A special point must be made about the educational programs and classroom applications of Title I-funded programs. There is a tendency to classify Title I programs as remedial and to look to other programs for more innovative and instructionally exciting practices. In fact, I would argue that Title I teachers, in conjunction with educational researchers and program developers, have pioneered in the development of exemplary and often exciting classroom approaches for teaching children who have found learning to be difficult. From Title I-funded projects has evolved much of the research on the interaction of effective instructional methods and on different learning styles; on the effective use of instructional time and its relationship to academic learning; on the testing and measurement of slow-learning children; and on the proper use of tests. In addition, the development and preparation of appropriate curricula materials for minority students and students whose home language is other than English have been funded by the Elementary and Secondary

Education Act Title I. To say that all programs, experiences, and curricula flowing from Title I classrooms are good or excellent would be patently foolish. It must be said, however, that the funding for this single title has made a significant improvement in the quality of and perspective on schooling for American children.

Title IV-C

Title IV-C of the Elementary and Secondary Education Act was designed to provide grants to states for the funding and support of activities that would improve educational practices at the local school district level. Funds were reallocated from the state to local school districts on a competitive basis. This title has undergone a series of transformations, from its designation as the original Title III of the Elementary and Secondary Education Act, to consolidation with Title IV-C (emphasizing "educational innovation and support"), and to Title IV-C in the Education Amendments of 1978 (emphasizing "improvement in the local educational practices").

Programs mounted under Title IV-C have been directed largely to fulfilling local school district priorities. Local superintendents, nationwide, consider the monies granted under IV-C the only federal funds over which they have had major control, notwithstanding state guidelines and monitoring. Nationally, projects developed under Title IV-C tend to focus on improvement of school-based instruction and/or organization. An earlier criticism of Title IV-C (Berman & McLaughlin, 1978) indicated that it did little to bring equity to disadvantaged children—that its funds tended to be allocated to middle-class and richer suburban districts that had staffs that could write sophisticated competitive grant applications. While I do not challenge this finding, I have found that in big cities with large minority populations, such as New York, Title IV-C funds do in fact benefit minority children, and that equity is not an issue. In New York City, applications for Title IV-C funding are initiated and prepared by the decentralized community school districts with technical assistance and support of the central Office of Funded Programs. With few exceptions, Title IV–C funds support projects for the gifted and talented as well as those that are designed to improve instructional practice and achievement in the basic skills.

Examples of the Federal Role in the Improvement of Educational Practice

Several programmatic efforts operating in the New York City school system serve to illustrate the essential role federal education programs can play in an urban school system—six exemplary programs form the basic instructional component of the Promotional Gates Program, while two others are school-based planning/improvement projects. Each of the examples has been federally funded, and validated, and has been measurably successful in improving the achievement of pupils in the New York City schools. The federally stimulated emphasis on program evaluation and the dissemination of validated educational programs has provided the basis for establishing quality in local school districts; the improvement of achievement outcomes is inextricably interwoven with the improvement of educational practice.

THE PROMOTIONAL GATES PROGRAM

In June 1980 Frank Macciarola, Chancellor of the New York City Public Schools, initiated the Promotional Gates Program. The program is based on a city-wide promotion policy that is directed at raising the educational standards by ensuring that all students acquire the basic skills of reading, mathematics, and writing. Students in the fourth and seventh grades who have not scored above the prescribed cutoff points on the California Achievement Test (CAT) in reading are retained in grade. The unique feature of the Gates program is a three-tiered educational treatment that has been designed to enable holdover students to meet the standards for promotion: first, the selection of exemplary programs; second, instruction by teachers experienced in remedial education who have been provided staff development training in the specific reading and mathematics programs to be taught in his or her school; third, assignment of the trained teachers to classes with no more than twenty students.

Although the Promotional Gates Program is supported by city taxes and state compensatory education funds, it is in the selection and designation of certain instructional programs as "exemplary" as well as in the format of the total program that the federal role in the improvement of education practice has emerged as a prominent factor. Many successful programs, funded by a number of different sources, exist in the New York City schools as they do in other urban systems; however, the only programs that have undergone a rigorous evaluation and validation process by both national and local standards are those that have been federally funded or funded by a combination of federal and state sources. Faced with the responsibility of identifying basic skills instructional programs of proven success, the Division of Curriculum and Instruction selected four validated reading programs and two validated mathematics programs to be used by the community school districts as their core instructional programs for the Gates classes. Each of the exemplary programs had been originally funded by the Elementary and Secondary Education Act Title I, or developed in Title I or Title IV–C projects. In reading, the programs are *Exemplary Center for Reading Instruction*, *High Intensity Learning System*, *Learning to Read Through the Arts*, *Structured Teaching in the Area of Reading*; and, in mathematics, *Diagnostic Prescriptive Arithmetic* and *Real Math* (for complete descriptions of these six programs, and evaluation information, see New York City Public Schools, April 1981). Several of these programs have been subsequently re-evaluated and validated by the U.S. Office of Education's Joint Dissemination and Review Panel and funded as developer/demonstrator projects by the federal National Diffusion Network (see Neil, 1981). In addition to the six exemplary programs, community school districts are permitted to submit additional program recommendations to the Division of Curriculum and Instruction based on similar evaluation criteria.

An additional feature of the Gates program which reflects the positive influence of the federal involvement on educational practice is the format of the total program. The design and format of the Gates program closely conforms to those characteristics identified as tending to enhance the potential for promising results: a discrete target population, specified expected outcomes, selection of treatment (exemplary programs) based on stated criteria, and an evaluation design with formative and summative components. Although the first complete annual evaluation of the Promotional Gates Programs is not yet available, of the original 23,500 pupils held over, 49 percent (11,500) had met end-of-year passing criteria by January 1982 (New York City Public Schools, January 1982). Preliminary statistics indicate that approximately 75 percent of the Gates students achieved the passing criteria by June 1982. Evaluations revealed the positive effects of the instructional programs within the overall process of implementing the Promotional Gates Program. The significant factor for this discussion, however, is that validated and successful federally funded instructional programs were available for the Gates program.

Two School-Based Planning and Improvement Projects

The School Improvement Project and the Comprehensive Planning Unit were initially funded under the Elementary and Secondary Education Act IV–C. Initiated on different educational premises, both projects are designed to make individual schools more instructionally effective through comprehensive planning.

The primary goal of the School Improvement Project is to heighten academic achievement in participating schools through a process of planned and coordinated self-development (see New York City Public Schools, August 1981, p. 2). Based on the effective schools research of Ron Edmonds, senior assistant for instruction in the New York City public schools from 1978 to 1981, the development of a total school improvement plan is the responsibility of several school-based planning committees composed of administrators, parents, and teachers. Each committee is responsible for making a needs assessment of their school in the five areas that were identified by Edmonds as distinguishing instructionally effective schools: strong administrative leadership; a school climate conducive to learning; schoolwide emphasis on basic skills instruction (in a comprehensive school plan); teacher expectations for high pupil performance; and a system for monitoring and assessing pupil performance tied to instructional objectives (Edmonds, 1979). A part-time liaison teacher, reporting to the central administration, works with the constituent committees in each school during the planning and implementation states of the project.

The 1981–82 school year represented the third year of the School Improvement Project for some schools and the second year for others. Preliminary reports based on the April 1982 administration of the citywide achievement tests indicate that the School Improvement Project schools, previously among the lowest ranked in their districts, significantly improved their citywide rank based on the percentage of students reading at or above grade level.

The Comprehensive Planning Unit, also centrally located and funded under the Elementary and Secondary Education Act Title IV-C, is a unit of the Office of Funded Programs. The Comprehensive Planning Unit was designed to help individual schools plan more effectively for the management of instructional programs. The state's program is titled Pupils with Special Education Needs. The state mandate was developed in response to the growing awareness that multiple federal and state programs often cause fragmentation and interruption of the basic educational programs at the individual school level, and further, that school districts, in an era of diminishing resources, have the obligation to make the best possible use of all available funds.

A study of the effect of programs funded by multiple sources in New York schools (Truesdall, 1979) parallels the findings of a Rand Corporation report (Kimbrough & Hill, 1981) which found that the combination of multiple-funded programs tended to fragment the instructional program of a school, resulting in program isolation. Both reports recommended the development of comprehensive planning practices for schools with multiple programs.

Employing a school-based planning model similar to that of the School Improvement Project, members of the Comprehensive Planning Unit provide technical assistance to the principal and teachers of the participating schools. A plan is prepared that integrates all instructional programs in the school, yet maintains the integrity of the programs' regulations and guidelines. The observable result of the plan is an instructionally integrated day for teachers and pupils and a more effectively organized school. The Comprehensive Planning Unit has completed its third year of operation in nine schools. Preliminary reports, based on the city-wide administration of the California Achievement Test, indicate that achievement has measurably increased in participating schools. The focus on a structured, combined instructional program must be credited as a factor in the improvement.

Conclusion

The primary purpose of this essay has been to argue that: (1) federal involvement in education has resulted in and positively influenced the improvement of educational practice; (2) the federal role in elementary and secondary education has been properly focused; and (3) the educational philosophy and purposes of the present administration, if continued and enacted into law by the Congress, will destroy the gains which have accrued to states and local school systems over the past twenty years.

When political scientists compare the respective roles of federal, state, and municipal government they tend to assign a redistributive role to the federal government, and a lesser redistributive role to the states and local governments. Peterson (1981) has argued that since redistributive policies are often at odds with the economic interests in a city, advocates for such policies frequently experience difficulty in organizing for their support (see also Brecher & Horton, 1982). Municipal governments are said to frame their obligations and allocations in terms of the tax-benefit truism that "those who pay the most taxes get the most benefits.'' The closest relationship between tax benefits and voter participation also tends to occur at the local level. It is through federal protection and intervention that rewards and sanctions are imposed upon both states and localities to encourage them to be responsive to the needs of their poorest and most disenfranchised citizens. This federal role must not be lost in education.

While educational researchers, psychometricians, and political scientists may question the value of the effect of the federal role on educational practice, each from his or her own discipline, several facts are clear to the urban schools practitioner:

1. Federal funding has allowed states and local school officials to focus attention on students who are the most economically and educationally disadvantaged, and those for whom the resources of the regular classroom are not sufficient.

2. Federal categorical funds have targeted students who are in greatest need. Although the sometimes rigid regulations that have accompanied legislation have caused political and organizational difficulties at the state and local levels, the money has reached the students for whom it was targeted and its purposes have been realized.

Regulations have been written in a highly restrictive manner for the purpose of targeting and carrying out the specific intent of the Congress. After seventeen years of experience with categorical educational legislation under the Elementary and Secondary Education Act there is no reason to assume that every state and locality will fit a ''worst-case'' description. Regulations can be written so that students who are eligible for services from several funding sources may receive them with a minimum of administrative burden on the school. In lieu of using program consolidation to make federal regulations less restrictive and more flexible, the administration should select fewer categories and fund them to the extent that all eligible persons can be served.

206 Education Policy in an Era of Conservative Reform

3. The federal government has encouraged effective educational practice, and has supported educational change based on research findings. Programs funded by categorical and competitive grants to states and local schools districts have produced measurable student improvement.

The federal role in education should continue to embody three concepts: equity, access, and improvement of practice. The achievement of equity and equal opportunity must be judged by achievement outcomes in the basic skills, in the arts and the humanities, and in students' abilities to acquire the skills necessary for living and employment in a continually changing, technologically oriented world.

The federal role must not be allowed to return to that of the Bureau of Education in 1967, whose only functions were to collect statistics, provide technical assistance when requested, and advise the President on education matters. The education of the nation's children is too important to be left to the diverse goals and priorities of the states without an active federal presence.

Aaron, H. J., *Politics and the Professors*, Washington, D.C.: Brookings Institution, 1978.

Berke, J. S. and Moore, M. T., "A Developmental View of the Current Federal Government Role in Elementary and Secondary Education." *Phi Delta Kappan* (January 1982), pp. 333–337.

Berman, P. and McLaughlin, M. W., *A Model of Educational Change, Vol. I, Federal Programs Supporting Educational Change: Implementing and Sustaining Innovations*, Santa Monica: Rand Corporation, 1974.

Berman, P. and McLaughlin, M. H., *Implementing and Sustaining Innovations*, Vol. 7. *Federal Programs Supporting Educational Change: Implementing and Sustaining Innovations*, Santa Monica, Calif.: Rand Corporation, 1978.

Berman, P., McLaughlin, M. W., Greenwood, P., Pincus, J., Pascal, A., Sumner, G., Wirt, J., Man, D., and Pauly, E.,

Board of Education). Center for Advanced Study in Education, Graduate School and University Center, City University of New York, May 1979.

Turnbull, B. J. and McCann, W., "The Elusive Experiment: A Critique of Grants Consolidation." In P. Kearney & E. VanderPutten (eds.), *Grants Consolidation: A New Balance to Federal Aid to Schools?* (Institute for Educational Leadership, Policy Paper No. 7), Washington, D.C.: George Washington University, 1979.

Vogel, M. E., "Education Grant Consolidation: Its Potential Fiscal and Distributive Impacts." In P. Kearney & E. VanderPutten (Eds.), *Grants Consolidation: A New Balance to Federal Aid to Schools* (Institute for Educational Leadership, Policy Paper No. 7), Washington, D.C.: George Washington University, 1979.

Wang, M. M., *Students' Educational Development During the School Year and the Effects of Compensatory Education* (U.S. Dept. of Education, Sustaining Effects Study, Report No. 10). Washington, D.C.: U.S. Dept. of Education, 1980.

Ward, J. G. and Gaeta, N. M., "Federal Education Grants Consolidation: Issues and Concerns." In P. Kearney & E. VanderPutten (Eds.), *Grants Consolidation: A New Balance in Federal Aid to Schools?* (Institute for Educational Leadership, Policy Paper No. 7), Washington, D.C.: George Washington University, 1979.

Wirt, F. M., Neoconservatism and National Schools Policy. *Educational Evaluation and Policy Analysis*, 2, (1981), pp. 5–18.

Wisler, C. E., Burns, G. P., and Iwamoto, D. "Follow Through Redux: A Response to the Critique by House, Glass, McLean, and Walker." *Harvard Educational Review*, 48, (1978), pp. 171–185.

INTRODUCTION TO PART IV

The essays in this book have provided empirical and descriptive analysis of the politics of retrenchment, using educational block grants as the public policy focus. Different themes have emerged as authors have chosen to concentrate on one or another aspect of the reduction of federal assistance to education and the broadened state discretion in distributing that assistance: the increased competition among educational interest groups, and between them and other human service interest groups; the severely deleterious impact that reductions in federal aid have had on large, urban, heavily minority school districts; the need for interest groups that had been accustomed to operating on the national level to develop access and skill to influence state legislators; the decreased concern with equity; and the diminished capacity for effective governance that has accompanied the block grant strategy. Rich in specific, empirical detail and analysis, the essays have dealt mostly with the effects of the reduced federal assistance to education and/or of implementing a block-grant strategy. None ask how groups with limited resources attempt to influence policy. In the concluding essay, Marguerite Ross Barnett provides a general theoretical summary of "the characteristics of the politics of scarcity under non-protest conditions" and questions some important assumptions about how the American political system operates.

Arguing the theoretical inadequacy of pluralist and stratificationist conceptions of the American political system, and the incompleteness of such suggestive models of protest politics as those of Piven/Cloward and Lipsky, Barnett substitutes role analysis and policy preference for the methodological individualism of both the pluralist/stratificationist and the protest models. The use of roles as the unit of analysis supplies a historical richness, specificity, and clarity that greatly helps in understanding the processes by which those with few resources can and do attempt to influence policy. At the same time, Barnett argues the usefulness of retaining Lipsky's idea of indirect access to political decisionmakers through alliance with supportive reference publics (e.g., in the media, among liberal political groups, etc.). The idea of "proxy politics," combined with role and policy preference analysis, yields a potentially fruitful hypothesis for understanding the politics of disadvantage: "When individuals with limited political resources seek public policies not on the 'normal' political agenda, and these policies require far-reaching and/or redistributive change, the likelihood is increased that some form of proxy politics will be characteristic of the process." Ultimately, such a formulation portrays a two-tier conception of American politics: a model in which the pluralist vision resonates with the reality of advantaged groups while stratification and proxy politics describe the reality of disadvantaged groups.

THE POLITICS OF SCARCITY:
NEW DIRECTIONS FOR POLITICAL SCIENCE
RESEARCH
ON GENDER, RACE AND POVERTY IN AMERICA

Marguerite Ross Barnett

Since the 1950s, pluralist theories of American politics have dominated the field of political science. Pluralists have argued that American politics (local, state, and national) is not controlled by any one group; that power is shared between the government and a myriad of interest groups and that a variety of groups with divergent resources influence specific public policies at different points in time. The pluralists believe that no one group and no one type of resource dominates the political process. Pluralist theory holds that even groups without high visibility in public policy-making have potential power and the possibility of increasing their access and of playing expanded roles in the political arena. Disadvantaged, seemingly powerless groups, that according to the pluralist framework may lack political resources[1] and/or skill to translate their resources into considerable power, are nevertheless, believed to be relevant and influential in the decision-making process.

Some critics of pluralist theory, specifically the stratificationists, have posited fixed, structured patterns of decision-making in which a unified elite group dominates across arenas of power.[2] Stratificationists have depicted the political process in ways which sharply deviate from the pluralists. Nelson Polsby, a critic of the stratificationists, has summarized their argument as consisting of five interrelated propositions. These propositions are: (a) the upper class rules in local community life; (b) political and civic leaders are subordinate to the upper class; (c) a single power elite rules in the community; (d) the upper-class power elite rules in its own interest; (e) social conflict takes place or potentially can take place between upper and lower classes.[3] In stratificationist theory, disadvantage is defined as mainly economic in substance and in general is equally shared by those at the bottom of what one might visually depict as a decision-making pyramid. Since the upper class rules in its own interest in stratification theory, everyone not in the upper class is disadvantaged to some degree.

Because pluralists believe the political system to be essentially fluid; accessible, with changing casts of actors depending on issues and circumstances, their methodology has emphasized the detailed analysis of specific decisions in order to illuminate the decision-making process. Stratificationists, on the other hand, have focused on structure, historical patterns, definition of group interests, ways in which certain kinds of issues are delegitimized and rendered politically unacceptable, and descriptions of key political actors belonging to the designated ruling class or dominant elite.

Both pluralist and stratificationist theories were developed in the earlier decades of the 20th century and came to prominence in the 1940s and/or 1950s when a simpler image of American life was not only tenable but widely shared. Blacks were, for many, an unresolved but invisible problem; many special-interest groups, now active, were not yet politicized; and women were rarely viewed as requiring analytical autonomy in theories of politics. Perhaps because of their historical roots neither pluralist nor stratification theory could adequately contribute to an understanding of the civil rights movement, civil disobedience, or the dramatic change in political actors, movements and political dynamics that took place in the 1960s. Pluralist theory could not explain why Black protest would be so prolonged and become violent. (After all, in pluralist theory, Blacks, like other disadvantaged segments, had potential access to the system. The only problem was to increase political resources and expand their influence.) Stratification theory, on the other hand, could explain why, but not how (given the total dominance of the ruling class) a significant protest movement could be mounted and achieve some success.

In the context of this theoretical vacuum, two types of middle-range theories were developed which sought to shed some insight on Black protest. One, typified by Frances Fox Piven and Richard Cloward's *Regulating the Poor*, focused on the impact of Black protest and by extension sought to answer the question why it developed.[4] A second type of theory, typified by the work of Michael Lipsky,[5] focused on process—what happened in specific decision-making situations. Both types of approach argue that there is a special, unique dynamic to the politics of the poor.

Frances Fox Piven and Richard Cloward, in *Regulating the Poor*, assert that government policy-makers respond positively to more strident protest on the part of the poor. They believe: "The key to an understanding of relief-giving is in the functions it serves for the larger economic and political order, for relief is a secondary and supportive institution. Historical evidence suggests that relief arrangements are initiated or expanded during the occasional outbreaks of civil disorder produced by mass unemployment, and then abolished or contracted when political stability is restored."[6]

Although their argument is specifically focused on welfare, there is an implication that civil disorder can be the most effective political resource of the poor. Michael Lipsky, whose work typifies a process orientation, also asserts that protest is a political resource for the poor. Lipsky's argument is, however, somewhat more sophisticated than the basic equilibrium model underlying the Piven and Cloward view. Lipsky argues that alliance-formation is critical for relatively powerless groups if they seek to join the decision-making process as participants.[7] He suggests that protest on the part of lower-class participants is an indirect process in which the effort is to form alliances with reference publics such as the media, liberals, etc., in order to use them as leverage to influence target political authorities. Reference publics, so the argument goes, will in turn be influenced by the actions of protest organizations and will convey their concerns to the target groups or individuals.

Although Lipsky is focusing on process, and Piven and Cloward on structural factors shaping public policy outputs, the distilled message is the same; protest is one of the most valuable, if not the most valuable political resource of the poor. If we combine Lipsky with Piven and Cloward, we derive the following mode: if A, who is poor, would like to bargain with B, a political authority, in order to secure public policy [p1], and A is relatively powerless, then A would take action against B through protest, taking care to inform and win the sympathies of reference publics C, D, and E. (C, D, and E being liberal organizations and/or individuals.) To effect material rather than symbolic change civil disorder on a large scale may be needed. This combined model points toward a conclusion that only civil disorder on a large scale would be capable of effecting major change and expansion of economic and other benefits.

At first glance the Piven/Cloward-Lipsky combined model seems to have great explanatory power. Some analysts, news reporters, and politicians have read recent history as showing a decline of protest by the poor as related to a decline in their political power. The unavoidable problem, however, would be to make a case for the decline in political power of the poor. Increasing numbers (since the 1960s) of Black elected officials, including Congressmen, state, and local representatives, would not support that case for Blacks, and similar empirical evidence exists for a wide range of groups.[8] Neither is it easy to reason backwards from policy by asserting that public policy decreasingly favors the interests of the poor, unless those interests can be specified and verified with concrete data. For example, the 1980–81 budget cuts of social programs created enormous problems for the poor, problems that have been documented by academics, politicians, and public interest groups. Are not these cuts, therefore, clear evidence of policy in conflict with the interests of the poor? No—not unless the poor themselves define the budget cuts in that manner. If one accepts the explanation, forwarded by many economists, that the cuts are necessary for the public good and indeed will benefit the poor in the long run, then the budget cuts should be seen as supportive of the interests of the poor. The point is not to argue any one singular partisan position here but rather to suggest the difficulty of analytically specifying what is in the "interests" of any group and the complexity involved in comparing the power of groups over time.

More important problems with these models exist, however. Both Cloward/Piven and Lipsky use the individual in all her/his combined roles as the unit for all phases of the analysis. The argument, therefore, assumes a zero-sum game quality that quickly generates counterexamples. An individual in even the poorest segment of society may have some part of his or her self-perceived political interests represented by existing lobbying organizations with direct access. Secondly, it is a mistake to assume that all or most of the protest in the 1960s was generated by poor communities or groups. On the contrary, the civil disobedience movement was generated by middle-class Black constituencies. Thirdly, some studies of the civil disorders showed those engaged in rebellion to be relatively better off than their peers.[9] These data lend credulity to an interpretation of rebellion from the comparative politics literature that suggests rising but truncated expectations and increasing social strain generated from asymmetries between real and anticipated socio-economic position are key causes of rebellion and social movement development.[10]

Fourth, neither theory sheds light on the normal political processes involving the poor. They fail adquately to convey how rare organized, continuing political protest is. Indeed it is extremely difficult to sustain such activity over long periods of time. In that sense the almost decade-long protest associated with the civil rights movement was an exception in American politics and must necessarily be studied as such rather than as the norm. The important question for understanding the everyday politics of the disadvantaged is: What resources do the poor and the disadvantaged have to influence politics when civil disobedience protest is not possible? What are the characteristics of the politics of scarcity and poverty under non-protest conditions?

Finally, the triangular model of political process (A = protestors; B = reference publics; C = target authority groups) is based on an assumption that key reference groups will be sympathetic to the protestors and that this will be reflected in the pressure they put on the target political authorities. While true at points during the 1960s, the relationships among reference groups, target groups, and protestors is not a given, stable factor but one subject to political shifts and transformation. Indeed, the more interesting question regarding the 1960s is why key reference groups were in some instances intermediaries applying leverage for the goals of the protestors. That question is the beginning of an analysis rather than a given element of a theoretical model.

Rather than rejecting the Lipsky and/or the Piven/Cloward model in its entirety, I would suggest that these and other existing models and theories of the politics of the poor and the disadvantaged need recasting, elaboration, and substantiation through additional empirical research. I shall outline a theoretical model for analysis of the politics of disadvantaged groups and suggest what a research agenda on this subject might look like. Special attention will be given to the particular problematic embodied in the confluence of gender, race, and poverty.

RETHINKING THE POLITICS OF DISADVANTAGE

A first problem in recasting theories of the politics of those in poverty is to be clear about what the unit of analysis is. Roles, not individuals, may constitute the most useful unit for theoretical purposes. Although the final goal is to clarify what happens to individuals, for the purposes of our initial analysis we might begin by segregating the role. This avoids denying roles which even very low income people might occupy that provide them or groups presenting their self-defined interests with considerable access and/or influence. A brief hypothetical example: An Appalachian coal miner and member of the local coal miners' union with a large family to support may be very poor, but in his role as worker and union member many of his interests, regarding both his job and public policy toward the mines, may be well-represented by lobbyists with political clout and direct access. This same miner may own a small amount of property. As a landowner he may face eviction and other problems not uncommon in that geographical area and often produced by the power of foreign-based conglomerates seeking expansion of their mining interests.[11]

In contrast to his role as miner, this same individual might find himself completely stymied in his role as landowner. It might be impossible for him to obtain or to effectively use direct access to public policy authorities who might mitigate policy toward small landowners. Furthermore, organizations with lobbying interests reflecting his own might be similarly effete. As a citizen, our hypothetical miner might have an ideology which dictated support for state ownership of the mines and redistribution of income. In that role not only might political access be virtually impossible but there might well be no effective groups representing his point of view. The point is obvious: the "power and influence" of our miner depends on the issue and the policy arena.

If role and policy preference become the center of analytical attention, how do conclusions about the power and influence of an individual, or conclusions about the structure of power and the process by which it is exercised change? Conceptual difficulties are inevitable. Pluralists, who focus on process, tend to capture the activities of visible interest groups representing broad constituencies and thereby give the impression of the wide power of individuals as organized into lobbying groups. And indeed, if all of each individual's political preferences were represented by equally powerful groups, their argument would have a good deal of validity.

Stratificationists on the other hand, focusing on structure, take a view of the whole that underscores the stability of a group's position over time. Groups at the bottom of society are then defined as having a political interest in issues and policies which would enable them to move upward. This approach highlights the policy preferences of groups which are defined out of the political arena and delegitimized. Involved here is what Bachrach and Baratz call "the other face of power."[12] In using the individual as the unit of analysis, the pluralist is led to conclusions of power or potential power while the stratificationist is led to conclusions of powerlessness.

A second problem in theory-building involves the need for clarification of the group being discussed. There is an unfortunate tendency to use interchangeably terms that require distinct and separate analysis. The politics of Blacks as a collectivity, the economically disadvantaged, other socially or culturally stigmatized groups might differ significantly. However, our use of roles as the unit of analysis may help clarify the issue. Our hypothetical example suggests that the role, the political access that role provides, and the degree to which the desired interest (defined as the self-perceived policy goal of the individual in a given role) deviates from the existing public policy agenda are all important factors in determining the power, access, and perhaps therefore the politics, associated with that role. Similarly, groups with equal income and economic resources might raise rather different kinds of issues in the political system. We might hypothesize that the more intractable, unprecedented and fundamental the issue raised, the greater the likelihood that individuals in roles that entailed raising that issue would experience limited access and influence.

Race, in the American context, carries a stigma of inferiority that has in the past infused political participation of Blacks with a special "system-challenging quality."[13] Gender, if politicized in ways which suggest more than limited representation of women in positions of power, also has important policy implications. However, for women who define their political self-interest in ways consistent with the current political agenda, it is quite possible that in the majority of the roles they occupy (if not all) their interests are well represented. On the other hand, a woman who might believe that women should be hired for academic, government and industry leadership positions according to their proportion in the population might find, like our Appalachian coal miner, that no group adequately represents her political interest and views. The point is that apart from the reality of individual, differentiated and segmented roles, there is also the reality of certain "epochal themes"; structural fissures in American society that are encompassing and create the potential for particular tensions, contradictions, and patterns of hierarchy and subordination.

Although hypothetically we might imagine a low income, Black woman whose self-defined political interests were identical with those of the majority of upper income, white males, in general the lower the income, the more stigmatized the group to which a given individual belongs, and the greater the policy deviation from the norm involved in the policy advocated, the less we would expect a large number of significant, powerful roles to be present. Therefore, analysis would focus on the kinds of roles that are possible, their access, influence and power; possible contradictions among roles; the totality created by the combination of all roles; and the comparison of the roles combined in various types of individuals and groups. What is known as "double or triple jeopardy" in political rhetoric would take on an analytical meaning when we consider that there are structural fissures in American society which create the potential for diminished numbers of significant; powerful roles.

A final issue has to do with the level of change required to translate a political interest into public policy. American public policy has often been characterized as incremental (favoring small alterations in existing policy rather than major breaks with precedent over policy requiring structural, systemic or fundamental change). Similarly, distributive policies (providing material benefits to all within a designated category) have been favored over redistributive policies entailing redistribution of benefits between or among classes, ethnic/racial, gender, or other collectivities. Redistributive, structural policies have always been more difficult to get onto the political agenda.

Having clarified some of the definitional and conceptual issues and having entered certain caveats regarding the Lipsky/Piven/Cloward model one finds it nevertheless important to retain what is valuable in their approach. The major thrust of the Lipsky argument is that protest politics involves indirect access. Protestors achieve political access indirectly through reference groups. Political resources of reference groups are used, according to the theory, to increase the influence of the protestors. Although Piven/Cloward and Lipsky focus only on protest and civil disobedience, I would suggest that a *proxy model of politics* (a useful term for the intermediate and indirect character of politics described by Lipsky) is a more general characteristic of the politics of disadvantaged groups. In other words Lipsky may have simply identified one instance of a more general phenomenon. That phenomenon is the need for and use of proxy politics by certain kinds of disadvantaged groups.

Therefore, the quick, brief, and simple answer to the question: What differentiates the politics of scarcity, the political experience of the disadvantaged—the answer would be the proxy politics, the indirect access, the need for political intermediaries and or legitimizers.

Combining the notion of proxy politics with the discussion of criteria for emergence of the politics of poverty and disadvantage we might suggest the following hypothesis: When individuals with limited political resources seek public policies not on the "normal" political agenda, and these policies require far-reaching and/or redistributive change, the likelihood is increased that some form of proxy politics will be characteristic of the process. Confluence of a number of variables that tend to reflect deep fissures, unresolved conflicts, and disadvantaged status increases the likelihood that far-reaching policy demands will be made. Blacks and women, because they are in societal roles that are defined as subordinate in one or more ways, are groups more likely to contain individuals with few or no roles that can be defined as powerful, with demands that stretch the boundaries of the normal policy agenda, and are therefore more likely to participate in proxy politics as part of their normal, everyday interaction with the political system.

THE "FOURTH WORLD" OF PUBLIC INTEREST GROUP LOBBYING: PROXY POLITICS IN ACTION

A brief example of non-protest, proxy politics would be informative and also helpful in defining new research directions and the arena of public-interest group lobbying provides such an example. Between 1975 and 1976, while conducting a study of Congress, I had occasion to interview a large number of leaders of what I began to call the "fourth world" of public interest lobbying groups. This name was derived from the metaphor of four worlds in the comparative politics literature. Among those conversant with international politics, there is often talk of a "first world" (western industrial nations); "second world" (socialist industrialized nations); "third world" (the 'elite' of the developing nations); and "fourth world" consisting of the poorest of the poor nations. The lobbying groups I will refer to in this brief example of the politics of the disadvantaged, will be from that "fourth world" of public-interest lobbying groups.

Most studies of interest group lobbying in Washington have concentrated on the largest and most visible lobbying organizations—groups perceived to be enormously powerful and skilled in the use of resources and influence. The Chamber of Commerce, the National Education Association, the oil industry lobbyists, the farm bloc, major labor organizations and so on are typical of the highly visible "first-world" groups that have received the attention of the media, academics, and the informed public. Some of the major public-interest lobbying organizations are less visible and/or less well described in the interest group literature but are nevertheless generally thought to be significant, influential political forces. The American Civil Liberties Union, The NAACP, The Leadership Conference on Civil Rights, Common Cause, Americans for Democratic Action, and so on fall into this category. In the category of lobbying organizations with secondary clout and modest visibility are individual labor unions, lobbyists for individual medium-sized companies; lobbyists for some of the large membership organizations—often their numbers suggest influence but they lack the resources to exert leverage as significant as that of the "first-world" organizations. Examples of the latter category would be the major church organizations, some of the large fraternities, sororities, environmental groups, and so forth. Although the literature has not adequately described the politics of these "second" and "third world" public interest groups, most of the large organizations (particularly those organizations that do not represent disadvantaged sectors) resemble the more visible, and more thoroughly researched organizations.

Without attempting to provide a summary of the literature on interest-group lobbying in Washington, it is possible to simply spell out the kinds of similarities I am suggesting exist among three levels of lobbying groups (highly visible, large, well financed groups; less visible, less well-financed but influential groups; and groups with some one resource which provides them with clout but without a developed infrastructure and a panoply of re- sources). On the most superficial level all of these groups have offices, staff, and a bureaucracy which provides some support for their lobbying activities. This includes some number of paid employees, money for printing, access to outlets for their press releases; and so on. These organizations also tend to have some one or several people who have direct access to most congressmen and senators as well as to officials in the White House and in the major federal offices in the bureaucracy. Someone in the organization can place a telephone call and have it answered. It may not always be the same person nor always the lobbyist—it may be an official of the organization. At the most superficial level, all of these organizations, although by no means equal, were at least institutionalized entities with the capacity to make an impact on the politics of the nation.

Organizations in the "fourth world" of public interest lobbying were differentiated in two major ways. First their resources were so limited that they could only be called lobbying organizations in the sense that they identified themselves as such. Often their staffs were all or nearly all voluntary. Without exception that meant that they were transient and not dependable. Often even the most basic resources were absent from their offices. Typewriters, telephones, paper were present in limited quantities and xerox machines and other slightly more advanced supplies usually not available at all. The total effect of the extremely slim resources was an overall sense of their transitory, non-institutionalized character. Most important was the difference in process. These lobbying organizations were engaged in a political process which was structurally similar to the model of proxy politics outlined above. The major difference was that the reference constituencies were other lobbying groups. Target authorities ranged from Congresspersons to major Washington bureaucrats and White House aides. The phenomenon of indirect lobbying follows the model of A, who seeks policy change (p1) and who is a lobbyist for a "fourth world" lobbying group, lobbying B, who is a lobbyist for another public interest lobbying group some distance from the major, leading "first world" lobbying groups, but with the access to "first world" lobbyists. B then lobbies C, who is a lobbyist for one of the most powerful, major groups, or lobbies Target authorities X, Y, and Z. B or C, in lobbying for A, can freely translate A's request since B and C are granting a favor and therefore engaged in a one-way gift relationship, not a bartering or exchange relationship.

Typically in the role of a B (reference lobbying group) would be an organization such as Common Cause, the Leadership Conference on Civil Rights, The Urban League or Urban Coalition. Often these organizations would then turn to the AFL-CIO for assistance on major problems. On legislation, it was always necessary to put together the entire progressive coalition which included labor, in a crucial role. One of the leaders of a "fourth world" group put the matter well. When asked how he spent his time he replied: "I spend my time trying to get other people to move on things. I don't go to Capitol Hill that much—I go to AFSCME (American Federation of State, County, Municipal Employees), over to see Ron (Urban League), or to the Civil Rights Conference (Leadership Conference on Civil Rights) when I want to get something done. I can't even get in to see Clarence Mitchell (major NAACP lobbyist at the time) most of the time."[14]

IMPLICATIONS OF PROXY POLITICS

The pattern of proxy politics described above has not been noted in the existing literature. For that reason, it is both theoretically important and suggestive of new research directions. To the extent that political pluralism has been presented, not simply as a theory of American politics, but as an intrinsic aspect of democracy[15] the identification of this pattern of proxy politics raises inescapable political theory issues. More directly, it raises questions regarding our perception of the American political system. Without exception both pluralist and stratificationist theorists discuss the American political system, the political process, and the distribution of power in uniform terms. The system is either pluralist or stratificationist for these writers. Even more recent authors, responding to this theoretical impasse, have either dismissed the debate as trivial or have advocated combining methodologies. Aggar et al., in a very innovative addition to this literature, suggested that if cities were examined comparatively and over time, both pluralist and stratificationist patterns of power distribution could be found to exist at different time periods.[16]

This article has suggested an image of American politics distinct from pluralists, stratificationists, and others contributing to the debate on the organization of power and the nature of the political process. Essentially a two-tier system has been described that includes the reality of the pluralist model for those individuals who, in all or most of their roles, have access to political authorities; and the reality of the stratificationist model for those who, in all or most of their roles, seek fundamental change, structural (systemic) innovation, redistributive policy capable of remedying collective disadvantage. For this latter group, proxy politics may be an important process of political representation.

Of critical importance is research on all of these issues. What are the implications of proxy politics for effective representation? Do messages become blurred, misrepresented, distorted through the proxy process? What happens when no group with political access exists which can transmit, represent a policy demand—that is, what happens when no reference group is available to provide access to the target authorities? What are the consequences of intermittent representation? When the weakest groups become so inert that they provide no representation at all for periods of time—that is, they become intermittent groups—what is the impact on representation? All of these are research issues that derive from our discovery of proxy politics. It is now important to learn more about how proxy politics works. This would include understanding when protest and civil disorders emerge. It may well be, owing to the intermittent, possibly inert character of proxy politics, that protest politics and civil disorders become more likely—whether or not there is a sympathetic reference public to transmit demands to political authorities. This would suggest a continuous framework of analysis, from proxy politics through civil disorders, relevant for those making fundamental demands on the political system.

For groups using proxy politics, dependence on reference groups is high, suggesting that inherent in a proxy political model is also a model of political dependency. Problems in a dependency model are numerous. For example, we might ask what happens to the policy preferences of dependent groups when the political access, influence, and power of the reference groups has been undermined? Or what happens when the reference groups are so busy defending their own policy preferences that they have no "political capital" to spend on proxy politics? We might add to our theoretical model by suggesting that in periods of economic scarcity, reference publics are likely to be less able to represent dependent groups. Proxy politics, therefore, become even more problematic than usual. However, all of these questions are matters for empirical study and should be on the research agenda of those interested in the politics of disadvantaged groups.

SUMMARY AND CONCLUSION

This article has argued that neither pluralist nor stratificationist theories of American politics have been adequate for explaining the politics of disadvantaged groups in the U.S. Both models are inadequate for understanding protest politics and could therefore offer nothing substantive in explanation of the civil disobedience or civil disorders of the 1960s. In addition, neither pluralist nor stratificationist models, taken alone, adequately explain normal politics for disadvantaged groups. Indeed, I have suggested a two-tier model, emphasizing roles rather than individuals, as the best way to envision American politics. This two-tier system allows for pluralism as a reality for advantaged sector roles and stratification and proxy politics for disadvantaged sector roles. A model of proxy politics extends the work of Piven/Cloward and Lipsky in trying to understand the politics of disadvantaged groups and suggests the process they found for the politics of protest has a more general reality.

The attempt to extend the Piven/Cloward and Lipsky models however, led to the rejection of their easy assumption that reference publics will assist the disadvantaged and will be readily available as transmitters of their policy demands. Also modified was the conceptualization of the unit of analysis. Using the role as the unit of analysis, it was suggested that there might not be an easy correlation between income and use of proxy politics, but that a notion of the self-defined political interest had to be introduced. It was suggested that some individuals in poverty might nevertheless have some roles that entailed representation by relatively powerful entities. Similarly, relatively well-off people could have self-perceived interests that entailed radical restructuring of the political system. However, the opportunities for significant roles involving political access and power diminished with low income and with membership in disadvantaged categories representing encompassing patterns of subordination in American life. Examples given were women and Blacks. For groups belonging in more than one disadvantaged category—that is, having a self-perceived policy demand requiring fundamental political change, belonging to a category of traditional subordination, and having low income status—the chances of significant, powerful political roles are slim indeed.

Finally, it was suggested that research is needed on the issues raised. This article has presented a new theoretical framework for viewing the politics of disadvantaged groups. Of necessity this framework has been presented in broad strokes and general terms that require further empirical verification. Of particular importance would be studies of interest groups representing the very poor; survey research of an innovative nature on disadvantaged sectors of the population; examination of the consequences of dependency inherent in proxy politics; and studies of public policy-making that go beyond process to examine structure. This kind of research agenda will provide the kind of data needed to illuminate the politics of scarcity in America.

NOTES

1. James Q. Wilson (*Negro Politics: The Search for Leadership*, New York: The Free Press, 1960), for example, makes this point in explaining Black politics.

2. Classical stratificationist theorists include: Floyd Hunter, *Community Power Structure* (Chapel Hill: University of North Carolina Press, 1953); Robert S. Lynd and Helen M. Lynd, *Middletown* (New York: Harcourt, Brace, & World, 1929): Robert S. Lynd and Helen M. Lynd, *Middletown in Transition* (New York: Harcourt, Brace & World, 1937.) See Terry N. Clark *Community Structure and Decision-Making: Comparative Analysis* (San Francisco: Chandler Publishing, 1968) for a clear, balanced discussion of the community power structure debate.

3. Nelson Polsby, *Community Power and Political Theory* (New Haven and Londen: Yale University Press, 1963).

4. Frances Fox Piven and Richard Cloward, *Regulating the Poor: The Foundations of Public Welfare* (New York: Pantheon Books, 1971).

5. Michael Lipsky, *Practices in City Politics* (Chicago: Rand McNally, 1970).

6. Piven and Cloward, op. cit., p. xiii.

7. Lipsky, op. cit., p. 169.

8. *National Roster of Black Elected Officials*, Volume 12, 1982 (Washington: Joint Center for Political Studies, 1982).

9. James S. Campbell, et al. *Law and Order Reconsidered* (New York: Bantam Books, 1970).

10. Ted Robert Gurr, *Why Men Rebel* (Princeton: Princeton University Press, 1970) and Marguerite Ross Barnett, *The Politics of Cultural Nationalism in South India* (Princeton: Princeton University Press, 1976).

11. John Gaventa, *Power and Powerlessness: Quiescence and Rebellion in an Appalachian Valley* (Urbana: University of Illinois Press, 1980).

12. Peter Bachrach and Morton S. Baratz. "The Two Faces of Power," *American Political Science Review*, 56 (1962), pp. 947–952; also Bachrach and Baratz, *Power and Poverty: Theory and Practice* (New York: Oxford University Press, 1970).

13. Marguerite Ross Barnett, "A Theoretical Perspective on Racial Public Policy," in Marguerite Ross Barnett and James A. Hefner, *Public Policy for the Black Community* (Port Washington: Alfred Press, 1976).

14. Interview with John Wilson, lobbyist for the National Sharecroppers' Fund.

15. Robert Dahl, *Pluralist Democracy in the United States: Conflict and Consent* (Chicago: Rand McNally, 1967).

16. Robert Agger et al., *The Rulers and the Ruled: Political Power and Impotence in American Communities* (New York: John Wiley & Sons, 1964).

CONTRIBUTORS

Marguerite Ross Barnett is Chancellor of the University of Missouri at St. Louis.

Samuel Bowles is Professor of Economics at the University of Massachusetts.

Marilyn Gittell is Professor of Political Science at the Graduate School and University Center of the City University of New York.

David M. Gordon is Professor of Economics in the Graduate Faculty of the New School for Social Research.

Charles Harrington is Professor of Anthropology and Education, and Director of the Institute for Urban and Minority Education at Teachers College, Columbia University.

Michael Lipsky is Professor of Political Science at the Massachusetts Institute of Technology and Lecturer in the Graduate School of Education at Harvard University.

Thomas K. Minter is Dean of Professional Studies at Herbert H. Lehman College of The City University of New York.

Gary Orfield is Professor of Political Science at the University of Chicago.

Thomas E. Weisskopf is Professor of Economics at the University of Michigan.

Philip V. White is University Associate Dean for Academic Affairs at The City University of New York.

Linda Faye Williams is Associate Professor of Political Science at Howard University and Senior Research Associate at the Joint Center for Political Studies.

Paul Ylvisaker is Charles Williams Eliot Professor of Education at the Graduate School of Education at Harvard University.

INDEX

Polsby, Nelson, 213
Powell, Lewis F. (Justice), 76, 78
Promotional Gates Program,
    200–202

R

Rand Corporation, 203–204, 209
Randolph, A. Phillip, 45
Rapping, Leonard, 8
Reagan, Ronald
    administration, ix, xii, xvi, 1,
        3, 12, 62, 81, 93, 103,
        104, 106, 118, 122,
        129–133, 137 ff,167 ff,
        177 ff, 190 ff
Rehnquist, William H. (Justice),
    76
Rockefeller, Nelson (Gov.), 108
Roosevelt, Franklin
    administration, 45
Rosenthal, Alan, 108
Rutgers University, 157

S

St. Louis, 127, 129
San Francisco, 134
San Jose, 124
School Improvement Project,
    202–204
Seattle, 129
Shils, Edward, 76
Smith, M. S., 201
South Carolina, 101, 105, 139, 142
Sowell, Thomas, 53, 76
State University of New York, 114
Stevens, John P. (Justice), 76
Stewart, Potter (Justice), 76
Stockman, David, 124

T

Taylor, Hobart Jr., 47–48
Teacher strikes, 152, 159–160
Tennessee, 136
Thompson, John T., 107
Tollett, Kenneth, 78
Troutman, Robert, 48
Truman, Harry
    administration, 46
Tuition tax credits, 5

U

Unemployment, 14–15, 49, 151
    black/white differentials,
        68–70
Urban decline, 115 ff, 134 ff, 150
    ff
Urban League, 225
U.S. Steel, 80–81
Usdan, Michael D., 107

V

Vermont, 107

W

Wall Street Journal, 93
War on Poverty, 172, 195
Washington, Harold (Mayor), 150
Washington, D.C., 157
*Weber (United Steelworkers v.
    Weber)*, 77, 79
Weiskopf, Thomas E., 9
White, Byron R. (Justice), 77
Wildavsky, Aaron, 180
Williams, Linda Faye, 9